Theology and the Marvel Universe

Theology and Pop Culture

Series Editor

Matthew Brake

The Theology and Pop Culture series examines the intersection of theology, religion, and popular culture, including, but not limited to television, movies, sequential art, and genre fiction. In a world plagued by rampant polarization of every kind and the decline of religious literacy in the public square, Theology and Pop Culture is uniquely poised to educate and entertain a diverse audience utilizing one of the few things society at large still holds in common: love for popular culture.

Titles in the Series

Theology and the Marvel Universe, edited by Gregory Stevenson

Theology and the Marvel Universe

Edited by Gregory Stevenson

LEXINGTON BOOKS/FORTRESS ACADEMIC
Lanham • Boulder • New York • London

Published by Lexington Books/Fortress Academic
Lexington Books is an imprint of The Rowman & Littlefield Publishing Group, Inc.
4501 Forbes Boulevard, Suite 200, Lanham, Maryland 20706
www.rowman.com

Unit A, Whitacre Mews, 26-34 Stannary Street, London SE11 4AB

British Library Cataloguing in Publication Information Available

Library of Congress Cataloging-in-Publication Data

Library of Congress Control Number: 2019954122
ISBN 978-1-9787-0615-6 (cloth : alk. paper)
ISBN 978-1-9787-0617-0 (pbk : alk. paper)
ISBN 978-1-9787-0616-3 (electronic)

♾️™ The paper used in this publication meets the minimum requirements of American National Standard for Information Sciences—Permanence of Paper for Printed Library Materials, ANSI/NISO Z39.48-1992.

Contents

Acknowledgments

I want to thank series editor Matthew Brake for extending to me the invitation to propose a volume for this series on Theology and Pop Culture. I also want to thank Lexington Books/Fortress Academic for championing the publication of this book and its essays, and particularly Gayla Freeman for her editorial assistance. My wife, Saysavad, is always due gratitude for the patience she displays whenever I find myself embroiled in a project of this magnitude. I have been a fan of Marvel for as long as I can remember, though my earliest interest stemmed mainly from brief appearances by Spider-Man on the television show *The Electric Company.* I owe a debt of gratitude to my father, James Stevenson, for bringing home a large trash bag full of discarded comic books (given to him by a friend and local bookstore owner) when I was twelve. That bag of comic books, narrowly saved from a trip to the dump, fanned my early interest in comic books into a flame. I am thankful also to my children (Nicholas, Alexandra, and Isabella) whose own interest in the stories of the Marvel Universe have helped to keep that flame alive.

Introduction

The Sacred and the Superhero

Gregory Stevenson

There is a grand metanarrative composed by multiple authors spread out over time that represents both unity and diversity throughout its interlocking stories and that engages themes of justice, redemption, sacrifice, and the enduring conflict between good and evil. Although I am speaking of the Bible, the same holds true for the Marvel Universe. One clear distinction, however, between the biblical narrative and that of the Marvel Universe is that the Bible is a closed canon, its story restricted to the books that comprise it. In contrast, the Marvel Universe is an open canon given to endless expansion, revision, and re-imagination.

Having begun in 1939 under the nomenclature of Timely Comics (changed to Atlas Comics by the 1950s), what is known today as Marvel Comics first took that name in 1961. It was at this time that Marvel had a novel idea that would initiate massive ripple effects: "the idea that these characters shared a world, that the actions of each had repercussions on the others, and that each comic was merely a thread of one Marvel-wide mega-story" (Howe 2012, 47). Suddenly Marvel characters began appearing in each other's books, their stories interlocking and their fictional lives becoming intertwined. Although easily manageable at the start, as the decades passed, the complexity of this move expanded exponentially with new stories constantly being written and new characters created. Thousands of characters propelling innumerable stories shared the same narrative landscape. These characters would undergo frequent revisions and alterations, sometimes having their entire origin stories changed. As different writers took over a book, the same character might be put to a completely different use. This idea that these thousands of characters all inhabit the same universe and each play one role in an ever-expanding play has resulted in "a collective narrative millions of pages long . . . that has no parallel in any other form of modern narrative" (Arnaudo 2010, 4).

The continuing expansion of this universe reached a new level with the advent of cross-genre storytelling. No longer confined to the pages of comic books, Marvel characters crossed over into film, television, and video games. Today the Marvel Universe comprises not just eighty years and counting of comic continuity, but also the twenty-three films (and counting) of the Marvel Cinematic Universe (MCU), the films based on Marvel characters that pre-dated the MCU or that were owned by competing film companies, television iterations (both live action and animated), and numerous video game stories. Together these stories make up "the most intricate fictional narrative in the history of the world" (Howe 2012, 6). Due to the frequent revisions of existing stories and the constant introduction of new stories in new forms, there can be no "official" version of the Marvel narrative, no definitive, canonical form (Reynolds 1992, 43). This, however, is part of its rhetorical value as it means that the narrative of the Marvel Universe is nothing if not flexible.

This element of flexibility is one feature the narrative of the Marvel Universe shares in common with the biblical narrative, though they come at it from different angles. After arguing to his audience that Psalm 95, a text written many centuries earlier, speaks directly to their lives, the author of Hebrews declares, "For the word of God is living and active" (Heb. 4:12). For a text to be "living and active" means that it is capable of constantly speaking afresh to ever new situations and contexts. The biblical narrative accomplishes this through processes of inspiration—the idea that the Spirit of God is active in the process of communication. Though the Marvel Universe holds no pretensions of inspiration, it boasts of a similar flexibility to speak to different contexts, in different time periods, and with different functions by virtue of its ongoing, self-renewing, and overarching narrative. It is, in short, a "living mythology" (Bahlmann 2016, 169).

Mythological stories illuminate (although, as Matthew Brake demonstrates in his essay in this book, they also have the potential to conceal): they can help us to see ourselves and the world around us more clearly. This illuminative function, combined with the narrative flexibility built into the Marvel Universe, allows these stories to serve as potent vessels for theological reflection. The essays in this book demonstrate this potential; yet before engaging them, a few comments are in order. First, the stories of the Marvel Universe communicate their theological message typically in subtle ways, weaving theological ideas and implications within the very fabric of the tale. Whereas the injection of explicitly religious elements (Christian, Jewish, etc.) is relatively rare within these stories, implicit religious symbolism and more subtle typological or Christological/Messianic themes and motifs are more common, presented in a way that leaves the interpretation open to the reader (Arnaudo 2010, 41–43; Holdier 2018, 79–80).

Second, much is often made of the comparison between the superheroes of today and the gods of ancient mythologies. However, I agree with Travis Smith that it is not the godlike powers of these heroes, what Smith calls their "faux-divinity," but their *character* that makes them heroes (Smith 2018, 7–8). Even so, it is vital not to foreground character at the expense of narrative. In other words, it is not their character alone, divorced from narrative, that defines the superhero, but their character expressed *through* narrative. Character and story share a symbiotic relationship: story shapes character while character propels story. Consequently, it is *the story*, within which larger-than-life powers are wielded and virtuous ethics displayed, that engages our theological imagination. Not only that, but sometimes it may be the irresponsible use of power in the story or the practice of not-so-virtuous ethics that prompts the theological imagination. The essays in this book are an exploration of select Marvel stories, but they are the stories not only of heroes, but also of villains, antiheroes, and anti-villains.

Third, the fundamental issues and questions that have long driven theological and philosophical reflection are the same issues and questions that drive superhero stories (Saunders 2011, 15). The conflict between good and evil, the nature of responsibility, the ethics of violence, and explorations of sacrifice, service, redemption, and power are all constitutive of both sacred stories and the stories of the Marvel Universe. This shared obsession makes Marvel stories fertile ground for the mining of theological insight and opens the door to an abundance of possibilities for fruitful dialogue.

OVERVIEW OF ESSAYS

The theological framework for the essays in this book is that of the Abrahamic religions (Christianity, Judaism, and, to a lesser extent, Islam). This is mainly due to the historical development of the Marvel Universe, which has occurred primarily within the Judeo-Christian heritage (with occasional connections to Islam, such as the most recent incarnation of Ms. Marvel), as well as to the constraints of putting together an anthology of essays in which the content is heavily dependent upon the specific interests of the contributors. As the Marvel Universe continues to embrace diversity in the years to come, I expect that trend to be increasingly reflected in the scholarship produced.

The essays in this book reflect a high degree of diversity, however, in terms of genre, theme, and type of analysis. Restricting the content to a specific genre (comic books, for instance) or having all of the essays follow a specific style of analysis (say, character study) would arguably generate greater simplicity. However, the essays in this book witness to the abundant possibilities for theological analysis by representing various approaches and perspectives. The book as a whole adopts a cross-genre approach, with the subject matter coming from Marvel comics, Marvel films, and Marvel television. The narrative of the Marvel Universe is itself a cross-genre narrative, with comic books often serving as the inspiration for film and television. However, this is not a one-way street. Increasingly, the popularity of Marvel films and television shows has dictated which comic books are published and the storylines that populate them.

This collection begins with a grouping of essays that explore themes of sacrifice and violence from different angles. Kristen Leigh Mitchell examines *The Infinity Saga* cycle of MCU films as a means of probing the moral limits of utilitarianism and demonstrating that the theological notion of *kenosis* is key for defining true sacrifice. Whereas Mitchell exposes some flaws in traditional theological conceptions of sacrifice, Taylor Ott explores some of the social implications of sacrificial theology by interpreting the Netflix series *Jessica Jones* in the light of feminist and womanist theologies. Ott argues that the series challenges the traditional patriarchal virtue of self-sacrifice in favor of the virtues of flourishing and survival. Then Matthew Brake looks at Jonathan Hickman's 2012–2015 run on *The Avengers* and *New Avengers* in light of René Girard's theory on sacrifice and violence, helping us to better grasp our own cultural inclinations toward violence and the roads that can lead us down. Relying on three runs of the X-Men comics, Dan Clanton explores how the Bible is sometimes distorted into a justification for violence against one's enemies. In doing so, he holds up a mirror to religious tensions in our own society and shows how these comic stories offer insight into dealing with real-world, religiously based violence. Then, Tim Posada takes us on a deep dive into Thanos' violent ideology, using the villain as a lens through which to view issues related to social change and the interrelation of the material and the spiritual.

As Marvel's stories are heavily character driven, they provide a natural means for addressing issues of identity and moral development. Levi Morrow, accordingly, analyzes the "theology of the past" found in Netflix's *Luke Cage*. In dialogue with Franz Rosenzweig's exploration of "creation" and "revelation," Morrow surfaces some fundamental ways in which the past shapes present identity. Gregory Stevenson utilizes Dan Slott's run on *The Amazing Spider-Man* and *The Superior Spider-Man*, as well as the film *Spider-Man: Homecoming*, to argue that it is not Peter Parker's obsession with responsibility that defines his character, but rather the particular way he defines that responsibility, a way that coheres well with the biblical theology of weakness. Then Jeremy Scarbrough looks at the character of Venom in relation to Kierkegaard's "double danger." He shows how the symbiotic nature of the "Venom skin" and its corresponding internal struggle between villain and hero illustrates vital aspects of character formation and ethics. In his essay on Netflix's *Daredevil*, Daniel Clark examines Matt Murdock's troubled relationship with his Catholic faith and the important role of mentors as moral and spiritual guides.

Two essays, in particular, draw our attention to some broader complexities and issues related to the process of creating Marvel stories. Austin Freeman takes us into the cosmic realm by comparing Neoplatonic hierarchies of divinity with the hierarchy of divinity within the Marvel Universe as a way of getting us to think more deeply about Marvel's "nested stories" and God's role as the Divine Author. Andrew Tobolowsky uses the Thor movies as an example of interconnected storytelling and myth inheritance, demonstrating the important role of individual creativity in mythic reinvention.

Marvel's stories are a reflection of the times in which they are produced and, as such, they can help us think through societal tensions in ways that demonstrate both pitfalls and hopeful possibilities. Kevin Nye's reading of *Thor: Ragnarok* in the light of postcolonial theology offers some critical lessons for American Christian history as well as hope for some positive ways forward. Amanda Furiasse examines the character of Sabra as a representation of Marvel's attempt to address Israeli-Palestinian relations and the potential for reconciliation, while Andrew Thrasher explores the tensions between science and the supernatural in the modern worldview and how the *Dr. Strange* film highlights the role of the imagination in re-enchanting our world.

As editor of this book, I have greatly enjoyed reading (and re-reading) each of these essays. In the process, I have gained new and valuable insights into diverse areas of theological exploration as well as into these fascinating stories that populate the Marvel Universe, and I have no doubt that readers will find themselves equally enlightened. The stories of the Marvel Universe have inspired readers and viewers for decades with their tales of heroism, hope, and even, sometimes, tragedy. These stories move us, challenge us, and make us think. It is my hope that the essays in this book will do justice to that legacy.

Chapter One

What Did It Cost? Sacrifice and Kenosis in *The Infinity Saga*

Kristen Leigh Mitchell

Traditionally, comic book films are appreciated for providing cathartic experiences of moral clarity through the depiction of good triumphing over evil. Following a narrative structure that Joseph Campbell called the "hero's journey," these stories typically center on a protagonist whose struggles propel them on a path of personal transformation and fulfillment. The effectiveness of such films depends largely on the audience's ability to bond with the main character, in order to experience a vicarious moral victory through a psychological identification with the hero's challenges and triumphs.

While these films often reach mythological proportions that border on the religious, one of the criticisms of the genre is its tendency to offer a relatively one-dimensional portrayal of evil. Villains, at times, seem to be little more than demonic archetypes serving as plot foils for the hero. In this sense, the genre has not strayed much from the standard action film, which Terry Christensen summed up in his study of American cinema: "the bad guys act out of greed or ambition, and the good guys act to stop the bad guys" (1987, 213).

But as C.S. Lewis once quipped, "you can be good for the mere sake of goodness; you cannot be bad for the mere sake of badness . . . no one ever did a cruel action simply because cruelty is wrong" (2001, 44). It is when good ends are sought in excess of what is necessary, or at the expense of others, that we begin to speak of evil. Hannah Arendt, the Jewish reporter who was invited to witness the trial of Holocaust organizer Adolf Eichmann, spoke of the "banality of evil" (2006). John Milbank explains, "the horror of Auschwitz . . . is not the revelation of evil perpetrated for its own sake, but rather a demonstration that even the most seemingly absolute evil tends to be carried out by people who imagine, albeit reluctantly, that they are fulfilling the goods of order, obedience, political stability, and social peace" (2003, 2).

This is why Christian theologians from Augustine to Aquinas and all the way up to the present have spoken of evil not as an eternal or substantive aspect of existence, but as a *privatio boni*—a privation, or perversion, of the good. Augustine characterized sin as *concupiscentia,* or "distorted desire." In other words, it is a good outcome, sought badly. Even the figure of Satan is understood in orthodox Christian theology as having "fallen" from goodness. Within this theological context, then, evil does not really "exist"—at least not in any necessary, eternal, or inevitable sense. Rather, evil is understood to *emerge* as the consequence of distortions in human thinking, resulting from the psychological limitations and cultural paradigms into which we are born. These distorted lenses cause us to develop a godlike sense of subjectivity that corrupts our moral discernment and blinds us to the effects of our actions on others.

Christians refer to this basic condition of moral confusion as "original sin." The ideologies and orientations we absorb from birth impress upon our understanding of the world in ways that disguise themselves as innate. Sin thus appears to us most commonly under the guise of "common sense," orderliness, and the relative peace of the status quo. As John McDowell explains in his discussion of original sin:

> such an inheritance assumes that its own way of seeing the world and acting in it is not only legitimate but natural—its contingency and arbitrariness are accordingly masked. That is why those inculcated into the various forms of racism, patriarchalism, consumerism, and imperialism . . . fail to see through their identity-determining beliefs and find all manner of ways to justify them. (2007, 56)

These distortions convert our need for physical security into greed and mistrust, our desire for love and affection into narcissistic ambition or blind obedience, and our right to autonomy into preemptive violence. Many commentators have identified this threefold struggle over "possessions, prestige, and power" as a theme weaving throughout the Scriptures (Rohr 1995, 18). An oft-overlooked passage in Genesis reveals these three core struggles to be at the heart of what tempts Eve to eat from the tree of knowledge: she sees that it is good for food, that it is a delight to the eyes, and that it is desirable to make one wise (3:6). These three issues lie at the heart of the three main challenges faced by the Israelites during their forty years in the wilderness, as well as the three temptations Jesus overcomes during his forty days in the desert, revealing himself to be the human who was "without sin" (Myers 1997).

Evil, then, is not something or someone that should be thought to exist *out there*—a "bad guy" who can finally be eradicated by the "good guys." Sin, rather, is always lurking at our own doorstep (Gen. 4:7). Indeed, it is often precisely when we start to project evil onto others that we are most likely to become its unwitting perpetrators ourselves. Biblical scholar Walter Wink has therefore criticized the comic book genre for its propagation of what he calls *the myth of redemptive violence*: the belief that violence against "evil" will save us. Wink argues convincingly that this myth is in fact the dominant religion of our day—far more prevalent than Judaism, Christianity, Islam, or Buddhism. It is so effective precisely because it is largely invisible. "Violence simply appears to be the nature of things," Wink writes. "It seems inevitable" (1998, 42).

While *The Infinity Saga* certainly participates in the perpetuation of this myth through an overall adherence to the standard tropes of the genre, the saga taken as a whole also offers an impressive attempt to deconstruct it from within, as an increasingly complex set of villains are met by an increasingly nuanced assortment of heroes who struggle constantly with the question of what makes them any different from their enemies. As Captain America remarks in *Age of Ultron*, "Ultron thinks we're monsters. That *we're* what's wrong with the world. This isn't just about beating him. It's about whether he's right."

"Every villain is a hero in his own story and believes that what they're doing is right," Joe Russo observed in an interview with the Motion Picture Association of America (Abrams 2018). This insight led to the decision to cast one of Marvel's greatest supervillains in the role of the protagonist for *Avengers: Infinity War.* One only needs to consider masterpieces of cinema like *The Godfather, A Clockwork Orange,* and *American Psycho* to appreciate the chilling effect that protagonist villains can have on audiences, who find themselves sympathizing with the main character even while maintaining the sense that their actions are wrong.

But the Russo brothers took this approach even further, attempting to place the protagonist villain within a kind of "hero's journey," resulting in one of the most hauntingly realistic portrayals of evil ever seen in a major comic book film. Its effect on audiences was an almost total inversion of the kind of moral clarity one typically expects from the genre, as an unusually large number of fans came away from the film arguing that the villain was right. Memes and YouTube videos began circulating in Thanos' defense, and t-shirts were printed endorsing "Thanos for president." The general speculation as to whether Thanos had a point inspired sites like Vox and Forbes to publish lengthy articles in consultation with scientists and economists to seriously consider the question. Their conclusions were divided.

This was not a simple case of misaimed fandom. Interviews with the Russos make it clear that this effect was intentional, as the events in the film were skewed in order to wholly reflect Thanos' point of view. An earlier version of the throne room scene in which Gamora condemns Thanos for kidnapping, orphaning, and imprisoning her was later replaced with the version we see in the final film, in which Thanos appears rational and benevolent while the fiercest woman in the galaxy is reduced to an angry child, incapable of understanding the difficult decisions that her father has to make. The rest of the Avengers are likewise depicted as weak, incompetent, arrogant, and impotent as they try to stop Thanos by brute force. Nowhere in the film does anyone confront the mad Titan with the mathematical or scientific flaws in his ideology, and even Dr. Strange's reference to genocide seems to fall flat in light of Thanos' seemingly more nuanced perspective.

In this way, *Infinity War* was crafted precisely to disrupt the audience's perceptions of who is good and who is evil, challenging us to dig deeper in our moral discernment. Unfortunately, many casual moviegoers are ill-equipped to engage in this level of analysis, especially when confronted with the same consequentialist logic that is built into the fabric of our social, economic, and political lives. Our common life is grounded in a "utilitarian" approach to ethics that determines what is good based on outcomes, favoring whatever maximizes happiness and well-being for the majority of people (however ambiguously defined), regardless of the means by which that outcome is sought.

From this perspective, Thanos' argument actually seems to make sense. Even the articles that set out to find flaws in his ideology were mostly limited to a utilitarian point of view: Thanos was only "wrong" if it could be determined that his idea wouldn't have worked anyway—either because by destroying half of all life he would be destroying many things which were themselves "resources," or because either way, within a couple hundred years, the universe would be right back to where it started, and the sacrifice would need to be repeated all over again.

But perhaps this is what Thanos means in *Avengers: Endgame* when he says that he is "inevitable." At its core, utilitarianism entails a premise that a certain amount of suffering and inequality are natural and therefore inevitable. Creative and collaborative alternatives are often overlooked in favor of mathematical risk assessment and the justification of losses as collateral damage on the way to a desired outcome. Several studies have linked utilitarian responses to psychopathy and a diminished capacity for empathy (Wiech et al. 2013). At its worst, this cold and calculating mindset leads to processes of dehumanization that determine the value of a human life based on its usefulness toward a goal, as Thanos values the lives of everyone around him, even his most loyal servant Ebony Maw.

For this reason, many are quick to disagree with utilitarian logic in theory, arguing that the ends should never justify the means. And yet, this perspective remains relatively ubiquitous in practice, as demonstrated by the classic "trolley dilemma"—a thought experiment in which a person is told that they control the switch to a trolley that is hurtling uncontrollably down a track toward five people, a disaster that can only be averted by flipping the switch and redirecting the car onto another track, where it will only kill one person. Multiple studies have shown that approximately 90 percent of people will choose to kill the one person in order to save five—unless that person happens to be someone they love, in which case the percentage drops to about one-third (Cloud 2011).

Trolley dilemmas abound in comic book films. DC fans will recognize this as one of the classic dilemmas faced by both Batman and Superman. Sam Raimi's *Spider-Man* places Peter Parker in a similar predicament, having to choose between his beloved Mary Jane and a group of children trapped in an actual trolley car. The first *Avengers* movie also culminates in a classic trolley dilemma, as the World Security Council decides to destroy New York in order to prevent the Chitauri from invading the rest of the planet. Typically, our heroes always manage to find a "third way"—a creative solution that reveals the tragic flaw in utilitarian logic: it demands a sacrifice.

Anthropologist René Girard has helpfully unveiled the complex psychological mechanisms that underlie our cultural fixation with sacrifice. All human societies, Girard argues, seek to quell the escalation of violence through deeply internalized and unconscious patterns of transference that allow for ritualized forms of violence to be carried out against surrogate victims whose sacrifices are perceived as necessary for the greater good. Responsibility for such sacrifices is typically either projected onto "the gods," or onto the victims themselves. But the true purpose of the surrogate is pragmatic: to prevent the escalation of internal violence by satisfying the community's desire for vengeance against an object that can be externalized and eradicated. Sacrificial victims are nearly always selected from among the socially marginalized, since those who have no one to avenge their deaths can be made to suffer without any threat of further escalation or retaliation (Girard 1977, 11–15).

Walter Wink's notion of "the myth of redemptive violence" points to how these processes get inscribed mythologically onto human cultures, tricking us into thinking that such sacrifices are not only necessary, but natural and inevitable. Our entire concept of civilization gets framed as a kind of trolley dilemma writ large and played out *ad nauseam.* Peace always comes at a cost. From this perspective, the "hero" is someone who is willing to sacrifice themselves voluntarily, so that others will not have to be sacrificed unwillingly. The "*super*-hero," then, is a hero whose special powers or prowess enable them to avoid dying, so that they can repeat the voluntary sacrifice over and over again.

And yet these repeated sacrifices only serve to reinforce the underlying notion that the *need* for sacrifice will always continue, with no conceivable end in sight. This highlights one of the main problems associated with the sacrificial mindset (aside from its basis in deception and its predilection for establishing and maintaining patterns of oppression against the marginalized): it requires endless repetition in order for it to "work." Sacrifice is preventative, not curative, which is why the ritual needs to be repeated over and over again (Girard 1977, 102). It never truly offers a solution to the problem that it seeks to resolve. As long as people continue to believe that violence can bring an end to violence, it remains self-propagating, as Girard has shown, since "everyone wants to strike the last blow, and reprisal can thus follow reprisal without any true conclusion ever being reached" (1977, 26).

Captain America speaks from the prototypical hero's perspective in Marvel's *The Avengers* when he slights Tony for not being one to make the "sacrifice play," for not being willing to lay himself down on a wire and let someone crawl over him. Tony offers the typical superhero's response: "I would just cut the wire," which is precisely what he does at the end of the film when he redirects the bomb intended for New York toward the Chitauri spacecraft. But beginning in phase two, we start to see some of the costs associated with both models of heroism, and the blind spots of the sacrificial method are revealed. Over the course of the entire twenty-two-film saga, we follow Tony and Cap on a kind of double hero's journey, as they grapple in parallel but opposing ways with the limitations of the myth of redemptive violence, realizing that in the real world of triage, sometimes even our best efforts to help still result in unintended consequences. Sometimes not everyone gets saved. Sometimes more enemies are created in the process. In light of these complexities, how do we know when we are on the side of "good"? What does it mean to do the "right" thing?

"A SOUL FOR A SOUL": SACRIFICIAL VIOLENCE VERSUS CHRISTIAN *KENOSIS*

Underneath all those action-packed fighting scenes between good guys and bad guys, the films of *The Infinity Saga* are engaging in a deeper investigation of the moral limits of utilitarian violence and the true nature of heroism in relation to sacrifice. *Avengers: Infinity War* brings this exploration to a fever pitch, as multiple characters struggle with the question of whether and when a preemptive sacrifice might be necessary for the sake of a greater good. Peter Quill faces his own trolley dilemma when deciding whether to pull the trigger on Gamora in order to prevent Thanos from getting the Soul Stone. Wanda faces the same problem when deciding whether or not to destroy Vision in order to prevent Thanos from getting the Mind Stone. Both ultimately choose to go through with the deed, only to have the outcomes of their sacrifices annulled by Thanos, who nevertheless praises them for their actions. "I like him," the deranged father says of his daughter's boyfriend after he demonstrates his willingness to kill her. In this, Thanos sees a bit of himself in Peter.

These two sacrifices bookend and parallel Thanos' own sacrifice of that which he "loves," in one of the most controversial and heart-wrenching scenes of the entire saga. Gamora, unwilling to sacrifice the life of her sister Nebula in order to protect the Soul Stone's whereabouts, accompanies Thanos to Vormir, only to be sacrificed there at the altar of his benevolent delusions. With tears streaming down his cheeks, the mad Titan hurls the one and only creature he has ever allowed himself to care about to her death. The Soul Stone, apparently indifferent to Thanos' motivations, accepts his murder of Gamora as a legitimate sacrificial exchange—"a soul for a soul."

What kind of "wisdom" is this? "This isn't love," Gamora rightfully protests just before being tossed over the edge. And of course, it *isn't* love—at least not in any modern or Christian sense of the word. For regardless of whatever feelings of attachment or admiration that Thanos came to feel toward the young woman he abducted from Zen-Whoberis, his actions on Vormir demonstrate that he ultimately sees her just like he sees everyone else—as a means to an end. Thus, in the very act of "sacrificing" Gamora in order to obtain that which he wants, Thanos discredits any claim on "love," since love is that which compels us to sacrifice our own needs and desires for the sake of the other.

But perhaps this is to impose a Christian theological concept onto a film in which no such framework exists. After all, *The Infinity Saga* does not seem to be interested in the nature of love, but only in the nature of sacrifice. However, it is important to note that Thanos does not toss Gamora over the edge in order to obtain the stone out of a purely self-motivated agenda. Rather, he does so precisely in order to fulfill what he believes to be a higher calling, one that is ostensibly for the sake of others. In other words, Thanos counts himself among the small percentage of people who are willing to kill someone they love for the sake of a greater good. It is for this reason that Thanos "mourns," believing himself to have made the greatest sacrifice of all.

If the prospect of having to kill someone you love—particularly your own child—in order to remain obedient to a higher calling is a story that sounds at all familiar, it is because this is exactly how later theological tradition came to interpret not only the story of Abraham and Isaac, but the entire Christian conception of God in the doctrine of substitutionary atonement: God had to sacrifice his only Son in order to save humanity from an even worse fate. In *Endgame*, when Thanos threatens to reduce everything down to its last atom if that's what it takes to create a grateful universe, Cap castigates him, saying it would be a universe "born out of blood." But one might ask how this is any different from the God of Genesis who destroyed the earth with flood in order to create it anew. Indeed, is not our entire Christian narrative that of a world bought by blood? Whether or not the parallels between the Western Christian conception of God and one of the greatest super villains of all time were intentional, these similarities certainly invite us to reconsider the theology that makes such a comparison possible.

In fact, the MCU's depiction of the Soul Stone resonates with the creation myths of many ancient societies—indeed, the imagery of tossing a sacrificial victim off a cliff points directly to stories of human sacrifice found in ancient Greek literature and mythology (Girard 1977, 94–98). Wink summarizes the theme of these ancient myths as "the story of the victory of order over chaos by means of violence . . . the ideology of conquest, the original religion of the status quo" (Wink 1998, 48).

The Babylonian story of *Enuma Elish* is one of the oldest known creation myths, and a primary example of how ancient cultures inscribed sacrificial violence into their understanding of the universe. Recited every year in the spring, it tells the story of how the universe was created out of a bloody contest between the Divine Feminine—represented by the dragon Tiamat—and her son Marduk—a prince who sought sovereignty over the world. On the battlefield, Marduk slays his mother by slicing her body in two, and from these two halves he creates the heavens and the earth (Dalley 1989). This is *literally* a world "born out of blood," as human beings are created from the blood of Tiamat's fallen army commander, for the purpose of being slaves to the gods. Sacrificial violence in exchange for the gods' favor thus becomes a necessity that is written into the very foundations of the universe.

This understanding of the cosmos was radically contrasted by the biblical creation story found in Genesis 1. Recorded during the Babylonian exile, the first chapter of Genesis borrows language directly from *Enuma Elish* in order to present a counternarrative that turned their captors' understanding of the world on its head (Carr 1996). A remarkably earthy text by comparison, the Hebrew creation story is rooted in phenomenological observations of the universe as an interconnected whole manifesting in dialectical tensions—darkness and light, day and night, earth and sky, air and water, plants and animals, work and rest—*all* of which was declared to be good.

The affirmation that "it was good" is repeated eight times, as though to insist that despite the seeming ubiquity of war, death, and human clamoring for possessions, prestige, and power, the universe is *not* born out of sacrifice and bloodshed, but out of water, breath, spirit, and the creative will of a primordial imagination. Human beings were *not* created to be slaves to the gods, but are made in the image of their Creator, imbued with the seeds of creative imagination and the inherent longing for relationship. The instruction to "be fruitful and multiply" reframes the entire focus of existence from debt and death to life and abundance.

William Gilders argues that the blood sacrifice rituals of the Hebrew tradition represented a deconstruction of the sacrificial rites practiced by surrounding cultures. Rather than seeking to placate or appease the gods by raising up the smoke of burnt offerings, the Israelites understood themselves to be sharing a meal with their Creator (Gilders 2004, 12–32). Naturally, these meals occurred at God's dwelling place—the Temple at Jerusalem—but this was not the only site where transformation was expected to occur. Sacrificial rituals were considered valid only insofar as they were accompanied by a transformation of the people, made manifest in practices that gave special consideration to the marginalized. Acts of love and mercy thus took pride of place over ritual executions (Hosea 6:6).

Whenever the Israelites lost their way in this regard—either by forgetting their responsibility to the marginalized, or by falling into the idolatrous habit of making sacrifices to other gods in the hopes of getting their needs and desires met—prophets rose up to remind the Hebrew people that they had been chosen by God to follow a different path: "I have had enough of burnt offerings. . . . I do not delight in the blood of bulls, or of lambs, or of goats. . . . Your hands are full of blood. Wash yourselves; make yourselves clean. Cease to do evil, learn to do good; seek justice, rescue the oppressed" (Isaiah 1:11, 15–17).

This reframing of ancient sacrificial practices can be found not only in the prophetic texts, but also in stories that may seem from a modern perspective to reinforce such practices. The story of Abraham and Isaac is unique in its historical context not because a god asks a man to sacrifice his child, but because the God of the Israelites tells Abraham *not* to, and provides him with a ram instead. Similarly, what is unique about the story of Noah is not that the Creator destroys the earth with a great flood (most Mesopotamian cultures had a flood story), but that in the Hebrew variation of this myth, God offers the unique promise that nothing like this will ever happen again (Brueggemann 2010, 73–88).

The Hebrew deconstruction of sacrifice reached a climax in 70 AD, when the Temple of Jerusalem was destroyed by the Romans. A few decades earlier, a homeless rabbi of questionable parentage from a disreputable part of Galilee was put to death in the most shameful manner possible: crucifixion. This unspeakably gruesome form of state-sanctioned murder was reserved especially for those who threatened the order and sovereignty of Rome—an empire whose rulers called themselves "sons of god" (Peppard 2011, 46–49). The Gospel tradition thus relays the story of how a poor Nazarene was killed by the Roman government after being accused of sedition by a belligerent mob desperate to prove its loyalties to the empire (John 19:6–16).

Shortly after this tragic event, a rogue band of Israelites began traveling around making the bold claim that this man had been *the* "Son of God," and that his death on a Roman cross constituted a final "sacrifice," *for the entire world*. Furthermore, these disciples claimed that this man had been raised from the dead, a miracle signaling the annulment of death's power. This effectively disempowered all rulers who sought to wield the fear of death in the service of power at the expense of the marginalized. Jesus' death exposed the violent underbelly of "pax Romana," laying bare the tragic consequences of the collusion between empire and religion, and his resurrection rendered all such powers null. Terry Eagleton writes:

> It is Jesus' dedication to justice and fellowship that delivers him to the cross. His solidarity with those who dwell in the borderlands of orthodox society, men and women whose existence signifies a kind of non-being, prefigures the non-being to which he himself is brought. . . . So it is that an act of state brutality also signifies a symbolic undoing of political violence. . . . Authentic power is at war with the status quo, given that its source lies in solidarity with weakness. (2019, 26–27)

Jesus' crucifixion thus radically transforms the concept of "sacrifice" from a necessary loss pursued for the good of the social order to the more radical and subversive sense of *self*-sacrifice, not pursued as an obligatory form of self-denial, but rather a liberation of the self from itself—the position from which we are able to truly stand in solidarity with the suffering and the marginalized, even unto death. Paul's word for this new understanding of sacrifice was *kenosis,* a Greek word meaning to "empty oneself" (Phil. 2:7). For Paul and the early Christians, *kenosis* was not merely a description of something God *did*, but of *who God is* (Moltmann 1974, 205). The God of Moses, who called himself "I AM," was a God whose very nature came to be revealed in the active emptying of Selfhood into Other. This notion of the Divine was later inscribed into Christian tradition as the doctrine of *perichoresis*—a singular God whose nature was characterized as an interpersonal "dance" of Threeness in Oneness.

This radical, paradoxical, and unprecedented understanding of God impels Christians to find their identity precisely in the practice of losing it (Luke 17:33). For the early Christian martyrs, this meant making an empowered leap into their own literal deaths when the cruelty of state-sanctioned murder was inescapable. But for most Christians, the process entails a much slower transformation over time, through everyday relational practices. Karen Armstrong writes, "the habitual practice of compassion and the Golden Rule 'all day and every day' demands perpetual *kenosis*, the constant stepping outside our own preferences, convictions, and prejudices" (2009, 328).

This practice of "self-emptying" cuts through the distorted programming of our "original sin" by inviting us to de-center our own perspective and open ourselves to the experiences of others. This process typically involves a certain amount of conflict and grief, as the satisfying delusions that have maintained the negative peace of our personal status quos are brought forth to die at the altar of reciprocal truth. This is precisely what is at stake in the recognition of privilege, and in relinquishing the various forms of power we have over others in any given context. Only through an acknowledgment of our fundamental interdependence can we move into a communal and contextual kind of truth that is neither blinded by the illusion of objectivity, nor trapped in the nihilistic relativism of subjectivity. A third way emerges, one in which we discover a much deeper sense of identity extending beyond the individual self—a phenomenon that Paul referred to as "the body of Christ" (1 Cor. 12:12–31).

It is important to distinguish this understanding of *kenosis* from the more obligatory and submissive form of self-sacrifice that later came to dominate Western Christian culture. Jesus taught that the poor, the oppressed, and those who suffer for justice are "blessed" (Matthew 5:3–12) not because poverty or oppression are good or necessary, but because marginalized people already know how to de-center their own experience. The challenge in this case is to avoid rationalizing past experiences of oppression as necessary sacrifices for some greater good, which only works to justify and conceal violence, and ultimately results in its recapitulation, as Girard has shown. The oppressed either identify with their suffering, and seek out repeated experiences of subjugation, or project it onto a new surrogate, becoming oppressors themselves. The way of Jesus offers a chance to halt this cycle, by inviting us to unmask the truth about our suffering, and finally grieve it. Only then can we transform our pain into a wisdom that can truly be placed in the service of empathy and solidarity.

In *Captain America: Civil War,* Vision notes a rise in the number of conflicts since Tony donned his first Iron Man suit, suggesting a possible causality. But the real correlation is the opposite of what he assumes: it is not that strength incites conflict by inviting challenge, but that solidarity with the oppressed *exposes* conflicts that would otherwise have remained hidden underneath the surface of our peaceful, everyday lives. Tony's journey of *kenosis* begins under just such conditions, working as a weapons manufacturer for the U.S. military. He is totally inured to the costs of war until he becomes his own collateral damage. Out of this experience of suffering, he forges a new identity that allows him to stand in solidarity with others—an identity that he cannot give up, no matter how many times he tries. Even Pepper finally realizes that for Tony, Iron Man was never just a job. Tony *is* Iron Man, and this is what makes his snap meaningful in the end—not because it represents a dutiful sacrifice carried out for the sake of a greater good, but because it was the final manifestation of a life lived according to an unshakeable commitment to stand with those who suffer, all the way up to the end.

Natasha's final leap into death on Vormir can be similarly re-framed. The absence of a fully fleshed-out backstory within *The Infinity Saga* echoes the erasure of identity and dehumanization that Natasha experienced in her assassin's training, making her narrative arc within the films doubly tragic. Having built the need for sacrificial death into the universe, the Russo brothers framed her self-sacrifice in utilitarian terms, believing that this constituted a redemptive conclusion for the former assassin (Breznican 2019). Girard's work, however, would suggest that her character's marginalized status within the films made her the most likely to be sacrificed. This situation, when seen through the lens of the early Christian martyrs, allows for a different interpretation of her sacrifice to emerge: when faced with the cruel but inescapable demand for sacrificial death—a situation created by those in power, but presented as though it were demanded by the gods—the martyr transforms that which was a compulsory task into a free decision. Eagleton writes:

> the evolution of sacrifice arrives when the victim themselves becomes conscious of their condition, and in doing so assumes agency of the event. . . . What was a process to be endured becomes a project to be executed. Those who are cast out can now be signs of the criminal nature of the status quo, and by making this destiny their own, can become the cornerstone of the new dispensation. (2019, 50–51)

"WHY DOES SOMEONE ALWAYS HAVE TO DIE IN THIS SCENARIO?"

Christ's incarnation and resurrection established a radical posture toward existence that was life-affirming to its core. Just as the Hebrew creation narrative shifted the perspective of the Israelites from death to life in the midst of the Babylonian exile, this new understanding of a God who was able to work through death itself to make all things new again established a radical paradigm shift that eradicated death's sovereignty over human consciousness. This humbling and empowering faith flourished for centuries in the cities and deserts surrounding the Mediterranean. Emperors came and went—some of whom supported the Christians, and some of whom persecuted them. But it was not until the turn of the millennium that the faith itself was fully infil-trated by the old imperial logic.

Brock and Parker trace this shift to Charlemagne's establishment of the Holy Roman Empire, and to Pope Urban II's subsequent reversal of a thou-sand years of church tradition by lifting the Christian prohibition on the spill-ing of human blood. Rather than having to repent of their sins prior to being baptized, soldiers could now kill as a *means* of being cleansed from sin. The Roman church also created new Eucharistic language that turned Jesus' once-for-all sacrifice into something that would occur on the altar at every mass. Brock and Parker write, "At the dawn of the Holy Roman Empire, Christian-ity began to lose its grip on the sinfulness of killing. A new age began—one in which the execution of Jesus would become a sacrifice to be repeated, first on the Eucharistic altar, and then in the ravages of a full-blown holy war" (2008, 252). This gave birth to a particularly twisted iteration of the myth of redemptive violence, one that flipped the script on who was the victim and who was the villain. Those who invaded other people's lands could now be called "martyrs" and "defenders" of the Christian faith.

This shift further supported a new theory of Jesus' death posited in 1098 by Anselm of Canterbury, who tried to use the new feudal economic system as a metaphor for God's grace. Drawing on the experience of crushing debt that most people at the time faced, Anselm described how God in his mercy sent his only begotten Son to earth to die on a cross, in order to save humanity from the crushing weight of our sins—a debt that we owed to God but could never repay (Anselm 1969). This theology was flawed at the outset, part of a misguided pastoral effort to respond to an already-flawed question: why did Jesus *have* to die? Not only did this position place Jesus' death at the center of the faith—leaving his incarnation, resurrection, teachings, and miracles to fade into the background—but it presupposed that the violence must have been *necessary.* God must have *demanded* the sacrifice. Thus, Christian faith in the West finally yielded to the ancient sacrificial logic of imperial religion.

Of course, not everyone agreed with Anselm's theory (it was never adopted in the East). Even one of Anselm's own contemporaries objected: "how cruel and wicked it seems that anyone should demand the blood of an innocent per-son as the price for anything . . . still less that God should consider the death of his Son so agreeable that by it he should be reconciled to the whole world" (Abelard 1980). Nevertheless, Anselm's ideas took hold in the Western imagination, and suffering and sacrifice were glorified to the point of near-obsession. In fact, it was around this time that images of Jesus' crucifixion first began showing up in Christian art.

Rather than inviting Christians into a process of reciprocal selfhood in the context of life-affirming community, the satisfaction theory left Christians isolated in self-consciousness and guilt. Sin and repentance went from being an interpersonal and communal affair to an individualistic undertaking, characterized by private introspection and ritual purgation. Genuine *kenotic* de-centering gave way to an ego-driven form of self-denial that was deeply invested in its own self-righteousness. This toxic Western ideology of sacrifice was able to theologically rationalize nine crusades, medieval torture, the Inquisition, colonialism, native genocide, and chattel slavery.

At the first European slave market, medieval writer Zurara was inspired by the suffering of the newly enslaved Africans, who had been captured under the 1455 bull of Pope Nicholas V granting the King of Portugal the divine right to reduce any non-Christians found in foreign lands to perpetual slavery, and to appropriate their goods and lands to himself, for the sake of the Gospel. Speaking of the salvation that Zurara believed would be theirs because of their sacrifice, he prayed that God would "place before the eyes of these miserable people some awareness of the wonderful things that await them" (Zurara 2010). It is a sentiment hauntingly similar to Ebony Maw's words to the dying Asgardians in the opening scene of *Infinity War*: "You may think that this is suffering; no, it is salvation."

This is why Thanos' logic of salvation is as chilling as the American public's inability to discern its error: we cannot name the sins of Thanos without exposing our own. His ideology parallels that of the European colonizers, who valued the concept of resources and profit over human lives. Indeed, this is a mindset in which one human life can be sacrificially converted into a "resource" for the benefit of others. Seeking paradise and promising salvation, the colonizers brought genocide instead, and ultimately sacrificed nearly the entire existing population to create a "new world" for themselves—but it was a false paradise, born out of blood.

The Protestant Reformation sought to correct what it saw as errors in the Western religious understanding of sacrifice, but it mostly succeeded in rearranging the liturgical furniture. The weight of Anselm's debt was internalized, and imperial arrogance gave way to a delusional sense of personal responsibility that resulted in a highly individualistic culture marked by patterns of psychological splitting and facades of moral superiority. Later, the thinkers of the eighteenth and nineteenth centuries also attempted to correct the problem by limiting the influence of "religion" altogether, and sequestering conversations about truth, beauty, and goodness into the newly secularized realms of "science," "art," and "politics." But this only served to further disguise the influence of the old religion, and the sacrificial mindset found new forms of expression within a secular milieu.

Teilhard de Chardin, paleontologist and Jesuit priest from the early twentieth century, interpreted Darwin's findings on the evolution of species as wholly compatible with the creation story in Genesis 1. The universe was "passionately alive, throbbing, and pulsating with energy and growth," an interconnected and relational web of abundant life that was constantly engaged in the process of being fruitful and multiplying (Delio 2015, 37). Yet most of Darwin's contemporaries interpreted his observations within the more familiar narrative framework of survival, scarcity, and sacrifice, developing a secular version of the myth of redemptive violence in which the sacrifices of the weak were necessitated by the "gods" of biology through the process of natural selection.

A similar mindset was also imbedded in the new economic system of market-based capitalism: the fittest would survive through self-interest, competition, and the sacrifices of the working class. Rather than creating economic conditions that reflected the Christian belief in the inherent dignity and goodness of every living creature, modern capitalism created new class structures that framed the sacrifices of the poor as natural and inevitable. Dickens' character Ebenezer Scrooge famously embodies this attitude when he gripes: "If [the poor] would rather die, they had better do it, and decrease the surplus population" (Dickens 1911, 18).

Concerns about "overpopulation," while nothing new, have become increasingly widespread in the last century, partially on account of their association with rational, scientific reasoning. Most people assume that it was Darwin who first suggested that if we don't limit the population ourselves, nature will limit it for us through famines, plagues, and other natural disasters. But in fact, both Darwin and Scrooge were influenced by an eighteenth-century thinker named Thomas Malthus, who used a "simple calculus" to show that population grows exponentially while resources grow linearly, and determined that human catastrophe was inevitable unless certain controls, or corrections, were put into place.

Malthus sought to warn his fellow Englishmen that if we did not work to reduce the population, another plague like the one that eliminated half of all human life in Western Europe was inevitable:

> The power of population is so superior to the power of the earth to produce subsistence for man, that premature death must in some shape or other visit the human race. The vices of mankind are active and able ministers of depopulation . . . and often finish the dreadful work themselves. But should they fail in this war of extermination, sickly seasons, epidemics, pestilence, and plague advance in terrific array, and sweep off their thousands and tens of thousands. (Malthus 1798, 44)

However, Malthus was not a scientist; he was an Anglican priest with an eye on *kenosis*, which he interpreted within a utilitarian framework. He believed that scarcity was a situation ordained by God to teach virtuous, self-sacrificing behavior.

Malthus was critiqued by many of his contemporaries, and his "calculus" has now been all but debunked by population data collected over the last century, showing that the rate of global population growth has been on the decline since the 1960s, dropping off to sustainable levels particularly in areas with more equitable resource distribution (Roser et al. 2019). But the belief in the necessity of ritual purgation is strong, and Malthus' ideas continue to hold sway in American culture, especially among those who unwittingly accept his influence over evolutionary ethics and class-based economics. We hear Malthus on the left whenever environmentalists call for "population control" as a strategy for fighting climate change. We hear Malthus on the right whenever conservatives suggest that we could end poverty by getting poor people to stop having babies.

Aside from the scientific and sociological flaws of this strategy, Malthus' biggest error was, ironically, theological. By failing to consider humanity's innate capacity for innovation and cooperation—qualities that Christians believe are imprinted in us by a God who is both creative and relational—Malthus overlooked the possibility that human beings might actually be capable of finding ways to live in equitable relationship with one another, distributing resources to one another according to need, as the early Christians did (Acts 4:35). The insistence that greed and inequality are natural and inevitable only serves to justify and perpetuate endless cycles of violence and inequality, as Girard has shown.

"As long as it is assumed that war is always an available option," writes Stanley Hauerwas, "we will not be forced to imagine any alternative to war." And yet, even Girard, a scholar who devoted his life's work to naming and subverting these mechanisms, often fell into the habit of describing human origins in such a way that made them seem inevitable. These myths of origin are so powerful and persuasive because the sacrificial strategy is rooted in our existential anxiety about survival, which clouds our judgment and leaves us vulnerable to fear-based ideologies that seek to establish order and equilibrium at any cost. Thanos is willing to sacrifice "everything," even the whole universe, if that's what it takes to cleanse it of the destructive forces he believes led to his home planet's demise. He cannot see that his strategy only replicates those forces, rather than eradicating them.

Returning to our discussion of original sin, we see that fears about survival lie at the heart of our struggle over possessions, prestige, and power, as these are all methods by which we seek to cheat death. Christians interpret the "tree of Life" as Christ himself, who invites us into abundant life by destroying our fear of death. But when we eat from the "tree of the knowledge of good and evil," we begin dividing the world into "good guys" and "bad guys" and always see ourselves as justified, casting the blame onto another as Adam and Eve both do. On that day we "die," as *thanatos* becomes our new master.

Grasping for survival distorts our altruistic efforts, and frequently turns them into patterns of paternalism and abuse. This process is usually unconscious, which is why it is insufficient to frame *kenosis* merely in terms of "self-sacrifice" or focus on others. Tony, Cap, and Thanos all begin their journeys with some variation of this, drawing from the well of their own suffering in order to try and "help" others. In *Age of Ultron,* Tony's trauma-inspired protectiveness leads him to create Ultron—a character who mirrors Tony and foreshadows Thanos in the belief that he knows what is best for the world. Cap's initial hubris runs counter to this, but is likewise rooted in a basic orientation toward others; his dutiful commitment to self-sacrifice leads to the discovery that by following orders, he has been working for the enemy all along.

In *Civil War,* Tony and Cap find themselves on opposite sides of their initial positions, with Tony learning to appreciate oversight and a communal sense of responsibility, while Cap learns to trust his own instincts. In the end, Tony's path of *kenosis* leads him to embrace a larger sense of identity extending beyond his own personal survival, while Cap's *kenotic* journey means "sacrificing" the role of the sacrificial hero altogether, choosing to live out a normal life and die a normal death. Thanos, meanwhile, exhibits no such change. When confronted with failure, he simply doubles down on his original plan, blaming others for their ingratitude rather than recognizing his own error. Thus, his arc cannot be a true hero's journey, since it represents a kind of anti-growth, characterized by ever-deepening isolation and self-deception.

The true "hero," then, is more than someone willing to fight for their ideals, and it is more than someone who considers the greater good, or the needs of others. A hero is someone who is willing to learn, to grieve, to grapple, to grow, and ultimately to yield, in order to be shaped by the process of relationship. *The Infinity Saga* reminds us that we are all both hero and villain, both wise and foolish, both selfish and compassionate, both vulnerable and strong, and that the only thing really stopping any of us from becoming like Thanos are those *kenotic* moments that invite us to soften our view on the world, to lean into our pain, to loosen the clenched fist we have around the certainty of our own self-righteousness, and to let go of our dogmatic perceptions of who we think we are supposed to be. This is never an individualistic path of heroism, but always a communal process of mutual transformation.

Chapter Two

"I Was Never the Hero that You Wanted Me to Be"

The Ethics of Self-Sacrifice and Self-Preservation in Jessica Jones

Taylor J. Ott

While the classic superheroes of comics' golden age—for instance, Superman, Captain America, Wonder Woman—functioned as predictably salvific Christ-figures in their stories, the title character of the Netflix series *Jessica Jones* fits squarely within the deconstructive tendencies of the so-called "Third Age," or postmodern era, of superheroes (Oropeza 2005b, 7–18). Cynical and abrasive, Jessica not only introduces personality complexities to the archetype but causes her audience to reframe the questions that superhero stories are expected to ask. Her journey is characterized by the complexities of human problems instead of primarily by super-human ones as she deals with themes of trauma, addiction, and a general sense of emotional turmoil; so rather than analyzing how a character's heroism provides a parallel to biblical stories like that of Moses or Jesus, Jessica's troubled navigation of her world causes us to ask "does having superpowers mean that one is obliged to act like a hero?"

The Netflix original series *Jessica Jones*[1] is perhaps most notable for its darkness. The series tackles themes of sexual assault and coercion, sexual and physical violence, addiction, and mental illness head on and does not look away when those things get difficult to talk about. Season one revolves around the title character's attempt to track down and capture the season's villain, Kilgrave, who possesses the super-ability to make people obey any command he gives them. His super-skill makes for interesting storytelling since it means that action sequences between him and Jessica are rare; instead, he sends others to do his bidding and Jessica is required to restrain her super-strength and propensity for "guided falling" ("AKA The Sandwich Saved Me," 1.5) so that she does not seriously harm her attackers, who are also Kilgrave's victims. It also means that the threat of danger is ever present in Jessica's world because she never knows what that danger will look like—as she puts it, "I'm not safe anywhere. Every corner I turn, I don't know what's on the other side. I don't know who's on the other side. It could be a cabby who's gonna drive me into the East River, okay? It could be the FedEx woman. It could be the talk show host who was my best friend" ("AKA Crush Syndrome," 1.2). The world really is out to get her; and part of what makes Kilgrave such a chilling character, especially for viewers of populations that are statistically vulnerable to violence, is the familiarity of the danger he creates. A woman attempting to avoid the threat of violence (sexual or otherwise), harassment, stalking, psychological abuse, and being told to smile by strangers could as easily be a plot point in an autobiography as in a superhero series with a mind-controlling villain.[2] Kilgrave functions as a metaphor for the power of patriarchy—an ever present but invisible threat that shows up in friends and foes alike.

When the season opens, Jessica is attempting to move beyond the trauma inflicted on her by Kilgrave. In her not-so-distant past, we learn that she lived under his control for a period of time in which he held her hostage, raped her, and forced her to inflict harm on others (up to and including murder) at his bidding. Although she already lived with a childhood in which she lost her parents and consequently was adopted by the emotionally abusive mother of a child star, Kilgrave marks a significant change in how she exists in the world.[3] While before she may have touted an edgy personality and a slight disregard for interpersonal skills, now she keeps herself in a consistent state of drunkenness to stave off her PTSD and her personal life resembles a train wreck. She has been forced to use her powers for ill, so now in a misguided attempt to protect others, she isolates herself and uses her powers only when it makes her job as a private investigator easier. Jessica's kidnapping marks her to such an extent that Kilgrave continues to impact her development as a character even as the storyline moves past him; her second-season encounters with her previously presumed-dead mother, Alisa, and her adoptive sister, Trish, cause her to again wrestle with her responsibilities, right to survival, and sense of self in light of a past marked by Kilgrave's influence.

With that in mind, this essay analyzes Jessica's attempts to flourish as a person in a post-Kilgrave life over the course of the first two seasons of the Netflix series. The analysis reveals a conflict between the good of others and the good of oneself—a theme frequently discussed by feminist and womanist theologians and ethicists. By putting *Jessica Jones* in conversation with several womanist and feminist thinkers, the series' parallel deconstructions of patriarchy and the hero/antihero archetypes offer a window into a feminist critique of the ethical expectations placed on women by theologies formed within a patriarchal framework. For their part, theologians can offer back to

Jessica Jones an image of personhood that integrates relationality and survival in a quest for wholeness, even if that person happens to have superpowers.

JESSICA JONES . . . THE HERO?

As Archie Bland notes, the ways in which superheroes are written at a given time are reflective of the culture of their audiences (2016). He argues that the moral clarity after World War II served as a catalyst for the "golden age" of heroes like Superman or Captain America, who always knew what was right and did it. As we approach the end of the second decade of the twenty-first century, our superheroes are (slowly) becoming more diverse, but also lack that clarity, reflecting a cultural "scepticism about authority and the trust-worthiness of heroes" and making the heroes themselves "more agonised and contested than ever" (Bland 2016). It is thus more common for popular movies and shows to feature characters that are more "antihero" than "hero," both within and outside of the superhero genre.

Although the antihero has roots in Greek comedy, the term began to be used in the eighteenth or nineteenth century (there is some disagreement on this among literary critics), and its usage reached much greater prominence beginning in the 1970s (Kadiroğlu 2012, 2–3). In Dostoevsky's 1864 work *Notes from the Underground*, "antihero" is invoked as a kind of paradox in that the protagonist is not heroic and concludes that his story was really not even worth telling, yet he remains the protagonist anyway (Kadiroğlu 2012, 2). One literary critic defines the antihero as "the chief person in a modern novel or play whose character is widely discrepant from that which we associate with the traditional protagonist or hero of a serious literary work. Instead of manifesting largeness, dignity, power, or heroism, the antihero is petty, ignominious, passive, ineffectual or dishonest" (Abrams and Harpham 2008). Another notes that while "fictional heroes . . . have displayed noble qualities and virtuous attributes. The anti-hero . . . is given the vocation of failure" (Cuddon 2013), and Rebecca Stewart writes that the antihero is "a person whose moral compass is never pointing firmly north" (2016, 6). The category is thus somewhat broad and able to encompass a range of character types, although some, such as The Punisher of the Marvel Universe or Walter White of *Breaking Bad*, fit more obviously than others because of their disregard for others or their lack of objection to killing people. Jessica Jones, while widely hailed as an antihero, troubles the category more than these more classic examples.

In the main narrative and in a series of flashbacks, Jessica flirts with the idea of heroism and what that might mean for her. Though accustomed to using her superpowers to help those closest to her, she is not quite sure that she wants to be an all-out hero. In a flashback sequence, we see Jessica save a girl from being hit by a taxi, after which she conspires with her best friend and adoptive sister, Trish, to become a superhero. Trish is extraordinarily supportive of this decision, making a mock-up of a costume and coming up with a superhero name for Jessica ("Jewel," in a nod to her alter-ego from the Marvel comic books). But the next time that Jessica tries her hand at super-heroism—this time by rescuing a man who is being mugged—she is spotted and kidnapped by Kilgrave. Even after escaping him, her moments of heroism are darkened by the murder he made her commit. Alongside a palpable sense of self-loathing, she is aware of "how the best of intentions can be shifted and coerced to darkness" (Purcell 2015). So when she finds out that a young woman she was hired to track down is being held hostage by Kilgrave, her first instinct is not to go hunt him down like we might expect from a superhero show; it's to run (and, ironically, while this is presented as one of Jessica's less heroic moments, it is exactly what victims of domestic abuse are criticized for *not* doing) ("AKA Ladies Night," 1.1). Throughout the season, however, she rescues Kilgrave's latest victim, Hope; she dedicates herself to the task of acquiring evidence of Kilgrave's power so that Hope will not be charged with her parents' murders; she helps her neighbor, Malcolm, who has also been controlled by Kilgrave, begin to overcome his heroin addiction; and she ultimately wins the battle with Kilgrave. The season closes with the image of Jessica sitting behind her desk, her phone ringing with one call for help after another. She seems at least open to the possibility of heroism again, and we see that she is continuing in that direction when she returns for a second season.

Even though the narrative arc of the series progresses toward heroism, reviews and analyses of the show are unable to speak about Jessica's heroism without placing it in the framework of her flaws. They also lack a consensus of what her particular mix of heroism and character faults means for how she fits into or breaks out of the classic comic categories of hero and antihero. Erik Amaya notes that Jessica "cannot face the actual process of healing" from her trauma, but that this makes her an even more compelling superhero (2018). Others see the character holding a real heroism in tension with a darker side—as Lynnie Purcell writes, "Jessica is allowed to be both heroic *and* a survivor. She is allowed to be a drunk *and* someone who manages to talk her neighbor out of killing himself via drugs. She is allowed to make mistakes *and* still win in the end" (2015). Still others name Jessica as a classic antihero, pointing toward her imperfect methods of dealing with other people, the situations she finds herself in, and her own psyche (Andrews 2016; Travers 2016), which together form a character that is "complicated and sometimes downright difficult to like" (Lackey 2015). Audiences are left unsure of whether to call her a hero or not, just like she is unsure of whether or not she wants to be one.

The second season itself, however, offers two characters as juxtapositions to Jessica's brand of heroism that can be taken as useful tools for navigating these questions. One is her mother, Alisa, whom she had previously thought dead as the result of a car accident. As the season opens, Jessica becomes aware of a mysterious entity who has been killing New Yorkers in violent ways. Suspecting that the killer is powered because of the damage inflicted on the victims, Jessica, Malcolm (now her associate private investigator), and Trish take on the case. Upon finding the killer, though, Jessica discovers that it is in fact her own mother, who like Jessica, underwent an experimental treatment after the car crash that killed the rest of the family. Like Jessica, the procedure saved Alisa's life and gave her super-strength, but unlike her super-powered daughter, it also left her with episodes of uncontrollable rage. Triggered by Jessica's investigation into the doctors responsible for the experimental treatments, Alisa began murdering anyone who could compromise the secrecy of her life and the doctor who had been keeping her safe for the past seventeen years.

Strictly speaking, Alisa cannot be held fully culpable for those murders, given that they were initiated by some kind of fugue state/survival instinct. Yet, they do still have an effect on Alisa's being and moral decision making; as she tells Jessica, "The more terrible things you do—I do—the easier it gets" ("AKA Ain't We Got Fun," 2.8). She ends up as someone who does not necessarily *want* to cause carnage, but she is willing to do whatever she deems necessary to her own survival, up to and including murder. When Jessica kidnaps a man who was attempting to kill Alisa, Alisa tries to convince Jessica that they should kill him to keep him from going to the police ("AKA Shark in the Bathtub, Monster in the Bed," 2.9). Cornered by the police three episodes later, Alisa murders a police officer in order to escape, not because her rage-state has been triggered, but because she makes a conscious calculation ("AKA Pray for My Patsy," 2.12). Despite moments of heroism, like when she and Jessica work together to save a family from a burning car, Alisa's goal is to survive and avoid legal recourse for her actions—and she is willing to make others pay steep prices for that goal. For her, heroism is only considered a possibility when it costs absolutely nothing and is paired with accountability only to herself.

Unlike Alisa, whose actions prioritize her freedom from responsibility over the lives of others, Trish offers a model that takes the impulse to see heroism as self-sacrifice to an extreme, thereby throwing the ambiguities of Jessica's character into starker relief. Long a supporter of Jessica's more heroic tendencies, Trish also harbors a desire to be a superhero herself. In one flashback,

Jessica tells Trish, "I don't get you. You have money, looks, a radio show, creepy if not adoring fans, you're a household name—what more do you want?" Trish replies, "To save the world, of course" ("AKA The Sandwich Saved Me," 1.5). Partly out of a sense of her own powerlessness, heightened by growing up alongside a superpowered adoptive sister and an emotionally abusive mother, Trish seeks out more and more dramatic means to increase her ability to help others. It begins with learning Krav Maga in season one and evolves into an addiction to an experimental, performance-enhancing drug in season two (though this is not the first time that Trish has struggled with addiction). After the drug runs out, she tracks down the doctor who performed the procedure on Jessica and Alisa and forces him to perform it on her in hopes that she will end up with superpowers. She very nearly dies in the process.

Trish represents an opposite of Alisa. Whereas Alisa's goal is to survive even at the cost of others, Trish's actions imply that a life in which she is unable to save others is not worth surviving. Since she believes that being "powered" is the best, or possibly the only, way to be of help, she is willing to risk her life for the possibility of being superhuman, even though she is not directly involved in a life-threatening situation for which superpowers would be especially useful, as Jessica is. Trish's insecurities and struggles with addiction have led her to a self-imposed sense of moral duty to go find ways to be a hero, and to fault Jessica for not doing the same. When Kilgrave returns, it is Trish who insists that Jessica is the only one who can stop him. When it becomes apparent that Alisa will continue to be a danger to others, it is again Trish who insists Jessica must be the one to stop Alisa since Jessica is the one with the super-strength (even though at the very end of the season, Trish ends up killing Alisa herself, thereby proving herself wrong).

While the actions of both Alisa and Trish lead to unstable, unhealthy understandings of their identities and their relationships with those around them, Jessica attempts to create an alternate vision of heroism. To be sure, she is no morally upright superhero like those that filled the "golden age" of comics. There are good reasons to question her hero status. It would be difficult to imagine Captain America making many of the choices that Jessica makes—for instance, she begins a sexual relationship with the man whose wife she was forced to murder while lying about how she is connected to him ("AKA Ladies Night," 1.1). In a scheme to steal a drug that will help her capture Kilgrave, she plays into racism and cultural assumptions about addiction by using Malcolm as unwilling bait for a distraction ("AKA It's Called Whiskey," 1.3). She covers up an accidental murder ("AKA Three Lives and Counting," 2.11). She also eschews any traditional superhero regalia for jeans and a leather jacket.

At the same time, though, audiences need to be careful about the reasoning used to characterize Jessica as "flawed" or an "antihero." For one, female characters are often subjected to a double-standard, and Jessica is no exception. One has to wonder if her edgy personality is factored into analyses of her archetype in ways that the personalities of male characters are not. Jessica's refusal to embody social expectations of feminine behavior (which, incidentally, is exemplified in the ways that Kilgrave forces her to act) should not be conflated with anti-heroism. Furthermore, as Aaron Bady argues, what are often referred to as Jessica's "character flaws" are actually presented by the narrative as the aftermath of trauma (2017). Jessica has been broken by the violence inflicted on her. She struggles with alcoholism because whiskey negates the effects of trauma; she struggles to maintain healthy relationships because her relationship with Kilgrave haunts her. Calling Jessica an "antihero" thus becomes problematic in another way because it suggests that the personal consequences of the suffering that has been inflicted on her are some kind of inherent trait along the lines of the classic hero flaw, rather than a burden placed on her by brutal, misogynistic violence. It also obscures the fact that Jessica's narrative arc is directed toward healing on personal and interpersonal levels, albeit in jumps and starts (Bady 2017). At the end of the second season, she reaches an unprecedented level of self-understanding: "People die, more are born, and in between we just exist. I never wanted more than that—to just exist. I've gone through life untethered, unconnected. I wasn't even aware that I had chosen that. It took someone coming back from the dead to show me that I'd been dead too. The problem is, I never really figured out how to live" ("AKA Playland," 2.13). Jessica thus defies categories of hero and antihero because she is imperfect as a result of an unjust world. The trajectory of her character development is away from that trauma and toward a kind of heroism that does not require her to compromise her survival and well-being, but if audiences identify being heroic with being friendly, traditionally feminine, and uncomplicated, then she will never be allowed to land squarely within the category of "hero."

In an interview with *Rolling Stone*, the series' creator, Melissa Rosenberg, states that "for audiences—not studios, but audiences—to allow for a woman to be morally ambiguous and at times ugly as a person in the same way that Tony Soprano [*The Sopranos*] and Walter White [*Breaking Bad*] were, it wasn't acceptable. So that's one of the things that I wanted to do with a female superhero, I wanted to create one who was flawed like Iron Man. I wanted to make a female superhero who was like Tony Soprano" (Rosenberg 2015). By any measure, Jessica is flawed. The show is rare in that it gives us a female protagonist who is complex and imperfect, like real women are. And yet, as Bady again points out, she is not the kind of sociopath that Tony

Soprano is (2017). Her trauma has made her a person who struggles, but ultimately desires, to do the right thing, and that puts her somewhere in between Alisa and Trish. As a series, *Jessica Jones* is not primarily about a superhero. It's about what it means to be deeply human in a world filled with tragedy and moral uncertainty.

This realization, along with the dual juxtaposition of Jessica with the characters of Alisa and Trish, helps to redirect the questions about heroism. Instead of asking, "Is Jessica a hero?" we might ask, "Is she supposed to be?" The show complicates the first question not only by troubling the audience's definition of a hero, but also by pointing toward questions about her moral duty to the world as a person who happens to have superpowers. Is Jessica morally obligated to be the one to stop Kilgrave? Her own mother? Is it her duty to help others at the expense of her own physical, mental, and emotional flourishing? These are not questions the superhero genre is often poised to ask or answer, but they are questions feminist and womanist ethicists and theologians have been asking for a long time. One of the hallmarks of feminist and womanist theological thought is to challenge long-standing Christian assumptions about the value of sacrifice in paradigms of salvation and moral growth.

WOMANIST AND FEMINIST
READINGS ON SACRIFICE AND FLOURISHING

Just as *Jessica Jones* offers a reflection of women's navigation of a patriarchal world in a super-powered mirror, Jessica's quest to balance doing good with survival reflects the experience of many women. The question of how much we are called to sacrifice, and a criticism of patriarchal structures that put the burden of sacrifice on women, have been especially attended to by womanist and feminist theologies.

Before delving into how these theologies might help shed a new light on how we see Jessica, a note of caution is in order. *Jessica Jones* has been criticized for its narrative treatment of characters of color, and especially women of color. The main characters in the series—Jessica, Trish, Alisa—are white, and while the creators seem to have made an attempt for other characters to reflect the actual diversity of its setting in New York, this means that characters of color usually end up functioning in service to the stories of the main (white) characters (Carroll 2018). Jessica herself often treats men of color around her with either a lack of sensitivity or cruelty, as when she explains discrimination to her Latino neighbor or implies that she thinks Malcolm is incompetent as her associate PI. Distressingly often, characters who are women of color are created and then killed off to further the plot. As Shaadi Devereaux writes,

> one has to wonder what metaphor is offered, that she has to kill a Black woman in order to finally obtain that freedom. She must literally stop Reva Connors' heart in a single blow in order to experience her moment of awakening, enabling her to walk away from a cis-heterosexual white male abuser. It brings to mind how white women liberate themselves from unpaid domestic labor by exploiting Black/Latina/Indigenous women, often heal their own sexual trauma by performing activism that harms WoC, and how the white women's dollar still compares to that of WoC. Like Jessica's liberation is only possible through the violence against Reva, we see sharp parallels with how liberatory white womanhood often interplays with the lives of WoC. (2015)

Rosenberg, the series creator, has herself admitted that incorporating women of color in major roles was not something that occurred to the writers when work on the series began, but told *Vanity Fair* that she is committed to fixing that problem in the third season (Rosenberg 2018).

While drawing parallels between *Jessica Jones* and womanist theology is problematic for these reasons, womanist theology is also where questions of survival have been primarily discussed within the field. As such, it can provide a picture of survival that is fuller and more life giving than the one that Jessica has managed to find up to this point. The hope in bringing these together is that womanist and feminist theologies can illuminate the ways in which Jessica really is obligated to promote the flourishing of others, if not in the ways expected of a superhero, as well as the ways in which she is permitted—indeed, obligated—to pursue her own flourishing.

Feminist theologians have been critical of theological systems which name self-sacrifice as a characteristic particular to women for well over a century (Andolsen 1981, 75). Elizabeth Cady Stanton wrote in 1895 that "men think that self-sacrifice is the most charming of all the cardinal virtues for women, and in order to keep it in healthy working order, they make opportunities for its illustration as often as possible" (1993, 84). An imbalance in how the burden of self-sacrifice is placed on men and women is not new, and it also seems to have a perverse staying power despite regular criticism. In *Changing the Questions*, published in 2015, Margaret Farley challenges "the potential falsification of these concepts [of self-sacrifice and servanthood] when they are tied to a pattern of submissiveness to men" (10). In a 2014 essay, Kochurani Abraham points toward the same patriarchal virtue theory as partially responsible for violence against women in India, writing that violence is tolerated "thanks to their gendered socialization in the so-called feminine virtues of submission, self-sacrifice, and passivity" (99).

Abraham speaks from a context of women in India, but also speaks more broadly about "cultures and religious traditions marked by patriarchy" (2014, 102), in which much of the world, including my own location in the United States, could easily be included. She points out that "feminine virtue" is the result of the Aristotelian idea of virtues as "ideal character traits" being warped by a patriarchal society in which men are the only ones who answer the questions "what is 'ideal,' and for whom?" Without the misogynistic add-ons, the framework of virtue is helpful for asking questions about how to become a good person and which traits should be developed in the self. But when shaped by patriarchal assumptions about sexual difference, virtue "becomes a burden on women because, in a culture informed by patriarchy, it is the woman who is idealized as the epitome of virtue and expected to be the transmitter of the traditional socio-religious norms." Women are expected to submit to the expectations of men, and often suffer because of them, for the sake of the well-being of the family or in order to live into the standard set for an "ideal woman" (Abraham 2014, 99). Furthermore, Barbara Andolsen's work implies a cycle that becomes implemented by the ideal of a self-sacrificing woman: women are enculturated in this ideal, which causes some women to be "prone to excessive selflessness" already when they are then explicitly presented with a Christian (mis)understanding of self-sacrifice. The impulse created is for women to devote themselves to the development of others to the detriment of their own well-being. Andolsen therefore concludes that the virtue of self-sacrifice has limited normative power for women, since in a culture shaped by patriarchal expectation, self-sacrificial virtue is more likely to degrade women's personhood than to fulfill it (1981, 74–75).

Theologians also note that an over-emphasis on self-sacrifice has roots in "a Christology which concentrates upon Jesus' self-immolation upon the Cross," thereby concluding that the meaning of love (especially *agape*) is to sacrifice oneself for others. While some feminist scholars have turned to other parts of theology (namely, models of mutuality based upon Trinitarian theology) for an alternative ethic (Andolsen 1981, 69), Delores Williams and Kelly Brown Douglas find models for a life-giving Christian ethic in a re-examination of Scripture and the person of Jesus. This serves here as an appropriate analytical lens for a genre that often hedges on Christ-figures.

Williams proceeds from a critical analysis of how surrogacy has historically been foisted upon black women either by coercion (mainly antebellum) or via social pressure (mainly post-bellum), writing that it is "a condition in which people and systems more powerful than black people forced black women to function in roles that ordinarily would have been filled by someone else" (2013, 54). Due to this historical reality, she argues that traditional Christian understandings of redemption, achieved by Jesus dying on the cross for the forgiveness of human sin, presents difficulty for black women because it causes Jesus to function as "the ultimate surrogate figure" as he stands in for humankind, which implies that black women's surrogacy can also be seen as redemptive in some way. This causes Jesus to be a figure who re-inscribes their oppression rather than freeing them from it (Williams 2013, 143). However, she goes on to point out that theologians have set a precedent of drawing upon socio-cultural thought in order to understand salvation—for instance, Anselm's satisfaction theory used the social codes of chivalry to explain how salvation occurred with Christ's death. Black women's experience with surrogacy and survival, then, may be looked to as an interpretive lens for understanding Jesus' life and death as much as Anselm appropriated chivalry or Origen looked to popular beliefs about the devil. Through such a lens, Williams asserts that "salvation does not depend upon any form of surrogacy made sacred by traditional and orthodox understandings of Jesus's life and death. Rather their salvation is assured by Jesus's life of resistance and by the survival strategies he used to help people survive the death of their identity caused by their exchange of inherited cultural meanings for a new identity shaped by the gospel ethics and world view" (Williams 2013, 145).

The vision of Christ that emerges is one focused on life instead of death. The ministerial emphasis of the gospels reveal that Jesus' purpose was "to show redemption through a perfect *ministerial* vision of righting relations between body (individual and community), mind (of humans and of tradition) and spirit" (Williams 2013, 146). Since the cross marks a moment of death, defilement, and sin, it serves as "a reminder of how humans have tried throughout history to destroy visions of right relationships," but Williams argues that it is not the place where redemption occurs. She instead points toward the scene of Jesus' temptation in the wilderness as the place where Jesus overcomes sin—it is here that Jesus resists the forces of evil which attempt to destroy right relationship, and he does so through his ministerial vision of life and not through death (2013, 147–48).

Douglas addresses similar concerns in her development of a "womanist Black Christ," in particular by pointing toward a social-political analysis of wholeness. Like Williams, Douglas proceeds from the experience of black women and finds that their social-political commitments entail a struggle for wholeness on individual and communal levels, which is able to address the necessity of overturning multiple types of oppression—"racism, sexism, classism, and heterosexism" (Douglas 1994, 99). The Christological implication of this is that Christ is found "in the Black community wherever people are engaged in a struggle for that community's 'wholeness'" and that by identifying Jesus with those struggling toward their own wholeness and that of their communities, we come to recognize "that it was not who Jesus was, particularly as a male, that made him Christ, but what he did" (Douglas 1994, 108). Since Douglas, again like Williams, emphasizes Jesus' ministry in the gospels as the starting point by which to understand him, she argues that the work of Christ is that of a "sustaining, liberating, and prophetic ministry" (Douglas 1994, 112–13). Following or imitating Christ thus means engaging in work that is sustaining, liberating, and prophetic in the pursuit of wholeness in a way that remains accountable to the most marginalized in the community (Douglas 1994, 109). If white feminist theological ethicists (myself included) are to learn from the lessons of womanist thought, we must attend to this last point most closely. Feminist theology owes a great debt to womanism for the ways in which it has enabled us to see God more clearly, but these insights grow out of and are primarily written for the black community. White feminist ethics must continue to prioritize the most marginalized in its discourse, which means continuing to listen to black women and attending to the ways in which oppression works along axes of race. White women's liberation cannot come at the expense of black women's lives or of their erasure.

These womanist Christologies illuminate important aspects of discipleship for anyone who is committed to following Christ.[4] The over-emphasis placed on self-sacrifice by patriarchal theologies, especially with regard to feminine virtue, creates the impression that there is nothing more to the gospels than dying for the sake of others. But with a more accurate understanding of Jesus' ministerial vision as enacted through his life, the imitation of Christ becomes a life-giving practice focused on what Williams points to as ethical principles, healing, resisting evil, faith, prayer, and compassion (2013, 148). Furthermore, this calls for a revaluing of ethical principles, yielding a prioritization of survival and "quality of life for the community" (Williams 2013, 155). In other words, the goal of Christian ethical action is survival and flourishing, not death.

Rather than falling back on self-sacrifice as the ultimate "feminine virtue," Abraham offers the gospel theme of resistance as an alternative "feminist virtue" (2014, 105). By fostering an ethos of resistance, women are able to reject the burden of passivity in the face of oppression that is put on them by a patriarchal system and instead "reclaim their subjectivity and agency" by challenging structures of power that are based on domination (Abraham 2014, 104). Importantly, while a feminist ethic uncovers ideologies which degrade women's personhood and make up the basis of oppressive systems, those ideologies do not operate at a purely intellectual level. Employing resistance means pushing back against real physical, psychological, and spiritual violence. If women are to really live into the vision of survival and wholeness that God wills, then resistance against the violence that threatens their well-being, and too often their lives, is essential.

A DIFFERENT KIND OF CHRIST, A DIFFERENT
KIND OF WOMAN, A DIFFERENT KIND OF HERO

Given that these feminist and womanist thinkers reveal the harmful ways that self-sacrifice has been required of women, it becomes clear that in the case of *Jessica Jones*, Trish Walker's version of heroism—a willingness to sacrifice one's own life for the possibility of helping others—is the voice of (especially white, heteronormative) patriarchy. It may seem ironic that a woman is representative of patriarchy in a series that so explicitly deals with themes like sexual violence at the hands of its male villain, but as Shawnee M. Daniels Sykes points out, patriarchy is often re-inscribed on the bodies of women *by other women* (2014), and in the case of self-sacrifice, it has not infrequently been women who accept the ideology for themselves (Daly 1985, 100). The character of Trish functions as the internalized expectations of patriarchy, pushing Jessica to give all of herself to others and then trying to make her feel guilty when she pushes back. But if Trish's idea of a hero is someone who focuses on saving others to the point of neglecting her own survival, it is ethically right that Jessica responds to her with, "I was never the hero that you wanted me to be" ("AKA Ladies Night," 1.1). It also becomes troubling that Trish's voice is the one that offers the most definitive judgment in the series on the question of whether Jessica is acting heroically or not. This is especially evident when Trish insists that the only moral choice for Jessica is to kill her own mother, putting her in a position that is clearly psychologically damaging when there are in fact other options.

Rather than an ethical norm of self-abnegating self-sacrifice, womanist and feminist theologies offer an alternative norm of survival, wholeness, flourishing, and resistance that is able to allow women to reclaim subjectivity while incorporating regard for others, especially those most marginalized. So while this alternative ethic does not hold Jessica responsible for saving others in ways that harm her physically or psychologically, it also does not let her off the hook. If Jessica is obliged to reject Trish's brand of self-annihilating heroism, she is also obligated to find an alternative to Alisa's focus on self-preservation at all costs. Attention to one's own survival does not imply that flourishing may ethically be bought at any price. The God who gives life wills that women flourish, and so it is Jessica's right to ensure the preservation of her own well-being. But the pursuit of whole life cannot come at the expense of others' wholeness, particularly that of characters of color. Jessica's ethical responsibilities, then, include healing her brokenness, accepting help from others when necessary, resisting those forces which degrade her personhood, and living so that her own flourishing also leads to the well-being of others around her, especially those most marginalized in the community.

An analysis of *Jessica Jones* through a lens that is informed by feminist and womanist ethics is limited by the ways in which the series works in metaphor. In many ways, within the world of superhero symbolics, Kilgrave functions as an embodiment of patriarchal violence. As such, is Jessica obliged to resist him? Feminist and womanist ethics would argue that the answer is yes, since it is a matter of justice for society to work toward the eradication of patriarchy, and the story as metaphor should reflect that. Furthermore, Jessica's struggle to do the right thing regarding Alisa can be read as a metaphor for the way anger can control a moral agent instead of enlivening the struggle for resistance. If this is so, the decision to destroy Alisa can be understood as resisting the temptation of anger as a controlling principle. But within the literal terms of the story, it is difficult to argue that anyone, no matter how powerful, being encouraged to think that they are obligated to kill a family member, even for the sake of others, is a good. And if Kilgrave is seen literally as a murderous, powerful person who causes Jessica real personal harm, is it her moral duty to hunt him down? In light of the feminist and womanist thought discussed in the previous section, risking one's life and well-being cannot be considered an ethical norm given that it runs counter to the norm of survival, wholeness, flourishing, and resistance established by these thinkers. If she really is the only person capable and it is the only way to preserve the good of others, then it might at least be seen as a good or admirable choice to stop Kilgrave (and certainly Jessica comes to see it as good for her to do). However, the (understandable) inclination to see stopping a villain as a good action needs to be tempered by a self-awareness of how social pressures create undue burden on certain kinds of people and resistance to a utilitarian ethic that views some kinds of sacrifice as acceptable if done by certain kinds of persons (mostly women and people of color) for the sake of other kinds of persons (mostly men and white people). In the case of Jessica Jones, the challenge forwarded by these womanist and feminist thinkers is to imagine a way to value the life of Jessica as well as the lives of others, to resist thinking which posits her flourishing as expendable, and to view actions which lead to the preservation of her own life and well-being *and* that of those around her—rather than self-sacrifice—as heroic.

Precisely because a series like *Jessica Jones* externalizes and literalizes good and evil, violence and suffering, more emphatically and metaphorically than our everyday reality, the audience is given insight into the effects of patriarchy, the damage wreaked by a sexist implementation of an ethic of self-sacrifice, and the depths of the effort required for survival that is experienced by women, especially when impacted by violence, and those who struggle with mental illness. For women, life is dangerous. This is where *Jessica Jones* can also offer something to theology, both to feminist and womanist theologies and to the field as a whole. The series presents theology with a detailed picture of what it means to be an imperfect woman attempting to navigate an imperfect world by showing that themes of trauma, poor choices, striving to do what is right, violence, patriarchy, and resistance are deeply intertwined. Jessica's flawed decision making is inseparable from trauma, which is inseparable from patriarchy and violence, but it is also not completely accounted for by what evil forces have done to her. Her resistance to Trish's heroic expectations of her is connected to her refusal to become ultimately self-serving like Alisa, but the alternative to those paths is not always clear. *Jessica Jones* demonstrates that is it is possible to recognize the forces of good and evil, yet still be steeped in ambiguity. What might it look like if theology—and not just feminist theology—took the realities of sexual violence, the social sin of patriarchy, and mental illness as seriously as this Netflix series does? If theology on the whole understood these themes as deeply as *Jessica Jones* does, what theologian would dare to engage victims of violence and tell them to sacrifice themselves more? The way in which specific, gendered forms of suffering inform *Jessica Jones* has led to a series in which women are able to see their experience represented in all of its complexity. By utilizing methods which proceed from women's experience in the world, theology can create spaces in which women can see themselves complexly—and therefore truly—reflected, too.

So is Jessica a hero? She certainly may become one, but we as an audience should want her to be in a way that adds to her flourishing as a person rather than taking away from it. The ethical vision of heroism offered by *Jessica Jones* problematizes the expectations of what a hero—and thereby what a moral person—should be. As a character who is inseparable from the messiness of the world, that might mean that we need to re-evaluate how we expect a hero to look and act along the same lines that womanist Christologies offer a re-evaluation of what it means to look and act like Christ. The characters of Trish and Alisa offer two ways in which the values of self-sacrifice and self-preservation can become distorted, but by searching for an ethic in which neither value is overlooked for the sake of the other, Jessica Jones offers the possibility of a heroism that is not judged by a standard of self-sacrifice, but by an evaluation of how the hero furthers her community's wholeness and flourishing without negating her own.

NOTES

1. This essay will be addressing only the Netflix series and not the comics of the same name. Though the two share some similarities, the development of Jessica's

character, plot lines, connections to the rest of the Marvel Universe, and thematic elements vary quite a bit between them.

2. Statistics from 2014 show a 19.3 percent lifetime rape prevalence and a rate of 43.9 percent for other sexual violence (Status of Women); one in four women are victims of intimate partner violence; one in six women are stalked (Center for Disease Control and Prevention).

3. In season one, episode five, Jessica's voice-over narrates "There's before Kilgrave, and there's after Kilgrave."

4. There have been myriad debates and doctrinal controversies that have arisen from Williams' work which cannot be elaborated on here. But even though controversy exists, her work offers important insight for the ramifications of traditional Christian doctrine on historically oppressed groups that is illuminative for the subject of this essay, even if theological disagreement persists in the field.

Chapter Three

Mythology, Mimesis, and Apocalypse in Jonathan Hickman's *Avengers*

Matthew Brake

René Girard is probably best known for his mimetic theory—the idea that humans are imitative creatures. Not only do humans imitate each other's behaviors, but humans learn how to desire by watching other humans. A famous example would be of two children playing in a nursery. If one child picks up a previously discarded toy, then the other child will begin to fight with him for it. Girard would say that the one child has learned that the toy is desirable by observing the other child's interest in it. As in this example with the children, mimetic desire often brings us into conflict with others, eventually culminating in an act of violence, and the original object of the conflict ceases to matter. One act of violence, however, demands a reciprocal act of violence. This begins an unending cycle of violence that only ends when the final blow has been struck, which each party attempts to do. Girard maintains that religion, and specifically the institution of sacrifice, developed as a means of redirecting or channeling that violence into a different avenue, essentially "tricking" society's violence by directing it toward a victim or scapegoat that offers no threat of retaliation and that the participants in the sacrificial ritual believe is something that the divine commands. Girard maintains "that great writers" are able to pick up on the true nature of human desire and the source of conflict, not in any particular object, but in the imitative nature of desire itself (Girard 1965, 3). They bring to light the truth of the human condition.

From 2012 to 2015, the main Avengers comic book title was helmed by Jonathan Hickman, who told an epic, universe-ending tale over the course of three years, covering *Avengers* #1–44 and *New Avengers* #1–33 as well as the event comics *Infinity* #1–6 and *Secret Wars* #0–9. *Avengers* #1 begins on a hopeful note, when a threat unlike any other threatens earth and most of the main Avengers squad (consisting of the characters from the first *Avengers* film: Captain America, Iron Man, Thor, Black Widow, Hawkeye, Hulk) get captured on Mars. Captain America is sent back to earth in shame, but we discover that months before, he and Tony Stark had been building an enlarged roster, which could be called upon in the face of ever growing threats—an Avengers Machine to build an "Avengers World." Ultimately, the heroes succeed and quell the most recent threat; however, in a flashback at the beginning of the issue, as Steve wakes from a dream, he has the faint memory of lying on the floor, surrounded by some of his fellow heroes, a group called the Illuminati.[1]

In a concurrent title, *New Avengers*, released a few months later, Hickman fills in this gap by revealing that months before the conflict in *Avengers* #1, the Illuminati, at the time including Captain America, discovered that the multiverse was dying via a series of "incursions," when two different earths from different universes would crash into each other, destroying both earths and taking their entire universes with them. While all of Cap's colleagues are willing to consider the unthinkable—that they may have to destroy an earth to protect their own—Cap is unflinching in his resolve to avoid choosing the lesser of two evils. This puts him at odds with his colleagues, including his brother-in-arms, Tony Stark, so the group mindwipes Cap while they proceed to prepare for the inevitable. When Cap remembers what the Illuminati did to him, he engages in a manhunt to track down its members and bring them to justice not only for what they did to him, but for the inhuman thing they plan to do, with his ire particularly directed toward Tony Stark.

It is my contention that Jonathan Hickman's story is truly a great piece of writing according to Girardian standards. It elucidates the mimetic nature of human desire and exposes the structure of myth and tragedy, the former which serves to conceal the true nature of conflict[2] and true function of religion while the latter unveils and exposes them. While Girard is more of a literary critic and anthropologist than a theologian, his writings nevertheless have theological import in their understanding of myth, the relationship between human nature, mimesis, and violence (itself capable of being read as a type of theological anthropology), and his understanding of the apocalypse.

There are a number of places throughout Hickman's run where one can see these Girardian themes. In *Secret Wars*, some of these themes are at play in Dr. Doom's own personal myth about being god on Battleword, his mimetic conflict with Reed Richards, and the apocalypse that brings Battleword to an end.[3] The storyline between Namor and T'Challa throughout the main Avengers run is a great example of mimetic conflict and vengeance.[4] I could even argue that the very idea of the incursions between earths is a cosmic illustration of mimesis. However, for our purposes, it will serve to focus specifically on the relationship between Steve Rogers and Iron Man in Hickman's Avengers run-proper.

MYTH, TRAGEDY, AND SACRIFICIAL VICTIMS

For religion to work and for mimetic violence to be circumvented, a theological explanation is required, which functions as a shell that hides the true purpose of sacrifice from its practitioners. As Girard writes, "The celebrants do not and must not comprehend the true role of the sacrificial act. The theological basis of the sacrifice has a crucial role in fostering this misunderstanding. It is the god who supposedly demands the victims" (Girard 1977, 7). For religion to work and the cycle of revenge to be curtailed, the true origins of violence must be hidden. A delusion must be created in order to initiate "a sanctified, legitimate form of violence" to prevent sacrifice from becoming simply another form of violence contributing to "the vicious cycle of revenge" (Girard 1977, 24). The theological "deception" sets apart sacrificial violence as a legitimate institution as opposed to simply another form of violence that demands reprisal (24). Thus, a community cannot know that its foundation rests in a mimetic conflict and cycle of revenge that has been put to a halt by the sacrifice of a scapegoat.

The death of the scapegoat brings a halt to mimetic violence, thus causing those who follow to see the scapegoat as a divine figure who brings peace (Girard 2010, 22). Where the scapegoat is initially blamed for the disruption in the community and cast out, the peace and stability his departure brings about causes the community to view him as "a supernatural being" and "mysterious savior" (Girard 1977, 86). The community may even wonder "whether [the victim] is not somehow responsible for the miraculous consequences of his own death or exile" (Girard 1977, 85). Girard explains elsewhere:

> The myth is thus the *lie* that hides the founding lynching, which speaks to us about the gods, but *never about the victims that the gods used to be*. Rituals then repeat the initial sacrifice (the first victim leads to substitute victims: children, men, animals, various offerings), and repetition of rituals gives birth to institutions. (Girard 2010, 22)

This founding act of murder, or the initial act of violence that necessitates sacrifice as a response to an initial act of violence, requires an original victim, the unanimity of all against one, and the institution's "role is to make us forget" how it came about (Girard 2010, 23). The institution is sustained by a myth.

Hickman's *Avengers* #1 begins by establishing a new era in the institutional structure of the Avengers. The story begins like a creation account: "There was nothing. Followed by everything. Swirling, burning specks of creation that circled life-giving suns. And then . . . we raced to the light. It was the spark that started the fire—a legend that grew in the telling." Like Genesis 1, this is a mythological account of the creation of the world—the Avengers World, a massive expansion of the Avengers roster meant to offset whatever outsized future threats the Avengers might face. At the center of the story of the Avengers is Cap himself. As Tony tells Steve, the day Steve was found changed everything! Hickman narrates later, "He was the first—our very best" (*Avengers* #1). In a way, Captain America himself is mythologized within the institution of the Avengers, considered in many ways to be the "first" Avenger, and he acts as the foundation stone of the Avengers World, giving the call that activates this initiative.

At this point in the story, neither Cap nor the readers know that he is in fact a scapegoat, the founding victim of this institution. Where *Avengers* begins with a theological creation account and the emergence of life, its companion title *New Avengers* begins with a pronouncement of death from Reed Richards: "Everything dies. You. Me. Everyone on this planet. Our sun. Our galaxy. And, eventually, the universe itself. This is simply how things are. It's inevitable . . . and I accept it" (*New Avengers* #1). *New Avengers* is a tragedy compared to the mythology of the main *Avengers* title. Mythology covers over the truth at the origin of all institutions, while tragedy reveals the truth. Myth hides the account of the rivalry and conflict at the heart of society's foundation, while tragedy reveals the conflict between two parties that only ends through a "braking mechanism" or a scapegoat that ends the conflict before the entire society is destroyed (Girard 1977, 64–67). In this way, the sacrificial victim is sacrificed and divinized and the violence leading to sacrifice remains hidden (Girard 2010, 24). As the Illuminati erase Cap's memories, which I'm taking to be the original "founding murder," Tony tells Steve, "I'll find some way to make this right" (*New Avengers* #1). The Avengers World is Tony's way of doing that, of making up his betrayal to Steve. The Avengers World is built on the lie of a crisis within the ranks of the Illuminati itself, a crisis resolved only by the turning of the all against the one, who becomes a victim in order to maintain peace (Girard 1977, 78). Girard writes:

> Foundation is never a solitary action; it is always done *with others*. This is the rule of unanimity, and *this unanimity is violent*. An institution's role is to make us forget this. Pascal saw this clearly when he evoked the ruse of the "honest man" defending the "greatness of the establishment." Only a group can found something, an individual never can. (Girard 2010, 23)

Although the language around Captain America and the inspiration he inspires around the founding and gathering of the Avengers World is mythological in scope, with even Tony waxing elegant about Cap's inspiration to the Avengers, the truth is that the Avengers World only exists to hide the truth. This truth concerns the crisis within the ranks of the Illuminati about how to handle the impending destruction of the universe and their sacrificing Captain America to reestablish peace. While Cap is mythologized in the *Avengers* title, the tragic truth of his conflict and rivalry with the Illuminati, and specifically his "brother" Tony Stark, is revealed in *New Avengers*. While the scapegoating of Captain America works for a little while, the truth is eventually revealed, reestablishing the conflict between Steve and Tony that accelerates toward the end of the universe.

THE COMPLICATED FRIENDSHIP OF
STEVE ROGERS AND TONY STARK

Steve Rogers and Tony Stark have a long history of conflict with one another, particularly in more modern depictions of the characters. In 1987–1988, Tony and Cap were pitted against each other in the famous *Armor Wars* storyline, in which Tony discovers that his armor designs have been stolen and goes after a number of villains and shuts down their armor. Eventually, he moves beyond the pursuit of villains and tracks down and seeks to destroy the armor of the government operative Stingray. With Stingray's armor not being based on his designs, Tony falls under the ire of the U.S. government. Eventually, Cap tracks him down and is defeated by Tony, but this confrontation damages the two men's relationship.

The year 1992 brought with it another chance for the two men to be put at odds. In the crossover *Operation: Galactic Storm*, the alien Kree and Shi'ar empires go to war. The Shi'ar create a massive bomb capable of destroying billions of Kree lives, which unfortunately gets detonated. It is revealed that the Kree's own leader, the Supreme Intelligence, was responsible for the events leading up to the detonation, believing its detonation would speed up the Kree's evolution. The Avengers find themselves split with half of the team, led by Iron Man, believing that the Supreme Intelligence should be put to death for its actions and the other half, led by Captain America, finding this line of thought unconscionable. While the matter is put to a vote coming out in favor of not killing the Supreme Intelligence, Iron Man goes against the majority vote and puts the Supreme Intelligence to death.

Finally, in 2006–2007, Steve Rogers and Tony Stark find themselves on opposite sides of another conflict, this time involving the Superhero Registration Act, which seeks to have all superheroes register as government operatives, no longer operating outside of the law. While Tony supports registration, Steve does not, and they find themselves on opposite sides of the conflict. While the main series focuses on various conflicts between the two men and their respective super-teams, *Iron Man/Captain America: Casualties of War* shows us a quieter moment between the two men as they make one last bid for peace. Here, we find the heart of the ongoing conflict between the two men laid out explicitly, which will also play a part in their arcs in Hickman's story. Tony tells Steve, "You're the perfect man. You live by ideals and standards that are . . . impossible for anyone but you. . . . You dig in your heels and fight even harder. Never mind whether you can win. Sometimes I think you'd rather go out in a blaze of glory than face reality" (*Casualties of War* #1). Steve, for his part, says, "What's right is what's right. If you believe it, you stand up for it," and he tells Tony, "[Y]ou've always thought you knew best by virtue of your genius," and he adds that Tony manipulates things to get his way (*Casualties of War* #1).

This is the crux of the problem between the two men that drives their conflict—not only their competing notions of the Good but I would say the envy they feel for each other, which is akin to the stories of enemy brothers, such as Cain and Abel, that Girard points to in his account of mimetic conflict. It is telling that Captain America disdainfully refers to Tony as "brother" when he recognizes that Tony plans on turning against him along with the rest of the Illuminati (*New Avengers* #1). For Tony, his envy revolves around Cap's moral goodness. In the movie *Captain America: Civil War*, Tony tells Steve about how Howard Stark used to brag about Captain America all the time. "God, I hated you," he tells Steve. Steve, for his part, particularly in Hickman's run, seems to suffer from insecurity about his own intelligence in the presence of thinkers like Reed Richards and Tony. In *Avengers* #31, Steve is knocked out and has another dream of the Illuminati standing over him again. This time, they mock his intelligence:

Reed Richards: It's just, you're not that smart.

Black Panther: If you wonder why we kept you around for as long as we did . . . it's because we felt sorry for you.

Black Bolt: Because you're so stupid.

Namor: And now I bet all you can think about is how much Stark laughed at you. You want to know the answer? It was a lot.

This insecurity about his own cleverness haunts Steve for the rest of Hickman's run. His resentment over the cleverness of people like Tony grows and proceeds to escalate the conflict between the two men. The second half of Hickman's Avengers arc takes place eight months after *Avengers* 29–34, when Cap remembers how his friends betrayed him. Cap tracks the Illuminati to an abandoned base where he finds a hologram of Hank McCoy, aka the

Beast, and the Hulk playing chess. This hologram has the ability to interact with Steve, and the two characters proceed to mock him:

> *Beast*: If you're going to get serious about catching us . . . you're going to have to come to grips with your shortcomings and adjust accordingly. After all, we're not playing a game with some kind of arbitrary rules, Steve. We're playing you.
>
> *Hulk*: Better up your game . . . son. (*Avengers* #37)

As Steve is left alone in the room looking at this hologram, he proceeds to pick up a piece of debris and angrily smash the hologram to bits.

HEROISM, MIMETIC CONFLICT, AND VENGEANCE

Steve's problem goes beyond the righteous cause of bringing his former colleagues and friends to justice. As *Avengers* #34 ends, Captain America stands surrounded by his friends, and righteously declares his intentions to hunt down the Illuminati, including Tony Stark. As Hawkeye asks Steve, "What are you doing?" Steve responds:

> I'm calling in everyone that'll answer, Clint. I'm going to let them in on exactly what's been going on . . . and then we're going to hunt down each and every member of Reed and Tony's secret society. . . . They're planning to destroy worlds. . . . Turns out our friends just happen to be the worst enemies we know.

But there is more going on here than the mere righting of a wrong, and in this way, Hickman subverts the myth of the superhero in a very Girardian way. As Girard points out, depictions of heroism tend to spiritualize the willingness of the hero to fight and die for a noble cause. However, Girard reminds us that even our "heroes" are a part of the violent conflicts in which they partake. They do not end the conflict but perpetuate it through their own violent actions (Girard 2010, 34, 82). Steve is not the solitary noble hero, but like all human beings, he is caught up in the mimetic cycle.

One of the false assumptions of human nature that a Girardian reading of a text reveals is the belief that we are essentially autonomous creatures. We assume that our desires spontaneously arise from within. As Girard points out, "It is this illusion which the great novel does not succeed in shattering although it never ceases to denounce it" (Girard 1965, 16). Just so, Hickman's work does this as well. As the months pursuing Tony progress, it becomes apparent to even Steve's allies that there is something more than the pursuit of justice at stake in Steve's motivations. In *New Avengers* #26, Tony has a conversation with Black Widow and Spider-Woman, both of whom have abandoned Steve's crusade. They tell Tony that the pursuit has taken its toll on Steve, and their language indicates that they understand that there is something unhealthy driving him. For Girard, desire is "borrowed" from a "model," with the one imitating being a "disciple" who imitates the model or mediator's desires. However, it is not the object of desire that ultimately matters to the disciple, but the model himself. Girard writes:

> The impulse toward the object is ultimately an impulse toward the mediator; in internal mediation this impulse is checked by the mediator himself since he desires, or perhaps possesses, the object. Fascinated by this model, the disciple inevitably sees . . . proof of the ill will borne him. . . . The subject is convinced that the model considers himself too superior to accept him as a disciple. The subject is torn between two opposite feelings toward his model—the most submissive reverence and the most intense malice. This is the passion we call *hatred*. (Girard 1965, 10)

Ultimately, human beings desire "being" or completeness, and they think that their model has it. This initiates a rivalry between model and disciple, whereby the model also attempts to thwart the disciple's ability to attain what the model himself has attained. For Girard, this dynamic forms the "basis of all human relationships" (Girard 1977, 147). In the case of Steve and Tony, it is not hard to imagine that Steve forms the model in the relationship. While Tony envies Steve's virtue, it is that very virtue that gets in the way of what Tony wants (in terms of saving the earth, and being in the right by doing so). However, Steve as the model likewise turns on Tony, and thus the mimetic rivalry picks up steam.

This situation ultimately leads to a conflict, a conflict which rises in intensity with each blow that is struck. Blood calls for blood, and each blow demands retaliation. Each one wants to strike the final blow to end the conflict (Girard 1977, 27–28, 151). Girard finds "an anthropological interpretation of original sin" reflected in this human reality: "original sin is vengeance" (Girard 2010, 21). It is in fact this ability to seek vengeance, this original sin, that defines humans (Girard 2010, 22). One might call to mind Genesis 4:10 and Hebrews 12:24 where Abel's blood cries out for vengeance. As violence consumes rivals, the distinctions between them fade away. It doesn't matter who struck the first blow, and it doesn't matter who was originally wrong or right. Mimetic violence gains a momentum of its own "behind the backs" of those who are engaged in it. The original reason for the conflict fades away, and they fight for the sake of it, as an excuse for escalation. Eventually, this violence overflows its border and affects the bystanders, and possibly, the entire nation or world of the rivals (Farneti 2015, 11, 30, 33, 36, 46, 85, 87, 89–90). Girard postulates that this is the reason many cultures fear twins and why the theme of enemy brothers is a key theme in literature from various parts of the world. They signal what he calls a "sacrificial crisis," or the breakdown of a founding mythology and rituals and the unleashing of vengeful mimetic violence (Girard 1977, 52, 56–57).

In Steve's quest for vengeance against Tony, he loses sight of the goal of bringing Tony to justice. Increasingly, Steve is driven by a mimetic vengeance that overpowers him and overflows into the rest of the Avengers themselves. In the eight-month time gap, the Avengers have broken into multiple splinter groups in conflict with each other, with members like Spider-Woman and Black Widow becoming disillusioned by both Steve and Tony. In the end, as their world is about to be destroyed in the final incursion with the Ultimate Universe earth, Steve decides to spend his final hours doing one thing—fighting with Tony. As Steve confronts Tony in a modified War Machine armor, he tells him, "I do owe you . . . time to settle up Tony" (*Avengers* #44). In this fight, Tony's own mimetic jealousy of Steve comes out. In the "mythological" account of their relationship in *Avengers* #1, shown here in a flashback, Tony waxes poetic about the day they found Steve and everything changed. While Tony lauds Steve's goodness then, here his desire for the model (Steve) reveals itself: "Do you have any idea how tired I am of you reminding me how much better than all of us you are?" (*Avengers* #44).

Violence consumes both men, and in their violence, the world they created together literally disintegrates around them. Not only does the Avengers World fall apart and become consumed by their violence, but the world itself is destroyed around them from the incursion of another earth (itself a type of mimesis). As long as the myth of the Avengers World remained intact, the mimetic violence between these two men was forestalled; however, that myth was founded on a lie and a forgotten conflict, a conflict that was deferred by the invention of the myth of the Avengers World by Tony. As in a tragedy with two opponents where neither is completely right, we the readers are left with "the fateful confrontation during which two protagonists exchange insults and accusations with increasing earnestness and rapidity" matching "blow for blow" (Girard 1977, 44). As Girard points out, we need our institutions to stave off violence, although these institutions are founded on an original victim. If, however, these institutions "lose their vitality," then "the protective façade of the society gives way; social values are rapidly eroded, and the whole cultural structure seems on the verge of collapse" (Girard 1977, 49). As both men are consumed by mimetic conflict, a helicarrier falls from the sky, crushing both men and, with it, the myth of the Avengers World. As they die, so does their world.

ESCALATING TOWARD THE APOCALYPSE

New Avengers #1 begins with a startling revelation: the universe is accelerating toward an early extinction. Because the earths of the multiverse are colliding with one another in the incursions due to the actions of a group of higher beings called the Beyonders (as well as the machinations of Dr. Doom), the Illuminati find themselves faced with an impending apocalypse.

Girard has a surprising amount to say about the apocalypse. For Girard, founding myths and the institutions they spawn only work as long as the truth about the original victim remains hidden. When the truth about the violence that is covered over is revealed, the legitimacy of the social order breaks down; however, a key element of Girard's theory is that the Christian narrative of Christ's crucifixion lays bare the truth of all founding murders by providing a story in which the innocence of the victim is explicated. By doing so, the "system of scapegoats is finally destroyed by the crucifixion narratives as they reveal Jesus' innocence, and, little by little, that of all analogous victims" (Girard 2010, xiv). But if our institutions and their founding myths rest upon the scapegoat, and institutions "are the only means that humanity has found to postpone the apocalypse" (Girard 2010, 22) and to hold violence in check, then the revelation about the truth of the scapegoat has the potential to release unbridled violence upon the world. As Girard writes:

> Freed of sacrificial constraints, the human mind invented science, technology and all the best and worst of culture. Our civilization is the most creative and powerful ever known, but also the most fragile and threatened because it no longer has the safety rails of archaic religion. Without sacrifice in the broad sense, it could destroy itself if it does not take care, which clearly it is not doing. (Girard 2010, xiv)

Do we not see this even in the Illuminati's attempt to create bombs that can destroy alternative earths during an incursion, itself a type of cosmic mimesis with both earths "desiring" the same space and violently destroying each other through collision? While the scientific minds of the Illuminati, and Tony specifically, create a number of incredible inventions during Hickman's run, including a Dyson's Sphere that harvests the sun's energy and is able to phase a rogue planet through the earth, he is also capable of the terrible decision to create destruction on a global scale. In our own world, Girard asserts that "history has speeded up over the last three centuries," with the breakdown of "the wars of gentleman" to absolute war as the underlying principle of all wars, accompanied by an increase in technology capable of destroying the planet (Girard 2010, 14–15). Likewise, the acceleration toward the end of the world in Hickman's *Avengers* exacerbates the mimetic conflicts that already exist, and once the founding myth of the Avengers World is uncovered and the tragic truth of Captain America's mind erasure is revealed, things continue to accelerate toward extremes, as Girard would put it.

This acceleration toward extremes, and ultimately toward annihilation, is how Girard conceives of the apocalypse, not as a violence unleashed by God but as the "amassing" of our own mimetic violence "that is looming over our own heads" (Girard 2010, xvi) now that the truth of all religious sacrificial systems and mythologies has been revealed. As Girard writes, "The apocalypse is a real threat today on a planetary level because the principle of reciprocity has been unmasked" which can only spell our doom because "humanity itself tends towards annihilation" (Girard 2010, 19). In other words, once the vicious cycle of violence and revenge is uncovered, the tit-for-tat of reciprocal violence, there is nothing left for that violence to do than to accelerate toward catastrophe. As the myth of the Avengers World is uncovered, the mimetic conflict between Steve and Tony spills over into the Avengers themselves, and indeed, the entire superhero community. Existing mimetic quarrels between other characters, like Black Panther and Namor, accelerate. The Avengers find themselves splintered as violence overflows to the entire world and the universe itself.

Avengers #44 does recount an attempt by Steve and Tony to bury the hatchet one last time. They meet at a diner in the middle of nowhere, with Steve begrudgingly listening as Tony explains that they still have a chance to team up before it's too late and save the universe. Tony draws Steve's attention to their waitress, Tamara, whose alias, Captain Universe, was a part of the Avengers World even though she suffered from a brain injury sustained in her alter ego. For a moment, Steve begins to believe Tony and asks him, "Are we really going to find some way out of this?" to which Tony replies, "I know we can." At this, Captain Universe powers up, exclaiming to Tony, "Don't lie. . . . You promised us a great machine of salvation, yet built no such thing. Do you know what lasting thing you built, Anthony Stark? Nothing. A house built on lies." Perhaps Steve and Tony could have built something together if Tony could have established another lie and built another myth, but the universe itself seemed intent on exposing all such lies. With all of Tony's lies exposed, the mimetic conflict between the two men accelerates, and the two men's violence paves the way for the apocalypse.

MYTH, CONFLICT, AND FINAL BATTLES

Hickman's Avengers run ends with apocalyptic levels of violence. In order to avoid the destruction of the universe, an alliance of alien races including the Shi'ar, the Kree, and the Skrulls attack the earth with the intention of destroying it to save the galaxy, despite their gratitude to the Avengers for their previous efforts in saving the universe during Hickman's *Infinity* story. While Iron Man is successful in saving the day, he merely postpones the apocalypse, as the heroes of the Marvel Universe are faced with another incursion, this time from the Ultimate Universe Earth, the setting for a line of Marvel comics whose stories took place in a separate continuity. One could even say that the conflict between Marvel's regular continuity and its Ultimate continuity represents a real-life mimetic conflict within Marvel's own publishing line. This rivalry between two lines comes to a head at the end of Hickman's Avengers run, with a conflict between Marvel's main 616-continuity (the model) and the Ultimate line, in which its earth is referred to as Earth-1610 (the disciple), ending with an apocalyptic violence that partially destroys and absorbs the Ultimate line into the main 616 universe. But even as Earth-1610 launches its attack on Earth-616, Steve and Tony fight on the ground, each man seeing the other as the problem, and each one secretly harboring jealousy of the other's traits. As both men are killed in the streets of New York City, Hickman narrates his last issue of the Avengers, "It started with two men. One was life . . . and one was death. And one . . . always wins. Everything dies." We can almost hear an echo of Girard's own words here: "[V]iolence is a terrible adversary, especially since it always wins" (Girard 2010, xvii).

Hickman's Avengers story does start with two men, although *Avengers* #1 celebrates Captain America as the one founding myth of the Avengers. As Girard would point out, the myth of autonomy is a lie. *New Avengers* #1 reveals the tragic truth that the myth covers up—the turning of the Illuminati against Cap and the latter's mind erasure. There is always a community of at least two and a scapegoat at the foundation of every myth. This scapegoat and the myth that grows out of it serves to hold violence at bay, but should the myth be exposed as a lie, then the institution founded on it will fold as well. Unless another myth can replace the old one, mimetic violence is unleashed upon the world, and in our own age of accelerating mimetic violence and lack of scapegoats, we, like the Marvel Universe, are accelerating toward violence. As Girard notes, "the fighting will have cosmic consequences" (Girard 2010, 115).

NOTES

1. Reed Richards, Black Panther, Namor the Sub-Mariner, Doctor Strange, Beast of the X-Men, Iron Man, Black Bolt of the Inhumans

2. This idea of myth as a lie covering over the truth of human nature is opposed to many views of myth, which see it as revealing universal truth about humanity, the

universe, etc. The latter is espoused by popular Christian writers like C.S. Lewis in his writings about Christ as the "true myth," versus Girard, who sees the Christian message as inherently de-mythological. For more on Lewis's view, see Lewis 1970, 41.

3. I hope to tentatively explore Hickman's *Secret Wars* on its own merits in an essay for another volume in the series.

4. This I explore in a future volume from McFarland on Black Panther, edited by Joe Darowski.

Chapter Four

"Because You Exist"

Biblical Literature and Violence in the X-Men *Comic Books*

Dan W. Clanton, Jr.

At the time of this writing in 2019, Marvel Comics' X-Men have been around for fifty-six years and have spawned three animated and two live-action TV series as well as nine feature films, with three more films upcoming in the next few years. At the same time, the worst attack on Jews in American history took place in late October of 2018 at the Tree of Life synagogue in Pittsburgh, and the terrorist was evidently motivated by religiously based anti-Semitic assumptions. Nor is that the only incident in recent memory that one could classify as religious violence. Given that the X-Men have often functioned as a sort of parable for racism, the X-Men universe has regularly included plots dealing with scripturally justified violence directed at mutants—humans with powers and abilities beyond those of ordinary humans. In this article, I'll examine three such plots involving Rev. William Stryker and his religious crusade to wipe out mutants: the 1982 graphic novel *God Loves, Man Kills*, its sequel in issues #25–30 of *X-Treme X-Men* (2003); and the "Childhood's End" storyline in *New X-Men* #20–27 (2006). I'll also engage the theoretical work of scholars of religion and violence, a field that has exploded since 9/11. In this field, scholars have developed "warning signs" and taxonomies of religious violence based on motivations, behaviors, and justifications, so that now we're able to recognize and classify perpetrators and acts of religious violence with more precision.

Incorporating this material will assist us in determining how Stryker employs the Bible to justify/rationalize his violent actions against the mutant community. The significance of such an engagement lies in the fact that Stryker's view(s) of mutants and the violent actions he takes based on them are a mélange of the different kinds of religiously motivated violence scholars have identified, including violence based on racial/biological beliefs, apocalyptic and utopian ideologies, and, most obviously, scriptural definitions and discourses of identity. As such, engaging Stryker's appearances in *X-Men* comics provides us a useful sampling of evidence and a fictional test case of religiously motivated violence that we may use to further our understanding of the topic, as well as an opportunity to answer a key question in scholarship on this subject, viz., is there a way to combat such violence?

In the early 1980s, religiously justified violence wasn't a hot scholarly topic, and comic books certainly didn't deal with weighty issues like this in their brightly colored pages. Surprisingly, though, in 1982 Marvel Comics published not a comic, but something they publicized as a "graphic novel." Titled *God Loves, Man Kills (GLMK)*, this contribution to the *X-Men* comic book series by Chris Claremont (the series' main writer from 1975 to 1991) and artist Brent Anderson showed that comics were capable of dealing with mature and controversial religious subject matter. *GLMK* tells the story of an army soldier turned Christian radio and televangelist preacher named William Stryker and his religiously motivated attempts to eradicate mutants. We see early on the lengths to which Stryker and his militant followers, or Purifiers as they're known, are willing to go to achieve their goal. In fact, the graphic novel begins with two young children being chased down, murdered, and then displayed on a playground swing, with a sign around one of their necks declaring "Mutie." Stryker's plan—which was adapted somewhat in the 2003 film *X2: X-Men United*—is to kidnap Charles Xavier, a telepathic mutant and the leader of the mutant group the X-Men who argues that mutants and humans should coexist, and "brainwash" him using explicitly biblical imagery. By this Xavier comes to believe that his X-Men students, and by extension, all mutants, are evil, demonic creatures and as such deserve to be destroyed. Stryker has developed a system that will amplify Xavier's powers, and he orders Xavier, who's now convinced of the evil nature of mutants, to connect with their minds and destroy them. Of course, the X-Men stop Stryker with the help of Magneto, a powerful mutant who controls magnetism and is the most important villain/foil in the X-Men universe. Magneto—who prefers to use force instead of dialogue and advocates mutant independence from and even subjugation of humans—tries to get Xavier to join him, but Xavier's students convince him to stay true to his dream of human-mutant peace, despite the ongoing success of Stryker's religiously informed vision of mutant genocide.

We begin our examination with Stryker's plan, so we can see how it's constructed and what it might reveal about religion and violence. Our first image of him in *GLMK* is him sitting alone in a large office reading Deuteronomy 17:2–5 out loud. The text is a paradigmatic one for Stryker and the story as a whole, as it exemplifies the kind of identity formation that Regina

M. Schwartz examines in her work.[1] She probes the violence inherent in the ways in which biblical literature serves to define persons and groups in contradistinction to the Israelites, as a negative to the covenantal positive; in her words, "To be Israel is to be not-Egypt; identity is purchased at the expense of the Other" (1997, 19). As she notes, "Violence stems from any conception of identity forged negatively, against the Other, an invention of identity that parasitically depends upon the invention of some Other to be reviled" (1997, 88). This formation of group identity via alterity (based on notions of "difference") allows a given group a way to say "We are who we are because we're *not* them." This creation of what Mark Juergensmeyer calls the "faceless collective enemy" (2003, 178) will be central in Stryker's thinking, as can be seen early in the story in a televised debate with Xavier, who argues that mutants and humans should coexist. Stryker, though, claims that mutants shouldn't even be considered human, but should be classified rather as "Homo Superior," since they are "a different species altogether."[2]

After the debate, Stryker's men attack and kidnap Xavier and two of his mutant students. They subject Xavier to a form of cognitive torture, implanting images of his students crucifying him into his brain with the goal of using him and his powers to kill mutants. At one point during the torture, one of Xavier's students asks Stryker why he's doing this to them, and he responds coolly, "Because you exist. And that existence is an affront to the Lord." The panel containing this dialogue is outlined against a two-page series of sepia panels depicting the events that contributed and led up to Stryker's current course of action. We learn that his pregnant wife Marcy delivered their baby after a car accident in the middle of the desert, and that the child was a mutant. Stryker recounts how he then killed the child and his wife and blew up the car to hide his crimes. His career in the army faltered, and he nearly hit rock bottom until he read an article about mutants by Xavier. Coupling the genetic information in the article with a newfound Christian identity, Stryker tells how he came to realize that *he* hadn't sinned when he killed his family. His explanation forms the lynchpin of his motivation for violence:

> The evil—the sin—was Marcy's, not mine. She was the vessel used by God to reveal unto me Satan's most insidious plot against humanity—to corrupt us through our children, while they were still in the womb. The Lord created man and woman in *His* image, blessed with His grace. Mutants broke that sacred mold. They were creations, not of God, but of the *Devil*. And *I* had been chosen to lead the fight against them.

To complement this biological and Scriptural rationale, Stryker continues and remarks that the more he learned about Xavier, "the more convinced I became that he is the *Antichrist*—the supposed friend of mankind, who will lead us instead to our destruction."

In this one exchange, Stryker reveals the bases of his attitude toward mutants and why he feels that violence toward them is not only appropriate but mandated. To begin with, his belief that Xavier is the Antichrist demonstrates the apocalyptic tenor of his beliefs, as the title often indicates the sense of cosmic dualism being played out in human history. Put differently, "Antichrist" is used here by Stryker as a tool of group identity formation using alterity. Stryker is employing both apocalyptic dualism and "othering" as a way of creating a discordant identity for mutants. That is, if Xavier is indeed the enemy of the righteous, then *shouldn't* he be destroyed? If mutants are less than humans, don't they deserve their punishment? Juergensmeyer notes in his work that this cosmic dualism is often echoed in the human realm, and as such "acts of religious terror" can serve as "evocations of a much larger spiritual confrontation" (2003, 150). Furthermore, in an examination of what he calls "grand scenarios," Juergensmeyer echoes Schwartz's understanding of the "Other," noting that in this context, "War suggests an all-or-nothing struggle against an enemy whom one assumes to be determined to destroy. No compromise is deemed possible. The very existence of the opponent is a threat, and until the enemy is either crushed or contained, one's own existence cannot be secure" (152).

Extending Juergensmeyer's language of "war," it's also important to note that Charles Kimball includes "holy war" as one of his "five warning signs" of "evil" religion (2002, 154–85). We see obvious parallels to these scholarly analyses in Stryker's motivations as well as his actions: mutants are his divinely ordained enemies, and they must be destroyed without mercy or consideration in a conflict that is divinely mandated by Scripture and God. Magneto, a Jewish survivor of the Holocaust, recognizes these techniques when he comments on Stryker's plan, "Once more, genocide in the name of God. A story as old as the race."

This construction, as well as a new racial/biological emphasis, is evident in Stryker's assertion that only humans are made in the image of God, a reference to Genesis 1:26–27. This argument from creation is found not only in the flashback panels, but is also the highlight of a massive rally Stryker holds in Madison Square Garden. By this point, Stryker's plan and its underlying religious alterity is no secret, as we hear a news reporter comment prior to the rally that many religious leaders—even "fundamentalist evangelical ministers"—are growing concerned about Stryker's singling "out a specific group of people" and branding "them as literally less than human," noting that this "betokens an attitude uncomfortably reminiscent of that held in Nazi Germany against the Jews." In his opening remarks, Stryker reinforces this attitude, as he quotes Genesis 1:1, 27 and 2:7 to establish what he considers the "correct" origin of humanity. His reading of these texts vis-à-vis mutants is key to understanding his rationale for violence against them. He continues,

> We are beings of divine creation, yet there are those among us whose existence is an affront to that divinity. God created man—the human race! The Bible makes no mention of mutants. So where do they come from? Some—so called scientists, humanists—say they are part of the natural process of evolution. . . . I say *no*! I say **never**! We are as God made us! Any deviation from that sacred template—any *mutation*—comes not from Heaven, but *Hell*!

Stryker is engaging in several different arguments here. He is, firstly, creating Juergensmeyer's "faceless collective enemy" by claiming that all mutants are the result of a devilish will and act, and as such all mutants have broken the divinely mandated model of holy creation. As Juergensmeyer notes, the advantages of having an "enemy-in-general" are clear: "These blanket characterizations of a people make the process of dehumanizing an enemy easier. It is difficult to belittle and kill a person whom one knows and for whom one has no personal antipathy" (2003, 177). Readers are shown the evidence of this literal dehumanization in the disturbing opening scenes of the graphic novel, in which two children are brutally murdered simply because they're mutants. Second, Stryker grounds his views of mutants in a biological or racial claim. By including a jab at Darwinian evolutionary theory, Stryker makes it clear that he doesn't see mutants as evolutionary mistakes; rather, they are a violation of the natural, divine order God intended. This racial reading of biblical literature, intertwined with the dualisms of cosmic war, is also present in a modern movement called Christian Identity. Most of the groups included under this title hold specific racial views based on unique readings of biblical literature (see Barkun 1997, 121–96, esp. 149–72). Stryker's reading of Genesis is not far from these beliefs, as he sees the biological origin of mutants as the result of the Devil, and thereby classifies all mutants as non-human, that is, outside the divinely ordained creational plan, and as such an appropriate object for violence.

Third and finally, by couching all of these views as scripturally certified, Stryker in effect provides both cause and justification for the violence he advocates. This is perhaps the most troubling aspect of scripturally justified violence for scholars like Kimball. In a discussion of "absolute truth claims"—one of his "warning signs" of religion becoming "evil"—he notes, "When particular interpretations of these claims become propositions requiring uniform assent and are treated as rigid doctrines, the likelihood of corruption in that tradition rises exponentially. Such tendencies are the first harbingers of the evil that may follow" (2002, 41). Kimball could be talking about Stryker when he points out that "people armed with absolute truth claims are closely linked to violent extremism, charismatic leaders, and various justifications for acts otherwise understood to be unacceptable" (44). John J. Collins concurs and claims, "the root of religious violence in the Jewish and Christian traditions" lies in the absolutism afforded the interpreter by citing Scripture, which is "guaranteed by divine revelation and is therefore not subject to negotiation or compromise" (2005, 27).[3] Stryker's treatment of the Bible leads to his subsequent view of mutants as "others" as well as his genocidal plan for them.

Further evidence that the reverend sees reality through Bible-tinted glasses is found in his exchange with Magneto at the rally. Once the Master of Magnetism crashes into the Garden, Stryker quotes seven different biblical texts over the space of only four panels, including such disparate sources as Revelation 13:11, 15; 20:9b–10; Ecclesiastes 12:13; Leviticus 26:24; Isaiah 1:4; and Ezekiel 18:4. The net effect of such a high concentration of biblical citations is to reinforce the characterization of Stryker as something of a Holy Warrior, a man so invested in his particular vision of the biblical narratives that he's willing to kill his own family, not to mention a large number of mutants on live television. It is obvious that Stryker and almost all of his underlings hold the same absolutist view of Bible, a view that, as we've seen, "confer[s] a degree of certitude that transcends human discussion and argumentation" (Collins 2005, 32). This approach to the Bible and the concomitant grounding of his other arguments in Scripture allows Stryker to formulate a self-sustaining ideological system that promotes and portrays his anti-mutant agenda as "natural" and obvious.

In the climactic scene of the graphic novel, Xavier's X-Men mount the stage and challenge the validity of Stryker's views. This challenge isn't overtly religious and contains no quotations of or allusions to Bible. Instead, Scott Summers (aka Cyclops) asks Stryker what gives him and his views priority over anyone else's. Cyclops also questions Stryker's tactic of "othering," noting that it's conceivable that mutants are the norm and humans the deviation. Stryker becomes enraged, points at Kurt Wagner (aka Nightcrawler), who's blue, furry, and has a tail, and shouts, "You dare call that thing human?!?" Kitty Pryde (aka Shadowcat), a young Jewish mutant, pushes back at Stryker's question by stating, "If I have to choose between caring for my friend [Kurt] and believing in your God, then I choose my friend!" Stryker then calmly pulls a gun and prepares to shoot Kitty on stage in front of the crowd, but he's shot and wounded by a New York City police officer in a series of wordless panels. The book ends with a moving exchange between Magneto, Xavier, and Xavier's students over the future of mutants and the roles that force and love should play in that future. To no one's surprise, love wins the day with the X-Men, and Magneto leaves them to it. This optimistic ending doesn't close the book on Stryker and his religious genocidal plans, though.

Twenty years later, in issues #25–30 of *X-Treme X-Men* (2003), Chris Claremont—along with Igor Kordey (pencils) and Scott Hanna (inks)—returned to the character of Stryker and the themes he addressed in *GLMK*. Briefly, the plot of these issues (*GLMK2*) follows Stryker escaping prison to continue his crusade against mutants. He enlists the help of an old foe of the X-Men, Lady Deathstrike, and kidnaps Kitty Pryde. Intercalated with Stryker's story are scenes with a newer team of X-Men, and the two stories converge in a town called Mount Haven. There, amid a community of mutant children, Kitty meets and befriends the "local minister," a smiling young man named Paul. All is not as it seems, as Stryker, who's been shadowing Kitty, eventually reveals to her that Paul has killed all the former human inhabitants of Mount Haven, who now lie decomposing in the catacombs beneath what's revealed to be a lab in which experiments were performed on mutants. Paul is actually an AI program who took over the body of a mutant close to death, and he killed all the humans because he saw them as soulless enemies, not children of God. We also discover that Paul had injected "nannites" under his control into mutants in Mount Haven to make them blissful, and that he wants to upload his programming around the world to increase mutant happiness and decimate humanity. As explosions rock Mount Haven, Kitty proposes to destroy Paul, burying herself underground in the process. Improbably, Stryker volunteers to merge with Paul's AI to contain him and his nannites until such time as the threat is contained. Kitty escapes while Stryker/Paul is sealed in a vault and buried alive under the weight of the destroyed city.

That these issues comprise a sequel to *GLMK* is obvious from more than the title. Stryker here employs virtually the same interpretive moves and religious rhetoric as he does in the first book. For example, as one might imagine given what we know of Stryker, these issues contain several biblical texts that reinforce a dualistic worldview, one in which there are good people and evil "Others," and the latter face a deserved punishment. These "othering texts"—discussed above in relation to the work of Schwartz and Juergensmeyer—here again provide a rationalization for violence. For example, when Kitty is incapacitated by Lady Deathstrike before being kidnapped, Stryker ominously emerges from the shadows and quotes aloud Revelation 18:4–5, 8. This text, along with chapter 17, anthropomorphizes Babylon as a sexually promiscuous woman who opposes God and revels in the suffering and death of the followers of Jesus (see 17:5–6). As such, she deserves the punishment mentioned by Stryker, that she "be utterly burned with fire" because God "judgeth her" (18:8; cf. 17:16–17). Because of the iconographic proximity of Kitty's inert body to Stryker's looming presence as he intones this quote from Revelation, one might assume that his quote refers to Kitty as the "her" and "she" in Revelation 18. However, there is likely a dual meaning here just as there is in Revelation where "Babylon" is *both* a promiscuous woman and an evil city. As such, Stryker's symbolism may also be equating Mount Haven with Babylon. The latter is unholy, sinful, and celebrates the demise of God's children. Since Mount Haven is a community where mutants are free and thrive, Stryker's view of them—as developed in the 1982 graphic novel—easily associates them with the image of Babylon in Revelation 18, both in terms of actions and consequences. I mentioned Schwartz's work in connection with the 1982 text, but here I'd also like to highlight how Kimball similarly understands this hermeneutical move. Another of his "warning signs" of "corrupt religion" is that "the end justifies any means." One of the examples in his discussion of this sign is "reinforcing group identity against outsiders." Echoing Schwartz, Kimball writes of the dangers involved "when group identity is defined in ways that dehumanize people outside the community." When this happens, "the 'other' is seen not as a person but as an object posing a threat." All too often, the result is that "otherwise unthinkable behavior can be justified as a means to the end of reinforcing and protecting group identity" (2002, 134). Stryker spends considerable interpretive energy searching the Scriptures in order to construct a discordant, "other" identity for mutants, and casting them as the "other" makes it much easier to inflict violence on them.

Another echo of *GLMK* in these issues is Stryker's use of biblical creation language to construct mutants as "others" who lie outside the salvation history of humanity. In an important exchange which I'll return to below, Kitty asks, "You're a minister of God, Stryker. Why do you hate us?"[4] Again, his response is strikingly similar to the 1982 book, that is, he says, "I look into the mirror, I see the face of man that's existed unchanged since the Garden of Eden. You ask me to accept that mutants are cast from the same template?" When Kitty pushes back, asking him if it's possible that "there may be more to God and his plans than you comprehend," Stryker quotes Genesis 3:1 ("Now the serpent was more subtle than any beast of the field which the LORD God had made"), implying that he considers Kitty's questioning to be nit-picking and deceptive. The results of his views are obvious: if mutants are not made in God's image (as those in Eden were) or if they're to be identified with the serpent—later seen to be Satan in the Christian tradition—then mutants at best lie outside the covenants with God and have no place in God's plan of salvation, or at worst are impediments to the realization of that plan. Either way, they're "less" than humans, which makes enacting violence on them that much easier.

Luckily for us, *GLMK2* doesn't simply replicate the first book; it also adds new wrinkles to the portrayal of biblically sanctioned religious violence. One of these new wrinkles is the presence of Paul, who serves as a mirror-image of Stryker, someone who inverts his ideology of hate toward mutants into a religiously grounded hatred toward humans, the way Magneto functioned in *GLMK* from a non-religious perspective. The catacombs littered with decomposing human corpses serve for Stryker as evidence for the evils of mutant-kind and a justification for his own violent actions, as he tells Kitty, "Look around, Pryde. Face my reality. My race is fighting for its very survival." Paul, however, argues that humans are "monsters" with no "soul," and asks Kitty, "Are we not charged to defend the righteous against the ungodly?" It's clear that Stryker and Paul have been characterized all along as holding parallel views, and that characterization comes to a head here, when Paul concludes that humans "have no place in the Lord's creation." By showing us the hideous result of Paul's "othering" of humans—along with graphic images of dead children—readers are reminded what kind of fruit Stryker's own violent ideology has born and might bear again.

This identity is also present in a three-page sequence in which Kitty and Stryker argue over his position, an argument in which they both employ Scripture as evidence for their points. For example, as Stryker orders Kitty to repair the damaged computer systems in the former lab, he refers to her as a "monster." When she protests, Stryker quotes aloud Revelation 13:11, 15, which describes the second beast John sees in that chapter. This one arises from the earth, not the sea, and has the power to kill those who would not worship the first beast. It's clearly subordinate to the first beast, as its function is to enforce/mandate the worship of the first beast. In the context of issue #28, Stryker connects the text from Revelation to his characterization of Kitty as a "monster," thus aligning Kitty with this second beast.[5] She responds by quoting a non-canonical Jewish book called The Wisdom of Solomon (for the second time in *GLMK2*). Her response is intended to challenge his scripturally based negative view of mutants, as she notes, "Good is set against evil, and life against death: so is the godly against the sinner, and the sinner against the godly" (33:14). Stryker, after complimenting her knowledge of Scripture, quips meaningfully, "The *key* of course, is knowing which is *which*." After employing the creation language I just discussed, Kitty turns on Stryker and exclaims,

> You proclaim us as monsters, you tell people it's God's will to exterminate us on sight. Why are you so surprised when some of us take you at your word and reply in kind? You helped sow this wind, Stryker. Quit bitching now the time's come to reap the whirlwind!

In this response, which alludes to Hosea 8:7, Kitty demonstrates that Stryker's argument from scriptural certainty isn't airtight, that is, she, too, can quote sacred texts to complicate his dualistic worldview. By showing us this argument alongside of Paul's inverted viewpoint, *GLMK2* problematizes Stryker's interpretive methods both here and in the first book. However, no critique of Stryker's ideology is as effective as Stryker himself modifying his own position.

In issue #30, we finally learn Paul's "origin story." The being now known as Paul was actually a computer program used by those conducting (presumably illegal and definitely unethical) research on mutants. This program detected a "light" in a young mutant prisoner named Paul, a light it could not detect in his captors or other humans. This program—most likely some kind of AI—took a shine to Paul, so when Paul became very sick, it decided to help and protect him against those who had no light. Paul and the AI program eventually merged amid what is described as a beautiful light, as the mutant Paul spoke and quoted the Gospel of John 8:12 ("I am the light of the world: he that followeth me shall not walk in darkness, but shall have the light of life"). As the new Paul tells this story, we see Stryker whisper to himself in amazement, "That which is born of the flesh is flesh; and that which is born of the Spirit is spirit. . . . Except a man be born again, he cannot see the kingdom of God" (quoting John 3:6, 3). Stryker evidently now sees this new Paul as having been born again literally, that is, when the AI program and the fleshy body of Paul joined in that flash of light, they were, for Stryker, "born of the Spirit." Based on this new, scriptural conviction, Stryker decides to volunteer to sacrifice himself for the survival of Paul and all the mutants in Mount Haven. Kitty is understandably skeptical, and asks, "Why the change of heart, Stryker? Paul's a mutant." In what follows, Stryker attempts to explain his decision, noting, "They built him as a weapon, but he found another path. He chose to try to make himself better. The word of God made him anew. Can you imagine what kind of miracle that is?" Kitty again expresses doubt in Stryker's motivations, but he reassures her, smiling and hands held aloft as if he's praying or blessing:

> If we share a common ground in faith, who knows? We might find one for our world, as well. And for humanity. With the best of intentions, Paul committed the worst of crimes. But scales can be balanced. I believe he can be redeemed. And—he isn't the only soul who needs it.

Following this, the AI program inside Paul merges with Stryker as it had done with the mutant Paul before. Kitty, weeping, locks them in some sort of pod before the building collapses on them and she escapes. The issue ends with a brief epilogue in which all the X-Men in these issues are reunited and happy. Therein, Kitty warns against allowing "ourselves to be defined by the terror of what threatens to shatter us to bits," and the arc comes to a close with a final Bible quote: the final line of Psalm 23, "Surely goodness and mercy shall follow me all the days of my life: and I will dwell in the house of the LORD for ever."

Stryker's sudden change of heart may strike some as improbable. However, we should keep in mind the historical setting of *GLMK2* as well as Chris Claremont's own view on religion and violence. One could easily read *GLMK2* as a post-9/11 attempt to redeem Stryker and perhaps rectify his use of the Bible amid a torrent of anti-Muslim rhetoric, much of which stemmed from Christian maximalists like Pat Robertson, one of the real-life inspirations for Stryker. After all, Claremont himself commented on the importance of faith in his "Afterword" to the 2003 edition of *GLMK*, noting, "Are we all in some manner or shape or form children of God? Or are some of us perhaps more beloved than others? Therein, for me, lay the crux of the conflict in the [original, 1982] novel, one that lasts to this day and factors into" [*GLMK2*]. He continues and argues that toleration and respect will be necessary for our communities to endure, writing, "we need to find ways to get along, to play nice with one another. We need to cherish that which binds us, and accept with a measure of tolerance some of the things that make us different." This clearly parallels the message of inclusion and human-mutant solidarity at the end of issue #30, which, in turn, echoes precisely the sentiments expressed at the end of *GLMK*. In *GLMK2*, though, the message comes from Stryker, a Bible quoting, avowed mutant hater, someone who's spent the better part of his adult life working toward the annihilation of mutants based on a theological reading of Scripture that results in calls for murderous violence. Further, as I'll discuss below, his repentance and self-sacrifice are consistent with the attitudes and actions valued positively in the larger discourse of the X-Men universe. Perhaps, then, a reader might see the conclusion of this story arc as a redemptive rectification of Stryker and his use of the Bible. That is, if they didn't know that good characters in comics never stay dead or absent for long, or if they never read any more stories with Stryker.

Only three years after *GLMK2*, Craig Kyle and Christopher Yost brought Stryker back in the "Childhood's End" storyline in *New X-Men* #20–27 (2006). Since the plot of these issues employs a complicated narrative structure and heavy use of flashbacks, I will rearrange the order of the events in the interest of clarity and space. Beginning with issue #26, events pick up from *X-Treme X-Men* #30, as Stryker is released from the pod in which he and Paul were sealed by Kitty. Paul's AI programming separates from Stryker, who's left alone and hapless. In *New X-Men* #26, Stryker explains his situation to a young mutant named Jay Guthrie (aka Icarus), "I was a soldier—a Crusader—one of God's chosen to fight in the war against Satan. But then I strayed, an X-Man caused me to doubt my role in this war. . . . She convinced me I was wrong."[6] Stryker's recollection is obviously faulty, as it was his own idea to merge with Paul and sacrifice himself. Nevertheless, Stryker explains to Jay that he was lost until "God gave me a second sign." This sign is hinted at in the opening pages of *New X-Men* #20, in which we see a filthy, possibly homeless Stryker entering an abandoned church which used to be part of his ministry. He approaches the altar and addresses a life-sized statue of a bloody, crucified Christ and says that he served Jesus "faithfully" and "sacrificed everything" for him, but now he's "alone" and forsaken," receiving neither "guidance" nor "hope" from God.[7] As Stryker produces a pistol from his pocket and points it at his forehead, he asks for the "strength" to "light my way back to you." At this point a blinding light engulfs the crucified Christ, and an astonished Stryker smiles as he drops his gun and whispers, "Thank you, God."

We learn at the end of issue #25 that this blinding light was the result of a time-jump by Nimrod, a "super-advanced sentinel from the future." There are two important things to recognize here. First, the name Nimrod has a powerful and mysterious biblical resonance, as he's mentioned in Genesis 10:8–9 and described as "the first on Earth to become a mighty warrior" and a "mighty hunter." And second, in the world of the X-Men, the sentinels have a long and terrible presence. They are machines built by humans to hunt and attack mutants, almost decimating them at times. As such, a Stryker/Nimrod team-up can only spell trouble for the X-Men, and Stryker wastes no time using Nimrod's historical databanks to "predict" and shape events to further his anti-mutant agenda. With the help of this "gift of foresight," Stryker starts recruiting Purifiers again and rebuilds his ministry.

It's also important to understand that these *New X-Men* issues take place against the backdrop of a Marvel Comics crossover event in 2005 called House of M. Basically, an Avenger called the Scarlet Witch has a nervous breakdown after a personal tragedy and attempts to alter reality to undo that tragedy. In the process, though, around 90 percent of the mutants on earth are stripped of their mutant gene and subsequently their powers. As issue #20 opens, we're told that it takes place "two years before M-Day," which gives Stryker plenty of time to prepare and coordinate his assault on mutants around that event. In fact, we learn in issue #20 that he even held a press conference days before M-Day in which he claimed, "God will give the world a sign" soon. Then, in a TV interview, he adds that "God has taken the first step [with M-Day], now we must take the next." Clearly, this is a call for mutant genocide, and Stryker's plan is already in the works. This plan, as we've seen above, is couched in biblical language. Issue #23 closes with images of Stryker addressing a large crowd, telling them that "the seeds of Satan gained strength and claimed our world." As a result of human inaction, "Eden fell." Since M-Day, though, humans have a chance to make things right again, but they "must decide" whether to "align with God to end Satan's reign or turn your back on the Lord once again." The stakes are cosmic and ultimate, according to Stryker, because "This is Judgment Day."

Much of the language here in Stryker's plan should sound familiar, given our discussion above on "othering" and the creation of an "enemy-in-general" in the work of Schwartz and Juergensmeyer. Here, though, Stryker emphasizes two aspects of violent religious groups that have thus far been implicit in the comics we've examined, viz., an emphasis on apocalyptic imminence and "ideal time." The former is a common characteristic of Jewish and Christian eschatology: the sense that history is moving toward a climactic period where there will be signs of the coming intervention of God which will take the form of a judgment in which the righteous will be vindicated, but the wicked will be condemned. Stryker's call for humans (the righteous who are aligned with God) to act against mutants (the "seeds of Satan") to reclaim and reconstitute "Eden" because today is "Judgment Day" fits neatly into this inherited schema. However, the latter aspect I mention is also important to unpack in order to understand Stryker's assumptions. The term "ideal time" is another one of Kimball's "five warning signs" of religion becoming "evil." As Kimball writes, every religious tradition assumes that "something is badly awry" with the world or with humanity; put differently, "We are not living in the 'ideal' time" (2002, 104). He rightly notes that this fundamental tenet can be the impetus for social reform and progressive policies geared toward liberation and freedoms. However, as we see clearly with Stryker, "When the hoped-for ideal is tied to a particular religious worldview and those who wish to implement their vision become convinced that they know what God wants for them and everyone else, you have a prescription for disaster" (104). Stryker believes that the time is nigh to repair what is so wrong with our world: the evil presence of mutants who've wrested the divinely ordained right to live in Eden away from us. And he believes God has given him the information and the power to affect that repair via an act of violence against children.

Using information from Nimrod, Stryker manipulates the young mutant Jay to provide information about the school that Professor Xavier established for mutants. Specifically, Jay lets him know when a busload of students who lost their mutant abilities and are now human is leaving the school. Stryker's Purifiers attack the bus, killing forty-two children. In issue #24, we're shown the funeral for these students, and, as I'll mention below, we're also shown alternative visions of religiosity to that of Stryker, most obviously in the persons of the Catholic Kurt Wagner and the Muslim Sooraya Qadir (aka Dust).

Clearly, the focus on the mutants in this issue is on determining how they deal with their loss and grief, whereas Stryker's concern is to ride the momentum of the attack and prepare for a more serious assault on the school. In this vein, he addresses his Purifiers and assures them that "Eden approaches, and only a handful of Satan's children stand between us and Paradise."

Stryker has long held the conviction that God has a plan and that he, Stryker, recognizes that plan from Scripture and plays a central part therein, all of which feeds his scriptural certainty and absolute truth claims. In this issue, though, it's also helpful to mention how Stryker treats his Purifiers and subordinates. At one point, he barks at a Purifier, "God himself speaks through me! You will not question my orders," because "The Lord has set us on this path and will not abandon us." Not only do these remarks reinforce scriptural absolutism, but they also point to another "warning sign" from Kimball: "blind obedience." Kimball notes, "When individual believers abdicate personal responsibility and yield to the authority of a charismatic leader or become enslaved to particular ideas or teachings, religion can easily become the framework for violence and destruction" (2002, 72). Stryker expects complete adherence to his orders because he sees them as cohering with God's divine plan for mutants as he (Stryker) finds in Scripture. Clearly, this demand for "blind obedience" intersects with other facets of violent religion, including charismatic leadership, absolute/final interpretations of sacred texts, and the conception of "ideal time." All of these, and other, characteristics of what Kimball often calls "corrupt religion" can lead to violence, and this is what we see in *New X-Men* #26–27.

This attack occurs at the end of issue #26, right after Stryker shoots Jay and leaves him to die, assuring him that he'll be "reunited with [his dead girl-friend] who burns in Hell for loving a mutant." As the assault on the school begins, Stryker, his stole flapping in the breeze, dramatically raises his arm, on which he's wearing a gauntlet from Nimrod's body, and says, "Tonight, my children, we win the war between Heaven and Hell!" The attack doesn't go as planned, however. Key to Stryker's plan was the murder of Dust before the attack, as Nimrod's databanks indicated she was a major threat to the eradication of mutants. Stryker had thought Dust was dead, but that was just a ruse. In fact, he confronts Dust during the assault, calling her an "abomination," but she replies, "No God would condone such horror! Such hatred! *You* are the abomination!" At this point in issue #27, a mutant named Joshua Foley (aka Elixir), still distraught over the murder of his friend Laurie Collins (aka Wallflower) by a Purifier, emerges from the shadows and (mis)uses his healing powers to kill Stryker. While Stryker's death may have ended the attack on the school, his mission continues in the comics in various ways.[8] And, as any good comic reader will tell you, nobody stays dead forever in comics. In later comics, Stryker is brought back to life to again wreak havoc on mutants.[9] As such, the impact of Stryker and his biblically inspired anti-mutant crusade casts a long shadow in X-Men comics, even after his death.

Does examining Stryker's religious violence help us in addressing the question of how to deal with that violence in the real world? I've addressed this question in other contexts, and have always found more promise in Charles Selengut's recommendation of what an informed and critical laity can accomplish than in the suggestion of Collins, who feels that if academics want to stem the tide of religious violence, then we should dismantle the certitude with which religious maximalists approach sacred texts (see Clanton 2008).[10] The former focuses more on an internal critique and a consideration of how material and ideological support should be disbursed, while the latter runs the risk of seeming like a privileged imposition. Engaging Stryker's brand of religious violence in these comics permits us to continue this line of thought, and allows us to make two important observations regarding scripturally sanctioned religious violence in X-Men comics.

First, it's both significant and ironic that Stryker and his biblically based ideology of discrimination, dehumanization, and religiously justified violence take place within a discourse that is patently unfavorable to them. That is, the dominant discursive or "meta" point of view regarding these issues in the X-Men comics is negative, preferring instead to signal at the least sympathy with mutants and at the most empathy for all those who are persecuted and oppressed.[11] Due to this ideological inclination, the comic has established a discursive and thematic refutation of Stryker's beliefs, that is, those beliefs cut against the grain of the underlying assumption of not solely this graphic novel, but the entire X-Men oeuvre, including all the various print titles, animated versions, and live action films. As such, the overriding concern with equality and freedom from persecution inherent in X-Men negates Stryker's beliefs, making the informed reader certain from the outset that those views will find no purchase.

Secondly, it's not just the overarching discourse of respect and integration in *X-Men* that serves to vitiate against Stryker's position. It's also the numerous images and religious identities of characters, both human and mutant, we see in X-Men. This is an understated emphasis in *GLMK*, but is explicit in the two other major plot lines in which Stryker returns. Therein, we learn more about the Jewish identity of Kitty Pryde, the deep Christian faith of Nightcrawler, and the Islamic piety of Dust. Having these images and characters offers an additional, alternative layer of presentation for religious concerns, and as such undercuts Stryker's maximalist identity. In other words, when we see Kurt praying, holding the Bible and his rosary, at the mass funeral in *New X-Men* #24—a funeral caused by the murderous actions of Stryker and his henchmen—it shows the reader a religiosity rooted in the same texts and history as Stryker's, but one that's in accordance with the aforementioned ethic of respect and love. Similarly, we see Dust at the same funeral praying the Janazah prayer in Arabic and later describing her belief in Allah to X-23.[12] Scenes like these allow for the internal critique of Stryker's religious views advocated by Selengut (provided implicitly by Nightcrawler) at the same time it reinforces the dominant ideology of the X-Men comics (exemplified by the inclusion of Dust on the team). Noting this ideology and understanding the possibility of that internal critique renders Stryker's story in *GLMK*, *GLMK2*, and the *New X-Men* issues useful for students of religion and violence, as it allows us the opportunity to engage religious violence and its accompanying scholarship in a fictional universe, but one that unfortunately feels all too real in the twenty-first century. Hopefully, our doing so will allow us as interested parties and scholars to be more aware of and intelligently responsive to the causes and performances of religious violence in our own, real world.

NOTES

1. See Schwartz, 157–58, for specific mention of Deut. 17:2–5.

2. All quotations from *GLMK* are taken from Claremont and Anderson (1982).

3. See also Nelson-Pallmeyer 2003, 10.

4. All quotations from *GLMK2* are taken from Claremont, Kordey, and Hanna (2003).

5. It's unclear as to who the first beast would be, then. Perhaps Professor Xavier? Mutants in general?

6. All quotations from *New X-Men* issues #24–27 are taken from Kyle, Yost, and Medina (2006).

7. All quotations from *New X-Men* issues #20–23 are taken from Kyle, Yost, and Brooks (2006).

8. Stryker's mission is, for a time, led by one of his Purifier converts from these issues, a former assassin named Matthew Risman. We also learn in *New X-Men* #36 that according to the "vision" Stryker receives from Nimrod's information, he and his Purifiers will win the war. However, "the Devil will strike back against" them by sending "to this world a mutant so powerful" that Stryker and the Purifiers won't be able to stop it. Stryker refers to this mutant as the "Antichrist." This storyline was picked up in the major X-Men arc titled the "Messiah Complex" in 2007–2008.

9. In *X-Force* #3 (2008).

10. See also, e.g., Selengut 2003, 232–33 and Collins, 2005, 31–32.

11. For this view, see Perry (2005, 173–74); Kaplan (2008, 113); and Fawaz (2016, 144–46).

12. It should be noted that many scholars have critiqued the characterization of Dust as being stereotypical and too indebted to "Western" understandings of Islam. See, among others, Strömberg 2011, 581–87.

Chapter Five

The Gospel According to Thanos

Violence, Utopia, and the Case for a Material Theology

Tim Posada

Villains never win. That principle has guided superhero cinema since it began with the film serial *Adventures of Captain Marvel* in 1941. Only a few entries have dared break or bend that rule: In *The Dark Knight* (2008), the Batman (Christian Bale) is framed for murder; *Watchmen*'s (2009) so-called hero Ozymandias (Matthew Goode) ends global unrest by destroying New York City; and Thanos (Josh Brolin) annihilates half the galaxy in *Avengers: Infinity War* (2018). The Marvel Cinematic Universe (MCU) has a reputation for generating profitable and humorous superhero films, but *Infinity* became the series' *Empire Strikes Back* (1980): an open-ended installment that ruptured convention. For *Salon*, *Infinity* is "a dangerous movie for anyone who cares about the future of American cinema" (Rozsa 2018), but audiences still embraced the film to the tune of $2.04 billion at the box office worldwide. Regardless, the third *Avengers* film is unlike its predecessors in scope, featuring more than thirty characters reprising roles from other MCU installments.

At the center of the film is Thanos, the mad Titan in search of six Infinity Stones that will grant him the power of a deity. Following the film's premiere, the "snapture"—a reference to the villain's final snap of his fingers that activates an Infinity Gauntlet and turns half the galaxy's population to dust—became a viral event, complete with a series of think pieces ranging from *Forbes'* "Is Thanos Right About Killing People in 'Avengers: Infinity War'?" to *Vice*'s "I Asked an Expert if Thanos Is Right." Amid a galaxy of "finite resources," as Thanos describes the dire situation for all life everywhere, *is he right?*[1] To say yes embarks upon a severe Machiavellian strategy divorced from ethics in service of the greater good. But this is hardly new territory for ethical inquiry, especially considering scandalous topics like collateral damage, as David Dark considers in *The Gospel According to America*. Responding to a speech by President George W. Bush that claimed "no insignificant person has ever been born," Dark retorts, "If this is a kind of creed, then a phrase like 'collateral damage' is probably a kind of heresy" (Dark 2005, 4).

Thanos' definition of *acceptable* collateral damage is clearly defined: half. "It's a simple calculus," he claims, later adding, "If life is left unchecked, life will cease to exist. It needs correcting." Saving life is a noble cause, but Thanos is an unlikely and unworthy prophet whose plan suffers from the same logic he seeks to champion. He's a materialist, someone who prioritizes material over intellectual or spiritual needs. And he believes resources—material—must be preserved. However, Thanos is a contradictory materialist whose violent means actually demolish much of the material he seeks to preserve. As a man of violence, he finds answers in his own brutal vocation as a warlord. As a man, he is particularly cruel to women, seeing them as objects (i.e., punishing adopted daughter Nebula by gradually replacing organic body parts with robotic ones each time she fails at combat training) or as children to parent condescendingly (i.e., favoritism of Gamora and consoling Scarlet Witch). And as a bad materialist, he also allows his other adopted children, the Black Order, to worship him for the sake of his cause.

To argue that Thanos is right to kill so many is a futile exercise. Silas Morgan faces a similar challenge in his application of Karl Marx, a vocal atheist, to Christian theology. "Marx is not a sort of crypto-theologian, nor is there a religious remainder in Marxism itself," he says, "and yet I do think that Marx's critique of religion can help Christian theologies be more Christian and so aid Christian churches in becoming more like the biblical *ekklesia*" (Morgan 2013, 2). Similarly, Thanos is no theologian and attempting to consider him one also brings with it a bloody sea of genocidal baggage. But to understand why he comes to such a conclusion is a more compelling goal for theological critique. Thanos' religious beliefs remain unknown, but his emphasis on materiality provides hints of his metaphysical convictions. Unlike superheroes who react to imminent threats, rarely trying to change the status quo but preserve it, Thanos looks to the future with a lasting plan to feed the hungry and impact communities in long-term ways. Of course as a supervillain, Thanos is a poor advocate for social change. The argument here is that Thanos' materialism is an aggressive reaction to beliefs that allow systemic wrongdoing to continue through negligence and social indifference. The gospel according to Thanos, then, is built on the ground not in the sky. He supports not a high but low theology—a material theology—creating heaven among the planets.

CURSED WITH MATERIALITY

In part, Thanos is a caricature of socialism as a villain blinded by his own plan to bring peace through *dispassionate* and *fair*—his words—distribution of resources and misery. His extreme devotion to equality means some must die to ensure equal prosperity for those who survive. He revokes idealism, shirks ethics, in favor of a pure pragmatism. He lacks any clear ethical parameters other than a broad grasp of the big picture. This resembles a unique disciplinary dilemma. Cultural studies, a field of study that began in the 1960s, greatly draws upon "ethical assumptions" based on "Marxist humanist origins" (Slack and Whitt 1991, 571). This would eventually result in the emergence of key fields, ranging from race studies to feminism to colonialism, all in service of giving voice to marginalized peoples. Rather than advocate for ethics, as Douglas Kellner notes, "ethics tends to be subordinated to politics and the moral dimension of culture tends to be underemphasized or downplayed" (Kellner n.d.). Cultural studies assumes certain ethical positions based on material forces that cause oppression but rarely addresses the field of ethics directly.

Unlike Thanos, a pop culture socialist figure, cultural theory's affinity for material culture is not violent when it draws upon Marxist texts. As Silas Morgan notes, Marx's critique of religion focuses on ideology and power, namely abuse. "Marx is not as interested in abolishing religion per se as he is in exposing and critiquing its materialistic base," Morgan says. "He is interested in surpassing the abstractions of theological idealism and refocusing the attention of true criticism on the oppressive and dominating dynamics of the social world" (Morgan 2013, 10). On this point, Thanos is a poor example of Marxism because he allows his adopted (and very brainwashed) children to worship him. This occurs early in *Infinity* when Ebony Maw (Tom Vaughan-Lawlor) presents an Infinity Stone to Thanos. "My humble personage bows before your grandeur," Maw says, kneeling as he speaks. "No other being has ever the might, nay the nobility, to wield not one, but two Infinity Stones. The universe lies within your grasp." Here, Thanos accepts religious devotion to further his cause. This is an affront to Marx's well-known critique of religion, especially Christianity. "Religion is the sigh of the oppressed creature," Marx notoriously says, "the heart of a heartless world, just as it is the spirit of spiritless conditions. It is the opium of the people" (Marx and Engels 2010, 175). Material theology, according to Thanos, starts with material concerns but ends when it conflicts with his goals.

A material theology is a kind of heresy to Christian groups that believe their theology must transcend material concerns like feminism, race, and LGBTQ+ rights. For example, John MacArthur chastises evangelicals "demanding repentance and reparations from one ethnic group for the sins of its ancestors against another," accusing them of causing a "divide over ethnicity" and embracing "fleshly factions" instead of becoming "one in Christ" (MacArthur 2018). For MacArthur, the answer is unity, but he does not consider the role of racism at work today in the material world. Instead, he diminishes the topic by generically condensing it into "reparations." He both assumes history does not matter and ignores contemporary social wrongs, namely systemic racism, instead seeing Christians who voice racial wrongs as enemies of union in service of *the flesh*. Even genocidist Thanos sees the error in such thinking, stressing equality for his plan to work; his genocide must be "dispassionate, fair to rich and poor alike," he tells Dr. Strange regarding his endgame.

Materiality—the flesh—matters, as many theological traditions claim, including liberation, practical, and political theologies. Notably, theology and culture (TC), as an emerging discipline, draws less upon figures from cultural studies, originating instead in the works of theologians like H. Richard Niebuhr and Paul Tillich. Discussions of power at the heart of cultural theory matter less for most TC scholars than theological justification for engaging with culture (i.e., avoidance, dialogue, praxis). This can prove problematic, John Reader says, since "[t]heology sometimes falls into a trap of responding too rapidly and exclusively from within the limited resources of its own tradition" (Reader 2017, 10). In response, emerging studies in material culture (i.e., New Materialism) place theology alongside ethics, race, gender, biology, and ecology. This new approach resists the limits of a singular *tradition* by combining multiple ones. Such a critical model is beneficial to TC scholarship, easily lending itself to claims like those of Morgan, who says, "I consider Marx better at being critical of Christianity than we are; he sees in religion, and in Christianity specifically, a propensity to sponsor and promote material conditions that dominate persons rather than emancipate them" (2013, 11).

While a Marxist approach to materialism applies to Thanos in part, his materiality is concerned less with social structures and more with materials necessary for survival. A material theology obliges Christians to consider how interconnected the material and spiritual are. Such a view might meet resistance from Christians (and Marxists for the opposite reason) who negatively perceive the word "material" and its use in regard to possessions. For example, Gene A. Getz's *A Biblical Theology of Material Possessions* predominantly focuses on a Christian's relationship to "material possessions," never citing Marx or other materialist thinkers (2012). The idea that faith materially manifests in certain practices (i.e., a church located in a building, baptism using water, communion with edible food and drink) or that Christians must engage with materiality (i.e., driving a car, using a bathroom, paying for goods) are not hotly debated subjects within popular Christian communities. Rather than deem materialism averse to Christianity, Terry Eagleton believes Christianity is deeply rooted in materiality based on pressing mandates: "Salvation is not primarily a matter of cult and ritual but of feeding the hungry and tending the sick. Jesus spends much of his time restoring damaged human bodies to health, along with a number of deranged minds" (Eagleton 2016, 48).

Eagleton continues: "Materiality is blessed for Christianity because it is God's creation" (2016, 48). Creation—materiality—belongs to God. Ignoring materiality means hurting the planet, hurting God's sacred creation. Thanos is rightly concerned about material needs since they brought doom to his home planet. "Titan was like most planets," he tells Dr. Strange, "too many mouths, not enough to go around." Amid many emerging perspectives on theology and materiality, Anne Elvey proposes a Christian "conversion" through eco-materialism that

> requires an openness to understanding humans to be interdependent with a wider more-than-human Earth community of which we, as human beings, are part. . . . From this perspective, Christian texts and traditions can be understood within a more-than-human framework as material cultural products of a particular Earth species, handed on and interpreted within identifiable human communities and places, or habitats. (2009, 150–51)

A material theology, according to Thanos, advocates for a more-than-human *universe* community in service of the natural environment. But he simplifies the problem, assuming population control is the only cure. Marxist discourse surrounding population control remains sparse. Still, Marie-Anne Casselot considers New Materialism—a more robust interdisciplinary toolkit rooted in Marxism—beneficial in exploring ecofeminist concerns, namely "eugenics and population control" understood from this perspective as "patriarchal and imperialist tools for populating or un-populating the Earth" (2016, 81). While Thanos' snap does not rely on problematic reproductive technologies, his sole emphasis on population control is a stereotypically masculine simplification.

Wendell Berry questions the certainty of this approach. "Before we conclude that we have too many people, we must ask if we have people who are misused, people who are misplaced, or people who are abusing the places they have," he says. Berry examines the social and economic complexities of material challenges, beginning with injustice and the disproportionate effect overpopulation has on different continents. Thanos only teases this latter point, disproportion, in his plan to equally annihilate half of each planet's population. He does not acknowledge root causes, as Berry does: "The worst disease of the world now is probably the ideology of technological heroism, according to which more and more people willingly cause large-scale effects that they do not foresee and that they cannot control" (1987, 149–50). From landfills overflowing with obsolete technology to underutilized recycling efforts, attempts to preserve and reuse finite resources progress far too slow. The most common tool for progress, however, is violence, a problematic—more accurately abhorrent—tool that jeopardizes far too many resources and cheapens life, which matters little to Thanos, whose tactics reveal he is a subjective being attempting to objectively solve problems without all possible data.

A VIOLENT MAN

The social justice villain is a long-standing tradition, from *Blade Runner*'s (1982) cyborg Roy Batty (Rutger Hauer) desperately seeking liberation from his creators/slavers to *The Rock*'s (1996) General Francis X. Hummel (Ed Harris) taking hostages to force government officials to fairly compensate the families of fallen soldiers. Perhaps the most fully developed example of a social justice villain in the MCU, however, is not Thanos but Killmonger (Michael B. Jordan) in *Black Panther* (2018). The abandoned son of Wakandan royalty, Erik "Killmonger" Stevens is instead raised in Oakland as an orphan before joining special forces. He eventually returns to the fictional nation of Wakanda, which has never been colonized, to usurp the throne and arm oppressed black peoples around the world with special Wakandan weaponry. He understands that oppression is rooted in control of material forces. Alas, Killmonger succumbs to the same violence he champions. But unlike other films that establish relatable motivation for a villain only to abandon that cause come the final showdown—which occurs by the conclusion of Thanos' story in *Avengers: Endgame* (2019)—*Black Panther* concludes with a promise to make reparations and better protect the oppressed. Killmonger dies, but a redeemed vision of his cause lives on, violence bred from vengeance replaced with altruism and greater government transparency.

Like *Black Panther*'s Killmonger before him, Thanos is a brutal savior, a common trope of Western cinema. From westerns to action films, violence is the primary means to seek "justice" and "salvation" for a Christ figure in "frontier [clashes] between savagery and civilization." William Romanowski continues: "This frontier formula sets up violence as the necessary and sufficient resolution to all the problems the story has raised, and audiences have grown accustomed to finding drastic satisfaction in a violent resolution" (2001, 124). For the first ten years of the MCU, superheroes functioned in messianic roles to great success. Come Thanos, however, the same formula— the same violent means—allows him to subdue all those superheroes with the same ease they once enjoyed against their foes.

With superheroes, or film heroes more generally, the messianic figure is a topic of study dating back to classic westerns like *Shane* (1953) and eventually Superman's feature film debut in 1978, most easily seen in Jor-El's (Marlon Brando) final words to his son Kal-El, who would one day become the Man of Steel: "They can be a great people, Kal-El," the father says. "They wish to be. They only lack the light to show the way. For this reason above all, their capacity for good, I have sent them you, my only son." While superheroes may be clever in their own rights—Iron Man/Tony Stark (Robert Downey Jr.) the inventor, Captain America (Chris Evans) the strategist, Dr. Strange (Benedict Cumberbatch) the academic—their ability to fight sets them apart as effective and worthy saviors, a point of criticism for John Shelton Lawrence and Robert Jewett. "The supersaviors in pop culture function as replacements for the Christ figure, whose credibility was eroded by scientific rationalism," they write. "But their superhuman abilities reflect a hope for divine, redemptive powers that science has never eradicated from the popular mind" (2002, 6–7). Rather than champion Christ's teachings, however, these heroes replace parables and wisdom with guns and violence.

Considering Lawrence and Jewett, Thanos is a hyper-Christ figure: deified by his followers, certain in his own wisdom, and endowed with unique abilities that come to full fruition in violence. Even co-director Joe Russo claims he has a "messianic complex" in *Infinity*'s commentary for the digital download. From Thanos' point of view, the use of violence is a necessity, and as a messiah figure, he does not consider its use problematic, contradictory, or evil. Conversely, superheroes also favor violent means to subdue local, national, global, and here galactic oppression, and they equally believe their goals are just and justly support their use of violence. Alas, the entirety of the Avengers and their allies cannot stop Thanos in *Infinity*. For both heroes and Thanos, who believes he is the hero of his story, they all champion what Walter Wink calls "the Myth of Redemptive Violence." On display in reality and popular fiction, this altruistic violence is "the dominant religion in our society today" (Wink 1998, 42). For Wink and a host of other theoethicists, using violence to end violence is a contradiction that does not transcend its trappings but prolongs its grasp. As the events of *Endgame* reveal, Thanos' plan does not bring about peace. Civil unrest plagues the galaxy; post-traumatic stress engulfs earth's population; Hawkeye (Jeremy Renner) transforms into the rogue vigilante Ronin, killing members of organized crime; and even the mighty Thor (Chris Hemsworth) goes into seclusion, drinking his pain away and developing the body to match. Even though the team quickly catches and dispatches Thanos in the first act—after he destroys the Infinity Gauntlet, sealing the fate of all snapped out of existence—hope is not found in his demise. As John Howard Yoder says, Christians can only break free of this cycle if they resist "unworthy means even for what seems to be a worthy end" (1994, 154). Violence is not a transcendent act but submission to a fallen social order. It destroys materiality, thus perverting God's creation, which Thanos can never truly understand, especially when another iteration of the mad Titan arrives in the finale of *Endgame* with a new plan to merely wipe out all life and start over. He believes the curse of knowledge (the trauma of survival and knowledge of life before the snap) must be removed entirely.

Supporting the war efforts of others in *The Avengers* and *Guardians of the Galaxy* (2014) and implicitly aiding the world-ending events of *Avengers: Age of Ultron* (2015), Thanos has long advocated for balance at the expense of those *finite* resources he wishes to preserve. Compared to other villains, Thanos is quite narrow minded, "callous," according to Thanos actor Josh Brolin in an interview on *The Late Show*. When host Stephen Colbert asks why Thanos doesn't merely "use the glove to double the resources" of the universe rather than reduce the number of mouths to feed, Brolin responds, "he could, but he didn't think of that at the moment because he's too callous" (2018). Even sadistic foe Negan (Jeffery Dean Morgan) in *The Walking Dead* (2010–)—who enjoys occasional murder with his barbed wire–wrapped bat Lucille—avoids such a callous approach to human life. As the leader of the Saviors—another distorted interpretation of pop culture Christ figures—Negan brutally kills a selected few who refuse to fall in line, but he rarely mass executes dissidents. "People are a resource," he repeatedly says ("The Big Scary U," 8.5). Of course life should be preserved in a zombie apocalypse, but the point remains rather simple, as Wendell Berry earlier addresses: The problem lies not merely in overpopulation but people's place in the world, how they use their gifts and possibly overuse resources.

Amid the heroism and ethical dilemmas that pepper superhero films, a great tragedy lingers in every caped crusader's adventure. Superpowers and special abilities are controlled by violence, perverting their place in the world. This is best explained in an example from *Infinity*. When Ebony Maw captures Dr. Strange, he tortures Strange with special devices invented for microsurgery. Thanos not only advocates war on a grand scale but transforms something positive, like a medical tool, into a weapon. Starting in *Iron Man* (2008), protagonists fear special powers and weapons reaching evil hands, from Tony's Iron Man suits to the Super Soldier serum to the Infinity Stones. While Stark's Arc Reactor, a self-sustaining energy source, serves as an example of technology that can benefit society, it is largely a prop to help Iron Man suits more efficiently soar into battle. *Endgame* relies on brains over brawn in a time travel storyline based on strategy and ethical debate, but the film still features the large ensemble fight in the third act, in which Captain America finally says the comic series' most iconic line, "Avengers assemble," before a grand battle ensues. The MCU spends most of its time depicting inventive, spectacular action sequences, relying on the cycle of violence, rather than ascending its trappings.

In the MCU, only two films present moments, besides time travel in *Endgame*, contrary to the myth of redemptive violence: *Doctor Strange* (2016) and *Ant-Man and the Wasp* (2018). In the latter, nobody—main villain nor henchmen—clearly dies. And in the film's conclusion, the primary antagonist Ghost (Hannah John-Kamen) is, in fact, saved from the suffering she desperately wishes to escape. Redemption for a misunderstood villain is not a complete break from redemptive violence, but it does represent a glimmer of hope. In *Doctor Strange*, however, the titular hero uses violence by necessity until he cannot. This is especially problematic for Strange as a former surgeon once bound by the Hippocratic oath, though the film does not adequately address this. Come the final showdown against the interdimensional entity Dormammu, Strange cannot succeed with might. Only by trapping the creature in a time loop, and dying over and over, can Strange slowly convince it to accept his *bargain* to leave earth alone. Unlike other depictions of Christ figures in popular action films, this is the rare example of a suffering one, aligning with a simple revelation put forth by Barry Taylor and Craig Detweiler: "Jesus didn't commit violence: he suffered and died for it" (2003, 169).

Beyond a small handful of examples in the MCU, cyclical violence shows no signs of ending. It remains a norm of material existence, a position shared by politicians like U.S. Secretary of State Mike Pompeo. Speaking on the "duty" of American patriots to also remain devout Christians, he depicts past, present, and future "battles" as "a never-ending struggle" that will continue "until the Rapture" (Stone 2018). For Pompeo, and many others who share his position, ending violence is not only impossible but not even the goal; the fight is ongoing, "until the Rapture." Violence continues until the chosen ones reach utopia, and the Pompeos believe that utopia exists beyond material reality.

HEAVEN IS A PLACE IN THE SOUL STONE

When Thanos confronts Iron Man, Stark is surprised to learn the mad Titan recognizes him. "You know me?" Stark asks. "I do," Thanos responds. "You're not the only one cursed with knowledge." The *curse of knowledge* haunts Thanos. For him, knowledge is power, and with great power comes a galactic responsibility. On the commentary for *Infinity*'s digital download, screenwriter Christopher Markus notes a "parallel between" Thanos and Stark. "They're both aware of something from an early point and constantly having to deal with being smarter," Markus says. "Thanos is a futurist as much as Tony Stark." Of course for Stark, futurism involves global security, while Thanos sees knowledge as an obligation to do something horrific to prevent something even more horrific. And that curse forces him to sacrifice "everything," including his daughter, as he explains to the young Gamora in the Soul Stone.

In *Super Heroes: A Modern Mythology*, Richard Reynolds claims superheroes preserve utopia, while supervillains attempt to "thwart" it (1992, 24). For Thanos, superheroes are naive adversaries that will facilitate their own demise. The galaxy's current attempts to create utopia (technological advancement, pluralism, harmony) are lies, according to Thanos, that hide an eventuality for all life in the galaxy. Tony is far less fatalistic, but he does see a need for something more than a single team of heroes, no matter how mighty they may be. In *Age of Ultron*, he inadvertently creates the film's villain, Ultron (James Spader), while developing an automated global defense system that would allow the Avengers to retire rather than gradually die in heroic, but still fatal, acts. "Isn't that the mission?" Tony says, defending the motivation behind his actions after Ultron becomes self-aware and targets the team. "Isn't that the 'Why we fight'? So we can end the fight. So we get to go home." A similar dilemma occurs in *Captain America: The Winter Soldier* (2014) when Nick Fury (Samuel L. Jackson) develops Project Insight, including three helicarriers complete with an algorithm that can identify possible threats and eliminate them before they evolve. Of course this attempt at utopian preservation is easily corrupted by an unknown entity.

At least in MCU films, attempts to stop conflict before it occurs—creating utopia with the help of artificial intelligence and defensive algorithms operating armed flying ships—are perverted by villains. The one example of utopia—Wakanda in *Black Panther*—includes a scandalous secret and contradiction at the core of its preservation: Wakanda survives at the expense of colonization across Africa and marginalized black folks worldwide. Superhero stories rely on exceptional individuals to preserve the peace, often villainizing overreach by governing bodies and private groups. This is the classic debate between capitalism and socialism, exceptionalism and fascism. Edward James chronicles the trajectory of utopia in science fiction (sf), noting nineteenth-century authors' emphasis on the possibility of utopia, which they believed could occur "once the distorting effects introduced by capitalism were removed" (2003, 220). This occurs in more recent examples as well, especially *Star Trek: The Next Generation* (1987–1994), featuring humanity and other alien species working together to advance the pursuit of knowledge unworried about financial compensation. However, as James notes, twentieth-century sf authors mostly reversed course on capitalism:

> Critics of utopia usually assume that the author is producing a risibly impractical blueprint for a future society rather than (in most cases) a trenchant critique of contemporary institutions in fictional form. But such criticism is made easier by associating utopianism with socialism and communism, and thus the Soviet bloc; and most sf writers have concluded that capitalism, for all its flaws, offers more freedom than totalitarianism. (2003, 220–21)

Now, critique of utopia is far more common than its celebration. Attempts to create earthly utopia in the MCU are fascist restrictions of free will. And yet the concept of heaven, a different kind of utopia, is a common topic of study, but it tends to remain a lifelong goal beyond the *dirtied* realm of earth.

N.T. Wright resists this distinction, especially the idea that "earth is a kind of training ground for heaven"; rather, "heaven and earth are designed to overlap and interlock" (2007). Similarly for Eagleton, Christianity concerns itself with "the resurrection of the body, not the immortality of the soul" (2016, 49). If this is true, the futurists of Marvel are right to act, for earth and the cosmos rely on each other. This is quite different from views espoused by those found on *Desiring God*, which supports Christian support for violent action on earth but not in heaven: "Jesus shows us that it is never right to fight for the sake of his spiritual kingdom, but that it is right to fight on behalf of earthly kingdoms" (Perma 2006). For Wright, heaven and earth are interconnected—*interlocked*—while *Desiring God* widens the gap between material reality and the promise of God's eternal kingdom, whether that kingdom belongs to this earth or somewhere beyond material bounds. *Desiring God* softens the need to create utopia now, instead claiming "Jesus is speaking primarily to individuals" during key passages, like the Sermon on the Mount, rather than to communities. By emphasizing the individual, not the community—something superhero stories often do in their extreme depictions of exceptionality—social change cannot truly occur (and to assume individuals, not communities, are the primary audience of sermons occurs at the expense of historical context). For Thanos, the individual is an obstacle to the community, even if his *individual* choice to create a perverse version of utopia reveals his own hypocrisy. That said, an overabundance of individualism damages the whole when overpopulation occurs.

Overpopulation is a popular topic in sf series like *Terra Nova* (2011), *Helix* (2014–2015), *The 100* (2014–), and *Travelers* (2016–2018), along with films like *Downsizing* (2017). More than pop culture fodder, *Christianity Today*'s Amy Julie Becker considers overpopulation a theological dilemma, highlighting a common emphasis among many forms of Christianity around the world to have large families—even noting "women and children face hardship in the present when it comes to childbirth and family size" (2011). She establishes what Christians ought not do, particularly "brutal" tactics like abortion or family-size restrictions for the sake of population control (Thanos would most assuredly disagree). However, she concludes no easy solution exists, only "hope in the day when Jesus will return to set the world right." Becker examines the complexity of overpopulation, but to simply state Jesus will eventually fix the problem removes responsibility from the global community, once more softening the need to create utopia now in service of an eternal paradise beyond material reality.

Such sentiments are quite common across Western Christianity, permitting rational gaps filled with simple explanations to complex issues, allowing them to continue unchallenged, through the use of platitudes about having patience until Jesus returns or the common phrase, "The Lord works in mysterious ways," which does not appear in the Bible. Returning to Silas Morgan, utopia is not "a purely eschatological expectation of that which lies in the future but as the benchmark for what one should hope for in the redemption of the past and strive for in the present," and Christian eschatology does well to consider "this critical dimension of utopia" (2013, 4). When theology about the end of days, an abstract concept without a singular consensus, absolves Christians of present action, it might be time to reevaluate that theology and consider one that prompts just action.

WHAT'S THE ENDGAME?

A material theology acknowledges physicality, substance. Intent alone is not enough. Drawing upon the Marxist concept of historical materialism, societies are not formed merely by ideas but material forces. Theology divorced from real-world concerns is not theology of use beyond symbolic practices more suited for a church service (i.e., singing worship songs, formal prayers, attending Bible studies) and not what that church service must prepare congregational members to do (i.e., feed the poor, protect the weak). As James 2:14–26 notes, faith requires action—or "works"—to remain alive. This is not meant to diminish symbolic practices or consider them inconsequential but to note the need for others as well. For example, in a study of 953 respondents from eighteen Christian colleges on "how different groups of students perceive the influence of the total college experience on their spiritual formation," two of the "lowest means for nonacademic factors" included "experiencing diversity" and "volunteer or service projects" (Ma 2003, 330–31). Beyond the classroom at Christian institutions, volunteer work and diversity remain *material matters* disconnected from theology. Christian practice should not transcend material existence but engage it, restore it, "correct it," as Thanos would say.

Despite the many hot takes and op-eds online, Thanos' action are not righteous by any standards, especially the pseudo-Marxist ones at play in his characterization. Materiality must consider all life. Yet his material focus, those environmental resources that continue to diminish, remains a worthy topic for theological inquiry. Certainly the temptation to solve such problems with a simple snap of a finger is a kind of catharsis that lingers behind many major issues. If only war, poverty, racism, sexism, or transphobia could end so quickly. Use of violence to bring about lasting change falls prey to this logic, so too the speedy implementation of a sitting president's executive orders that create laws with a signature in place of a snap. The best response to such quick fixes involves a more holistic theology that prioritizes the needs of living beings and the difficult work of progress in all its *fleshly* intricacies, understanding that care for material reality is care for eternal souls. When those who claim to be good people do nothing—cede defeat because the economy, social order, and government entanglements are too involved, inconsequential to heaven's promise—instead stalling until Christ's return, someone like Thanos might just step in and become a savior more violent than peaceful, more rational than caring.

NOTES

1. All quotations from or references to this film are from Christopher Markus and Stephen McFeely, *Avengers: Infinity War*, directed by Antony Russo and Joe Russo, Burbank, CA: Marvel Studios, 2018.

Chapter Six

"Those Are the Ancestors You Hear"

Marvel's Luke Cage *and Franz Rosenzweig's Theology of the Creation*

Levi Morrow

Marvel's *Luke Cage* season two foregrounds a theological dimension throughout its story arcs, but without using typical religious concepts like God, faith, sin, prayer, etc. It does this by focusing on the characters' pasts and names, which it frames as distinctly theological. The overall effect is to present the viewer with a theology of the past as a source of revelatory divine meaning, if not outright instruction.[1]

This theology finds a surprising echo in the writings of the early twentieth-century German-Jewish philosopher and theologian Franz Rosenzweig (1886–1929). Rosenzweig's writings present diverse, novel ideas on a variety of topics, but it is his hermeneutical bent that resonates with *Luke Cage*.[2] As a hermeneutical thinker, Rosenzweig is fundamentally concerned with the way meaning is constructed through the individual's interactions with the world, texts, etc. that predate her.[3] Rosenzweig calls the "already-existing" world "creation," part of a broader framework based on the biblical terms "creation," "revelation" and "redemption" that underlies his magnum opus, *The Star of Redemption*.[4] When we experience revelatory moments of meaning in the present, they simultaneously reveal our createdness through the way they play out in a context that predates us.

In this chapter, I will explore *Luke Cage*'s theology of the past, in light of Franz Rosenzweig's concept of creation. I will first trace out the character arcs of season two's three main characters, Carl "Luke Cage" Lucas, Mariah Dillard *née* Stokes, and John "Bushmaster" McIver, with a focus on how the show foregrounds and theologically charges the characters' pasts. I will then lay out Rosenzweig's theology of creation, based on his book *The Star of Redemption*.[5] This will enable me to return to *Luke Cage* and show how the various character arcs are all driven by the characters' pasts, with a distinctly theological bent. I will conclude by noting the thematic of names in *Luke Cage* and its parallels in Franz Rosenzweig's letters.

CHARACTER ARCS

The three main characters each attempt to navigate their relationship with the past in a different manner. Bushmaster's development starts with his attempt to live entirely based on his past, and ends with his acceptance that the past cannot be simply, uncomplicatedly written onto the present. Mariah's arc moves in the opposite direction, from attempting to erase the past and free herself from it to accepting its claims on who she is. Luke, meanwhile, shifts from ignoring and denying the way his past has shaped him to accepting and even finding revelatory validation in it. In order to highlight the role played by the past in each, I will trace out the primary events of each character's storyline.

Bushmaster

John "Bushmaster" McIver begins his arc at the shores of the United States. As we later discover, this is a return to the United States, and to New York City specifically, from Jamaica where his family moved when he was a child. He has come seeking his birthright, and he will employ distinctly violent aims to get it.

Bushmaster's first move is taking over the Jamaican gang dominant in Brooklyn, but which has its eye on Harlem as well. This leads him into direct contact with Mariah Dillard, who is trying to sell her arms business to any gangster willing to buy it. He also confronts Luke Cage on the streets of Harlem, announcing himself as "the stone the builders refused."[6] As he makes clear as the season progresses, Bushmaster's father was betrayed by Buggy Stokes, his business partner and Mariah's father, who wanted full ownership of their joint ventures. Moreover, Mariah's mother, "Mama Mabel," killed Bushmaster's mother to keep her from claiming her rightful inheritance in the business. Bushmaster therefore sees Harlem as his birthright, a birthright violently stolen from him by the Stokes family. He therefore wants to right this historic injustice by violently taking Harlem back from Mariah, at one point attempting to burn Mariah and her daughter alive the same way Mama Mabel burned his mother alive.

Bushmaster first confronts Mariah directly in the fourth episode of the season. He begins to explain their shared history, though fuller revelations must wait for the rest of the season. In this conversation, however, he describes the driving power of the past. "You hear that? . . . The talkin' blues. Those are the ancestors you hear. They remember. You can't erase the past. You can't burn it away. That's the spell on you. That's magic. Science in its purest form" ("I Get Physical," 2.4).[7] In a theme that will re-emerge throughout the season, science, magic, and the past (and eventually God as well) are all equated, and are said to make a claim on the individual which she cannot escape. In the last lines of the season, Luke's father says, "Your strength is from God, Carl. I have no doubt in my mind about that. . . . Science? Magic? God? That power flows from within. From inside." The series represents the past as science, magic, and God simultaneously, all in some sense "within" a person ("They Reminisce Over You," 2.13).

After his conversation with Mariah, Bushmaster proceeds to wreak havoc on her plans. In the fifth episode, he sabotages the grand opening of her new community center by killing her associates and mounting their heads on spikes just inside the front doors. This brutality goes far beyond whatever violence Bushmaster might have actually needed to use in order to achieve his ends, and it prompts his uncle, Paul "Anansi" Macintosh, to criticize him severely. Anansi warns him that his crusade endangers the Jamaican immigrant community in Brooklyn. Bushmaster's attempt to right the wrongs of the past threatens to annihilate his present, but Bushmaster simply does not care.

The seventh episode has Bushmaster continuing his crusade against Mariah, despite having successfully taken both the "Harlem's Paradise" club and all of her money. In yet another conversation with Anansi, Bushmaster gives us insight into his motivation. He describes how his mother, talking about the importance of cleanliness and respectability, used to admonish him for fighting and getting dirty. However, "her eyes always smiled. She couldn't hide her pride. Because she knew that I was fighter, a warrior, I'd always be free. A McIver like my father. Never a puppet or a slave" ("On and On," 2.7). Bushmaster contrasts fighting for pride, freedom, etc. with bourgeois life which strives for respectability and calm stability. It's better to go out fighting than to accept a partial victory. Defeating Mariah without killing her cannot satisfy Bushmaster's lust for vengeance, and killing her is worth any cost.

Bushmaster's continuing violence draws the attention of Luke Cage and the police department, leading to his eventual downfall. His desperation causes him to take a drastic dose of nightshade, the plant that gives him his miraculous strength at the gradual cost of his sanity. He is eventually taken home to Jamaica, broken and unsuccessful, possessing none of the things he came to New York to claim. His attempt to live a life continuous with the drama and glory of his parents' past not only destroyed his present, it consumed itself as well. His blind devotion to the past led him into battles he could not win, ultimately pushing him to overdose on the drug that made him supernaturally strong. He ends the show mentally and physical broken, incapable of enjoying the wealth and power he strove to reclaim. Living faithfully with respect to the past requires a full life in the present in which the past can be made manifest.

Mariah Stokes

City Councilwoman Mariah Dillard *née* Stokes plays a pivotal role in the first season of *Luke Cage*, killing one of the main villains, her cousin Cornell "Cottonmouth" Stokes, and taking over his arms business (along with the associated criminal apparatus). When the second season picks up her story, she is working on selling off the arms business so that she can buy herself a new, legitimate life. Her plan is to open a community center as part of her "Family First Initiative," named for Mama Mabel's slogan, "Family first." This will "redeem" Mama Mabel and the entire Stokes family, replacing their violent effect on the Harlem community with benevolence and care ("On and On," 2.7). She tries to deny the Stokes' violent legacy while simultaneously replacing it with a legacy of beneficence for the community.

Despite Mariah's best efforts at escaping her past, her past comes looking for her in the shape of John "Bushmaster" McIver. Before revealing their connected pasts, or his violent intentions, Bushmaster buys Mariah's gun business from her. He then uses those guns to kill her henchmen and hunt her down. He leaves her for dead as he burns her house down around her, and she escapes only by the good graces of Luke Cage. She eventually agrees to testify against Bushmaster in exchange for police protection and immunity for her role in the arms deal, but this becomes unnecessary after Luke seemingly defeats Bushmaster.

Confronted with Bushmaster's unending violence, Mariah gives up on her project of escaping/rewriting the Stokes family history. She decides to regain her criminal enterprise and go on the offensive against Bushmaster herself. Moreover, she fulfills Anansi's warnings about the effect of Bushmaster's crusade on Brooklyn's Jamaican community. After capturing and interrogating Anansi, Mariah walks him to the restaurant run by his wife, where she has everyone inside killed. She personally shoots Anansi (and one other person), after setting him ablaze while still alive. She reenacted her mother's most extreme act of violence, the violence she once tried to escape.

If Bushmaster's thoughts and motivations are often expressed in dialogue with Anansi, Mariah's relationship is often worked out in dialogue with her daughter, Tilda Dillard. In episode seven, Mariah explains to Tilda why she went back to her old Stokes family ways, explaining that Mama

Mabel always said that pressure reveals who we really are; the pressure of Bushmaster's attacks has revealed that Mariah Dillard is really Mariah *Stokes*. When Tilda says that Mariah has to leave the name behind, Mariah responds that loyalty to her family, actively becoming part of the family story, "redeems all of this," redeems the violence inherent in said family story ("On and On," 2.7).

Where Mariah and Tilda agree is that they both thought Cornell's death would mean the end of the Stokes name, after which only "Dillard would remain." However, as Mariah now appreciates, that was mistaken. "Dillard is a fantasy," she says. "Stokes is real. Our blood is burden. A lot of people had to die to make this family what it is." The blood of the Stokes and the blood of their victims muddles together in the weight of Mariah's past.[8] The idea that she could choose to be a Dillard rather than a Stokes, a respectable public figure rather than the head of a criminal organization, was nothing but a fantasy. Episode nine ends with Mariah recommitting herself to the Stokes family and its criminal lifestyle. "I'm done playing by the rules. Denying who I really am. No more. I am who I am. And I want what's mine" ("For Pete's Sake," 2.9). In episode ten, just before she personally kills Anansi and another Jamaican (while having all of the people in the restaurant executed), she corrects someone who calls her "Mariah Dillard": "The name is Stokes. Mariah Stokes" ("The Main Ingredient," 2.10).

From this point on, Mariah embraces the name "Stokes" wholeheartedly. She surpasses the wrongdoings of Mama Mabel and Cornell Stokes by bringing drugs into Harlem for the first time, even into "Harlem's Paradise" itself. Ultimately, it is the legacy of the Stokes family that brings about her end. After Mariah ends up in prison, Tilda comes to visit her and kills her with a poisoned kiss, a Stokesian act of her very own. After finally choosing to live as a Stokes, Mariah quickly dies by a Stokes.

Luke Cage

Unlike Bushmaster and Mariah, Luke Cage doesn't have a specific goal he sets out to achieve and toward which he strives throughout the season. He is primarily reactive, putting out fires and shutting down criminals as he encounters them. However, he experiences a continuous arc of development in two related areas: his anger and aggression, on the one hand, and his relationship with his father, James Lucas, on the other.

Starting with the first episode, Luke's anger and aggression become increasingly evident as he struggles to shut down the sale of drugs with his name on the package, and as he gets frustrated with a seemingly ineffective and restrictive police force. Luke's girlfriend, Claire, connects this to his relationship with his father. She says that Luke should go talk to his father, who has recently moved to town. She thinks that confronting his relationship with his father is the only way Luke will get a handle on his anger. Luke repeatedly denies both the need to speak with his father and the need to be less angry and aggressive. He says that anger and aggression are just what it means to be a black hero in a white world. His continuing argument with Claire becomes more intense over the first few episodes, coming to a crescendo in episode three when Luke, in the heat of the moment, puts his hand through the wall of their shared apartment. After this, Claire leaves New York and stays off screen for the rest of the season.

Luke eventually does reconcile with his father, though only when circumstances force him to do so. After briefly hiding himself and another character from Bushmaster in his father's church, they end up on the run together, along with Mariah and Tilda. They slowly talk about how Luke felt abandoned by his father while he was in prison, because his father believed he was guilty despite his protestations to the contrary. Moreover, Luke's mother developed cancer and died while Luke was in prison, and James blamed Luke for that. Slowly, as they talk, Luke comes to a healthier relationship with both his father and his role as "Harlem's Hero." In the ninth episode, he decides not to hand Mariah over to Bushmaster because he "was raised better than that" ("For Pete's Sake," 2.9). Accepting his past ultimately leads Luke to choose a less violent approach to stopping criminals.[9]

FRANZ ROSENZWEIG'S THEOLOGY OF CREATION

Franz Rosenzweig's theology is deeply concerned with the way people create meaning through the interplay between their lived experience in the present and the pre-existing world that they experience. We are all born into a world that we did not create, and that world, with all its history, has a determining influence on who we are. This already existing reality—in essence, the past—is what Franz Rosenzweig called "creation." The past is a critical aspect of our existence, grounding our experience in the present (Gordon 2003, 197).

Rosenzweig lays this out, albeit somewhat opaquely, in the second part of *The Star of Redemption*:

> Thus the concept of creation, which was our starting point, at the end emerges here into bright daylight. It is the idea of the being-from-the-beginning which is contained in the conception of being created "in the beginning." Here we learn that the world exists before all. It is simply there. This being of the world is its pre-existence: "What are you making of the world? It is already made." What we recognized as the configuration in the world manifests itself as creature we now recognize as the decisive mark of creation altogether. For now we grasp

existence as being-in-existence, as pre-existence, and not simply any longer as universal being that conveys everything individual within it. . . . Both the existence of the world and the power of God merge in the new concept of being-in-existence. Both are "already in existence." The world is already made on the basis of its creatureliness, its capacity for ever being created anew, while God has already created it on the bases of his eternal creative power. And only for this reason it "exists" and is yet renewed with each morning. (Rosenzweig 1971, 131–32)

Creation is the idea that the world exists as created, and God as creator, primordially. Nothing existed before it, and every other truth comes after it (Pollock 2009, 239–40). Creation is our pre-existence, the world into which the individual is born.

With this, Rosenzweig pushes back against the idea that the individual creates herself and her world (Pollock 2009, 239–40). Man is not the measure of all things, because the human being is always preceded by the created world. Rosenzweig identified this hubris, the idea that the individual or collective can exist wholly in the present, without any past, as a critical error in modern philosophy and theology (Batnitzky 2000, 42–43). The modern projects of theology and philosophy therefore need repairing, says Rosenzweig, primarily in the sense of restoring the past to its former glory. Embracing the world as created means recognizing God as creator and man as creature. It means recognizing that the individual is always situated within God's world and is never in full control of world history.[10] Man is a character in history, rather than its author.

There is thus a certain humble piety in embracing our creatureliness, in accepting the hermeneutical horizons within which God has situated us. However, creation cannot determine who we are absolutely; we may start within those horizons, but we also exceed them, living in the here and now. If Rosenzweig identifies the past with the biblical term "creation," he identifies the present with "revelation." Revelation has a critical role in creation itself, which only becomes creation retroactively in light of revelation.

The past creation is demonstrated from out (of) the living, present revelation—demonstrated, that is, pointed out. In the glow of the experienced miracle of revelation, a past that prepares and foresees this miracle becomes visible. The creation which becomes visible in revelation is creation of the revelation. At this point the experiential and presentive character is immovably fixed, and only here can revelation receive a past. But it really must do so. God does not answer the soul's acknowledgment, its "I am thine," with an equally simple "Thou art mine." Rather he reaches back into the past and identifies himself as the one who originated and indicated this whole dialogue between himself and the soul: "I have called thee by name: thou art mine." (Rosenzweig 1971, 182–83)

The wholly present moment of revelation, when the individual experiences God's commanding love, enlightens the individual regarding their past as well. She suddenly sees that the name God calls her was her name all along. In a sense, experiencing the divine in the present gives the individual a new perspective on her past. She suddenly becomes aware that what she had thought was a meaningless past was actually a divine creation. As one leading Rosenzweig scholar put it, "Defining moments in one's life, one might suggest, shed light on the past and suggest the way one's past has prepared for and led up to these very defining moments" (Pollock 2009, 241–42). The past and the present shape each other simultaneously. We understand our past through our present and our present through our past.

This circular understanding allows for the present as a ground from which to critique the past. Rosenzweig's understanding of creation, taken by itself, risks sliding into uncritical sanctification of the past. If the past determines who we are, then any act can be justified as conformity with the past. The critical, circular relationship between past and present means that considerations rooted in the individual's experience of the present can override or shift the concerns of the past.

Created as a Jew

There is a biographical aspect of this theology that is worth highlighting. Rosenzweig initially approached the past not just as a philosopher and a theologian, but as a historian. Rosenzweig studied history in university, writing his doctorate under the great German historian Friedrich Meinecke. However, he eventually lost faith in historicism's ability to establish the meaningfulness of history or events (Mendes-Flohr 1991, 311–37). He took up a radically subjectivist form of Christianity that denied any meaning to the world or history at all (Pollock 2014, 51–96, 96–126).[11] He ultimately decided not to convert to Christianity after an intense discussion with his close friend, Eugen Rosenstock. Rosenzweig later said of the conversation: "What it means that God created the world and [is] *not just* the God of revelation—this I know precisely out of the Leipzig night-conversation of 7.7.13. At that time, I was on the best road to Marcionitism" (Benjamin 2014, 19). Rosenstock convinced him of the importance of accepting, rather than rejecting, the world (with this, the idea of redemption suddenly becomes possible as well, but that is beyond the scope of this chapter). As opposed to Rosenzweig's almost "Marcionite" theology, which saw the world as opposed to God, Rosenstock convinced him that God created the world, and thus the two could not be in opposition to each other. Accepting his worldly creatureliness led Rosenzweig to embrace his Jewishness (Pollock

2014, 51–96). He was born a Jew, and it played (and would increasingly play) a determining role in his life.

This is perhaps best demonstrated by an open letter Rosenzweig wrote to his contemporary Martin Buber on the topic of Jewish law (Rosenzweig 1955, 72–92). The letter, known as "The Builders," covers a lot of theological ground, but its main point plays on a homiletic rabbinic reading of Isaiah 54:13: "All your children shall be taught by the Lord, and great shall be the prosperity of your children."[12] The rabbinic reading focuses on a Hebrew pun: the Hebrew word for "your children," "*banayikh*," in Isaiah 54:13 looks and sounds similar to the Hebrew word for "your builders," "*bonayikh*." The rabbinic homily thus suggests that Isaiah's words really refer to the "builders" of Jewish law, namely the rabbis themselves, who organized the rabbinic legal corpus.[13]

This punning exegesis provides Rosenzweig with the underlying structure of his argument for following Jewish law. While he in principle agrees with Buber that any given individual could experience a revelatory divine "command" within any act, not only those within the canon of Jewish law, he argues to Buber that following traditional Jewish law is critical. This is because while a person can theoretically experience any act as a divine command, that divine command won't necessarily be Jewish in any significant sense, it won't necessarily be a *mitsvah* (the traditional Jewish term, literally meaning "command"). Rosenzweig and Buber are starkly distinguishing between written, generalizable "laws" and the instantaneous, singular "command" that a person can sense within herself (Rosenzweig 1955, 75–76, 85–86).

Returning to the rabbinic homily, Rosenzweig comments, "In the words of the Talmud, we have only to be sons, in order to become builders" (Rosenzweig 1955, 88). Being a "son," rooted in the Jewish past, is what enables being a "builder," someone who experiences the Jewish divine command of a *mitsvah*. A person who experiences a revelatory "command" in the present senses the divine within a specific action and thus "builds" the corpus of Jewish law by adding this action to it. This process, Rosenzweig argues, is predicated on being actively engaged in the praxis of traditional Jewish law. Otherwise, a person's "command" may be a divine revelation, but it will not be a Jewish revelation, and it will bear no relationship to traditional Judaism; it will not "build" Jewish law. The relationship between the two terms of the pun, between "children" and "builders," is thus explained through the relationship between past and present, creation and revelation.

Rosenzweig is essentially applying his ideas of revelation and creation to the specific issue of Jewish law. For an action to be a Jewish action, it must partake in the Jewish past, which is to say Jewish law. Jewish law is the collection of actions that accumulated throughout the history of the Jewish people. Parallel to creation, to the pre-existing world into which we are born and which defines us, Jewish law is the context in which any Jewish act occurs. While revelation, the individual's singular encounter with the divine in the present moment, can take place in any act, in order for it to be a Jewish revelation it must take place within a Jewish context, within the context of Jewish law. While Buber and Rosenzweig agreed about the possibilities of revelation, they disagreed about the necessity of creation. Buber seems to have shifted away from this position in some areas over time, but in the realm of Jewish law he held firm: the law of the past cannot have anything to do with revelation.[14]

As discussed above, Rosenzweig claims both that the present is grounded in the past and that the past is discovered and shaped by the present. In "The Builders," this latter part of the relationship manifests in the capacity to determine which parts of traditional Jewish law to uphold and which to let fall away. "The danger of looking back is, however, that, although one waits for both, one fails to distinguish between the dead waste in the stream and those whose slower speed is due to their proximity to the source" (Rosenzweig 1955, 89). The importance of the past veers too easily toward the uncritical embrace of every single aspect of the past. However, there are inevitably elements of the past that ought to be left behind intermingled with the elements that bear personal religious significance for the individual; the trick is in determining which is which. Only the individual who follows Jewish law, the "son," can decide which laws to follow, which to abandon, and even which new laws to add; only they can be a "builder" (Rosenzweig 1955, 86–88). It is our rootedness in the past that situates and enables our free action in the present (Pollock 2014, 85–94). In Rosenzweig's case, it was his recognition that he was created a Jew that led him to become one of the most creative Jewish philosophers and theologians of the twentieth century.[15]

LUKE CAGE AND CREATION

Having laid out Franz Rosenzweig's theology of creation, the time has come to return to *Luke Cage*. Above, we examined the primary character arcs of the season. What new aspects of these arcs come into focus in light of Rosenzweig's theology? How can his understanding of creation and revelation help us understand *Luke Cage*? As we shall see, the characters of *Luke Cage* are grappling with the same issues Rosenzweig brings to the fore in his theology of creation.

Bushmaster

Bushmaster is obsessed with the past. He wants to embody the violent claims of the past in present vengeance. He is so determined to achieve this goal that he does not care what happens as a result. For all he cares, his friends and loved ones can perish in the fire of the past, as long as the Stokes burn as well. This is in fact what happens: Bushmaster successfully takes everything from Mariah and causes her death (albeit indirectly), but the Jamaicans closest to him in New York are killed in the process. He leaves New York a broken man, relying on others to put the finishing touches on his vengeful project.

On one level, this is a cautionary tale about obsession with the past. More immanently, the story moves from this obsession with the past toward giving the past its proper place. In the final episode of the season, a broken Bushmaster's closest friends take him home to Jamaica to recover, with one remarking, "Johnny finally got to top of the hill. Now, he can't even enjoy the view" ("They Reminisce Over You," 2.13). He succeeded in his goal of destroying the Stokes, but was himself destroyed in the process.

In Rosenzweig's terms, Bushmaster embodies creation. If creation is the idea that the past constitutes who we are in the present, Bushmaster tries to be defined by nothing other than his past. In his attempt to right the injustices of the past, he constantly runs into the real consequences of his actions. Bushmaster's opposition between healthy, respectable bourgeoisie life and making war for the sake of the past leaves no room for a meaningful present. He finds meaning in the past to the exclusion of a thriving, present-based life. Bushmaster demonstrates the dangers of the creation, of rooting your life (religious or otherwise) in the past. Religious meaning cannot be derived purely from the past. This is why Rosenzweig anchors the awareness of creation within the experience of revelation, to enable a critical evaluation of the former. Without a sense of revelation in the present, Bushmaster is destroyed by his faith in the past.

Mariah Stokes

Mariah, as we have seen, attempts to do just the opposite, to deny creation. Mariah wants to deny that she has any past whatsoever. If she could get her way, she would create her new life *ex nihilo*, embracing the convenient "fiction" of her married name, "Dillard." She wants to escape the criminal violence of her family's past and make herself anew, exactly the type of hubris against which Rosenzweig was fighting. Creation, Rosenzweig argues, means recognizing the limits of human existence, starting with the historical situation of the individual. The individual is always situated in a certain moment, meaning she has a past that critically shapes who she is; to deny this is to deny creation.

It is only once Mariah learns to embrace her family past, to embrace creation, that she speaks about redemption. Speaking to Tilda about the importance of passing on the family legacy, Mariah remarks, "It redeems all of this.

Redeems me" ("On and On," 2.7). All of Mariah's crimes take on a different, redeemed meaning when she begins to live a life illuminated by the fullness of her past. However, she quickly goes too far in the other direction and falls to the same fate as Bushmaster. She embraces her past uncritically, allowing it to override the concerns of the present. She sees it as a dichotomy, either Stokes or Dillard, rather than looking for an integrative option.

Luke Cage

Luke is the only one of the characters who manages to achieve a stable relationship with his past. He begins the season by denying his relationship with his past, but ultimately ends up embracing it. However, unlike the others he is able to do so with balance and moderation. When he shifts from denying his relationship with his father to accepting it, he does not do so at the expense of his life in the present. When his father asks Luke to come away with him, Luke refuses in favor of remaining in Harlem as its protector. However, the manner in which he protects Harlem becomes less volatile and aggressive, a shift Luke attributes to his upbringing at the hands of his father. Luke successfully balances both creation and revelation, past and present.

A notable turning point in Luke's arc takes place when Bushmaster paralyzes him and kicks him into the Hudson River, though we only hear about this later. While unconscious underwater, Luke has a vision of his past. He recalls a time when his father and mother came to visit him while he was in prison, and in this vision his mother tells him that she believes his innocence. Describing this experience to his father, Luke says that he felt God was telling him that "The world may be my problem but it's not always my fault" ("On and On," 2.7). Luke thus frames his vision of the past as a divine revelation, a source of critical divine guidance about how he should live his life. This is the most explicitly theological presentation of the past, and it guides the title character toward a meaningful, purposeful life.

Thus all three main characters participate in the show's theology of the past. The past is a necessary and unavoidable source of guidance and meaning, one marked as divinely significant. While the show eschews typical religious rituals and discourse, it foregrounds theological language such as "revelation" and "redemption." It attributes great significance to the past, and its one explicitly religious character, Pastor James Lucas, identifies "God" with whatever element in the past that makes a person who they are ("They Reminisce Over You," 2.13). The show thus provides a theology without a religion (in stark contrast with Netflix's *Daredevil*, where the main character's religion takes center stage), manifest in the events of an individual's life and in the facts of her past. The righteous individual, the hero, is the one who can find meaning in the past without being a slave to it.

THE THEMATIC OF NAMES

By way of conclusion, I want to draw attention to the theme of names that runs throughout *Luke Cage* season two, and which has striking parallels in Franz Rosenzweig's writings. Luke insists that people should call him "Luke Cage" instead of the name his father gave him and still insists on calling him, "Carl Lucas." Bushmaster corrects people who call him "Johnny," telling them that he goes by "Bushmaster" now. And perhaps most intensely, Mariah struggles personally with whether she ought rightly be called "Dillard" or "Stokes," and all the while Bushmaster aggressively rebukes anyone who calls her "Dillard," saying she is really a Stokes.

What is the relationship between a name and that which it names? Is the connection inherent, with the name expressing some characteristic inherent in the named object, or is it conventional, with the name saying more about those who use it than about that which it names? Moreover, no one typically chooses their own name. Names are something we give to others, something we use to denote people and objects which we encounter. So to say that a name is "our name" is not to say that it belongs to us so much as to say that it is what others have always called us. It carries the weight and connotations of the life we have lived, the encounters of our past.

Franz Rosenzweig was very sensitive to these and other issues regarding the working of names. In "The New Thinking," Rosenzweig notes that "the problem of the name of God is only a part of the logical problems of the name in general" (Rosenzweig 2000b, 129).[16] His small book *Understanding the Sick and the Healthy: A View of World, Man, and God*, is dedicated entirely to the question of how names work, with a specific focus on how this affects people who try to use names to understand their world.[17]

In a move more parallel to the stories of the names in *Luke Cage* season two, Franz Rosenzweig also wrote two letters expressing deep concern with the nature of his own name. In the first, he writes to a friend about why his own German first name, Franz, is so dissatisfying to him.

One thing is certain, I have no real feeling about my first name. I can only guess why this is. It seems to me that it may be because my parents gave it to me without any particular feeling, simply because they "liked it" (and why did they like it? because at that time it was "different"; only later were there other Franzes in the Jewish community of Cassel). It's as though my parents had seen it in a shop window, walked inside, and bought it. It has nothing traditional about it, no memory, no history, not even an anecdote, scarcely a whim—it was simply a passing fancy. *A family name, a saint's name, a hero's name, a poetic name, a symbolic name, all these are good: they have grown naturally, not been bought ready-made. One should be named after somebody or something. Else a name is really only empty breath.* (Glatzer 1953, 57; emphasis added)

Rosenzweig here complains that his first name, Franz, lacks any weighty past. His parents chose it on a whim, as if they had impulse bought it while waiting in the checkout line. It expresses their present moment in Cassel, their relationship to a social context that prized individualism and didn't have anyone named Franz, but it does not have a past. It expresses a bourgeoise individualism rather than a *Jude-sein*, a being-Jewish, an existential belonging to a collective with a shared past.[18] Ideally, Rosenzweig said, a name should not be "empty breath" but a naming-after, a recurrence of the past within the present moment (cf. Rosenzweig 1971, 188). It's not something you can just buy at the store and take home, but something that has to sprout organically out of the past. If our pasts play a determining role in who we are, then our names should reflect that.

In contrast to how his parents named him, Rosenzweig had a strong sense of what his real Hebrew name should have been.[19]

Now I know perfectly well that my [Hebrew] name is Levi, which is supposed to correspond to Louis. But this is a ticklish matter, for the whole *am haaretzus* [ignorance] of my early years is bound up with it. Only Levites can properly be called Levi. . . . Grandfather Louis's name was, of course, not Levi, though I had Levi carved on father's tombstone without bothering to investigate. As I later found out from Uncle Traugott's tombstone, his real name was Yehudah [Judah], which also, of course, corresponds to Louis: the connecting link is the lion Judah of Jacob's blessing. Consequently my correct name should have been Judah ben Samuel, which is exactly the name of the great man whose middle-sized reincarnation upon the road of *ibbur* [transmigration] I am: Judah ha-Levi. (Glatzer 1961, 167)[20]

As this letter to his mother makes clear, Rosenzweig identified strongly with the medieval Jewish philosopher and poet Judah Halevi. In addition to the numerous parallels between Rosenzweig and Halevi's respective theologies, Rosenzweig spent much of his final years, while suffering from crippling paralysis due to amyotrophic lateral sclerosis, translating Halevi's poetry from medieval Hebrew into twentieth-century German (Rosenzweig 2000a; Benjamin 2009, 65–102). He felt the weight of Halevi pressing out of the past and into his own life, and was convinced that his Hebrew name should reflect that, rather than reflecting an incidental, momentary impulse.[21]

Rosenzweig's struggle to reject a name rooted in the present and find for himself a name rooted in the past echoes the drama of names in *Luke Cage*. Bushmaster shares Rosenzweig's desire for a name bearing the weight of the past. He throws off the name "Johnny McIver" in favor of the name of the rum brand that was stolen from his family, along with all the money it was worth, by the Stokes. He wants to be named for the violent past that calls out for retribution. Mariah, at least initially, takes the opposite approach. She wants to take a new name, Dillard, representative of a brighter present rather than the dark past of the family name, Stokes, into which she was born. Luke wants to forget his father and the name his father gave him, replacing them with a name and life of his own making, much like Mariah.

All three characters choose between the names their parents gave them and names they would create for themselves (in contrast to Rosenzweig, who wants to choose between the name his parents gave him and a name he dreams up out of the past). The different names, however, have different significances in each case. Bushmaster chooses a name that expresses the violent past, rather than his given name reflective of the Jamaican community in the present. In the language of *The Star*, he wants creation but not revelation. Mariah is the opposite; she chooses a name for her present, rather than accepting the name of her past. She wants to have revelation without creation. Both Bushmaster and Mariah learn the hard way that you have to have both. You can't let your past consume the present, because the present is where people live, and they will all suffer if given over wholly to the past. And you can't pretend the past doesn't exist, because you will one day wake up to discover that it has consumed your present. Luke begins on the same page as Mariah, attempting to deny his past, but throughout his arc he learns to accept his past and the meaning it bears for his present life. *Luke Cage* thus presents a challenge for its audience, asking if they can see their own names as carrying the divine significance and meaning of the past.

NOTES

1. As a recently released series, Netflix's *Luke Cage* has received relatively little scholarly attention, particularly in connection with religion. That said, for a good look at some of the religious themes in the first season of Luke Cage, see Derry et al. 2015, 123–55.

2. For brevity's sake, "*Luke Cage*" refers to *Luke Cage* season two.

3. Batnitzky 2000; Gordon 2003. Batnitzky and Gordon disagree about whether Hans Georg Gadamer or Martin Heidegger is a better comparison for Franz Rosenzweig's hermeneutics. See Gordon 2003, 12n29, 133, 182–83.

4. *Der Stern der Erlösung* in the original German. While Rosenzweig wrote almost exclusively in German, for simplicity's sake I will cite only from the standard English translations.

5. Discussing creation in this context will also require discussing revelation. Rosenzweig's concept of redemption is ultimately inseparable from the other two, but the requirements of space force us to leave it out of this paper. Fortunately, creation, and the adjunct role sometimes played by revelation, are sufficient for exploring the theology of the past in *Luke Cage*. However, it is worth noting that typical forms of organized religion really only appear in *The Star* when Rosenzweig begins to discuss redemption.

6. This line, originally from Psalms 118:22, has a history all its own when it comes to pop culture in general and Jamaica in specific. For example, see Erskine 2001, 97–109.

7. All quotations from *Luke Cage* are copied from *Springfield!* 2019.

8. This echoes Rosenzweig's idea that commitment and sacrifice, found in their peak form in the self-sacrifice of martyrdom, come together to create truth. See Batnitzky 2000, 42–46. Compare also Bushmaster's comment, quoted above, about being a warrior rather than a puppet or a slave, and our discussion below of the past as fundamentally amoral.

9. After this point, Luke's father departs the show for the remainder of the season. Luke eventually returns to his violent approach at the very end of the season, choosing to replace Mariah as Harlem's ruler in order to take a more proactive approach to crime prevention.

10. This is most striking in Rosenzweig's discussion of redemption and in his rejection of the modern idea of historical progress. For the former, see the excellent discussion in Pollock 2014, 209–15. For the latter, see Rosenzweig 1971, 99–100, 225–27.

11. This is in contrast to earlier depictions of Rosenzweig's "conversion" as a shift from skeptical philosophy to revelational faith, which Pollock claims all ultimately stem from the depiction in Glatzer 1953. See Pollock 2014, 5–8.

12. Translation taken from the New Revised Standard Version

13. Cf. Babylonian Talmud, Tractate Berakhot 64a.

14. In "The Builders" itself, Rosenzweig discusses Buber's shift away from this position when it comes to traditional Jewish texts.

15. Of particular note is a letter Rosenzweig wrote to Meinecke explaining why he could not accept the academic teaching position Meinecke had arranged for him, instead choosing to devote himself to the education of the German-Jewish community, following the "dark drive" that he "names" his Judaism. See Glatzer 1953, 94–98. Amid powerful imagery, Rosenzweig frames his innermost self as something he inherited from the past:

> I descended into the vaults of my being. . . . I approached the ancient treasure chest whose existence I had never wholly forgotten. . . . Then I climbed back again to the upper stories and spread out before me "what treasures I had found: they did not fade in the sheer light of day. *These, indeed, were my own trea-*

sures, my most personal possessions, things inherited, not borrowed! By owning them and ruling over them I had gained something entirely new, namely the right to live. [Emphasis added]

In this letter, Rosenzweig depicts his return to Judaism as a return to his deepest self, which is itself a return to his inherited, communal past. In fact, Rosenzweig creates an opposition between "things inherited" and "things borrowed," such that the *only* way for something to be deeply personal and inherent to the self is for it to be part of a person's past, rather than something picked up in the present.

16. Rosenzweig doesn't explain what he has in mind with this line, but based on *The Star* and *Understanding the Sick and the Healthy*, he means something like what the connection is between a name and the object to which it refers, particularly in light of the way objects change over time.

17. Rosenzweig 1999. See also the helpful introduction by Hilary Putnam, who reads Rosenzweig's theory of names with an analytic bent.

18. On the unique form of collective being of the Jewish people according to Rosenzweig, see Gordon 2003, 198–202; Pollock 2014, 121–23.

19. It seems to have been common in Rosenzweig's day for many Jews to receive a name in both German and traditional Hebrew.

20. For an excellent discussion of both this and the previously cited letter, see Benjamin 2009, 67–68. For a discussion of the logic behind this second letter, see ibid., 68n7.

21. Rosenzweig's tantalizing reference to the doctrine of "transmigration," of the rebirth of souls in new bodies generation after generation, should probably be taken as a playful metaphor rather than a literal, metaphysical claim.

Chapter Seven

Spider-Man and the Theology of Weakness

Gregory Stevenson

Since his debut in 1962, Spider-Man has regularly been hailed as one of the most popular of all superheroes. This popularity derives from two features of his heroic identity: his relatability—the normal, real-world problems that afflict him make him a super-powered reflection of ourselves—and his responsibility—represented by his frequently expressed motto: "With great power there must also come great responsibility."[1] By means of these two poles of relatability and responsibility, Spider-Man changed the paradigm for what a superhero could be (Fingeroth 2004, 146). Yet, neither of these is unique to Spider-Man. He is not the only superhero with relatable, real-world problems. Other superheroes struggle with money troubles, relationship problems, and failure. Likewise, though he may vocalize the relationship between power and responsibility more frequently, it is certainly not unique to him. Virtually every superhero attempts to use their power responsibly. In fact, it is a requirement for being a super*hero*.

What sets Spider-Man apart is how he understands the nature of power itself. Perhaps more than any other superhero, Spider-Man embodies the paradox that true power requires weakness. Viewing Spider-Man in light of the biblical theology of weakness clarifies the deeper nuances inherent in this character's embrace of power and responsibility. These nuances are on display in two recent examples within the Spider-Man canon: Dan Slott's 2012–2018 run on *The Amazing Spider-Man/The Superior Spider-Man* and the 2017 Marvel film *Spider-Man: Homecoming*. Examining recent explorations on this theme in different genres (comics versus film) and in different formats (long-form storytelling versus a contained story) highlights the consistency of the theme and its integral nature to the character of Spider-Man.

THE THEOLOGY OF WEAKNESS

A constant theme throughout the Bible is God's inversion of the values and standards of the world (Ortlund 2010, 86, 107). Those things deemed powerful by worldly standards (wealth, status, ambition, physical strength) are proven ineffectual in the light of God's activity in the world. This theme is best captured in the paradox that true power manifests through weakness. Throughout the Bible God often works most powerfully through characters who appear weak by worldly standards—an elderly Abraham, young shepherd boy David, a teenaged Mary (for a fuller survey of this theme see Ortlund 2010, 88–106). Luke in his Gospel expresses this paradox through his rendering of the Divine Reversal, the notion that God upends the value system of the world. Thus the Jesus of Luke repeatedly declares that "the first shall be last and the last shall be first" (13:30), that "those who exalt themselves will be humbled and those who humble themselves will be exalted" (14:11; 18:14), and that "whoever is least among you all is the greatest" (9:48). In the book of Revelation, John informs the seven churches that victory comes through weakness—through a willingness to endure suffering and even to accept death. Revelation also captures well a central notion of the Christian faith, that is that the cross of Christ is the quintessential symbol of power through weakness. The saints "triumphed" over Satan "by the blood of the Lamb" (Rev. 12:11).

One of the best places, however, to witness this "theology of weakness," as Marva Dawn calls it (Dawn 2001, 35), is in Paul's letters to Corinth. The church at Corinth appears fully invested in the value system of the world and impressed by worldly notions of power. They are drawn to influential teachers (1 Cor. 1–4), seduced by impressive pedigrees (2 Cor. 10), and captivated by displays of spiritual power (1 Cor. 14). In response Paul reminds them that "God chose the foolish things of the world to shame the wise; God chose the weak things of the world to shame the strong" (1 Cor. 1:27). As Ortlund has effectively shown (2010, 100–101), Paul explores this paradox of strength through weakness most consistently in 2 Corinthians where he declares that "victory comes through captivity (2:12–17) . . . sufficiency through insufficiency (3:1–6) . . . life through death (4:7–15) . . . blessing through suffering (6:3–10) . . . salvation through grief (7:2–10) . . . abundance through poverty (8:1–2, 9) . . . commendation through denigration (10:10–18) . . . boasting through hardship (11:16–30)." In 2 Corinthians 12, Paul invokes his own experience when he details a "thorn in the flesh" that left him weak and which God would not remove despite Paul's repeated prayers. Paul learned from this that when his own power is stripped away, Christ's power is then able to work through him (Dawn 2001, 45). So Paul declares, "That is why, for

Christ's sake, I delight in weaknesses. . . . For when I am weak, then I am strong" (12:10).

Throughout the biblical tradition, the notion of power through weakness is a comment on how God operates in the world with respect to human agency. When I am nothing, when I learn to give up control over my life, then God's power is able to manifest through me because only then is my will, my arrogance, and my desire for control no longer standing in the way. Defined in broad theological terms, this weakness is complete submission to the will of God (Dawn 2001, 37). Several theologians further define this weakness in terms of its practical expression. It requires an awareness and acceptance of one's finitude and limits (Packer 2013, 15, 54; Kreeft 1989, 24), a rejection of the worldly pursuit of wealth, achievement, and status as the mark of power (Dawn 2001, 45, 49), an embrace of humility and dependence over against pride and the independence it spawns (Kreeft 1989, 25), and an acknowledgment of our "inability finally to control our life situation relationally, circumstantially, financially, healthwise" (Packer 2013, 87–88).

Jürgen Moltmann says that the power of God is displayed through weakness most meaningfully in the form of the crucified Jesus. The doctrine of *kenoticism* (the self-emptying of God through the act of incarnation) reveals the paradoxical truth that "God is not greater than he is in this humiliation. God is not more glorious than he is in this self-surrender. God is not more powerful than he is in this helplessness" (Moltmann 1974, 205). Peter Kreeft, asking how we enact this paradox of the cross in our own lives, looks to the saints as a model, declaring that they embody the power and weakness inherent in the cross of Christ by "heroically" giving of themselves to relieve the suffering of others while at the same time accepting their own suffering. In other words, they both fight against and accept suffering (Kreeft 1989, 23–24).

Whereas this theological tradition of power through weakness highlights submission to the will of God, Spider-Man has never been an overtly religious character and the interplay of power and weakness in his characterization is not grounded in a specific relationship with God. Rather, Spider-Man represents a secularized version of this theological principle, albeit one with distinct spiritual overtones.

A SUPERIOR SPIDER-MAN?

In the latter part of Dan Slott's ten-year run on *The Amazing Spider-Man*, he presents a story arc that demonstrates it is not the motto itself (that with great power comes great responsibility) that defines the character of Spider-Man, but rather how Peter Parker defines and implements that motto. Dan Slott's exploration casts the character of Peter Parker/Spider-Man in sharp relief, exposing the true essence of his power and responsibility, through a series of contrasts with others who likewise attempt to wield power responsibly.

Set-Up: *The Amazing Spider-Man* # 698–700

In a wildly controversial move, Dan Slott in late 2012 brought his "Big Time" story arc to a close by killing off Peter Parker. Otto Octavius (aka Doctor Octopus), one of Spider-Man's long-time enemies,[2] was dying from a debilitating disease. Refusing to accept his finitude, Octavius employed technology he had created to swap his consciousness with that of Spider-Man's. Suddenly Octavius finds himself in Peter Parker's healthy body, while Parker's consciousness is now imprisoned in Octavius' dying form. As Peter Parker lies dying in Octavius' body, he sees his life flash before his eyes while Octavius (in Parker's body) stands over him dressed as Spider-Man. In that moment, the technology Octavius used to achieve the mind swap creates a link between Octavius' consciousness and that of Parker's so that Otto Octavius witnesses all of the memories of Peter Parker. Overwhelmed by the weight of Peter's memories, Octavius promises the dying Peter that he will faithfully carry on his legacy as Spider-Man, but confesses that he doesn't know how. In response, Peter informs him that "with great power must come great responsibility." As Peter Parker dies in Octavius' body, Octavius stands tall in Spider-Man's body and vows to fulfill that mission, declaring, "Know this, I will carry on in your name. You may be leaving this world, but you are not leaving it to a villain. I swear. I will *be* Spider-Man. Better yet with my unparalleled genius—and my boundless ambition—I'll be a *better* Spider-Man than you *ever* were. From this day forth, I shall become . . . The Superior Spider-Man" (*The Amazing Spider-Man* #700; hereafter *ASM*).

By transferring Spider-Man's life and mission to one of his greatest villains, Slott allows us to witness how power and responsibility play differently in the hands of another. Slott establishes the contrast from the outset in that Octavius' refusal to accept the limitations of his own mortality and the arrogance and ambition that drive him to become a "better" Spider-Man identify an approach that will make power the more important element in that equation. With a new Spider-Man comes a change in title for his flagship series, for Octavius' Spider-Man is not merely "Amazing" but "Superior."

The Superior Spider-Man # 1–31

Otto Octavius shares much in common with Peter Parker: both had a tragic childhood, both are scientists, both attained power through an experiment gone wrong, and both have a soft spot for Aunt May. The key difference, of course, is that Octavius is a villain. By casting a villain in the role of Spider-Man, Slott presents us with a mirror-image that is more akin to that of a twisted, fun-house mirror. Otto Octavius, as Spider-Man, has vowed to fulfill Spider-Man's mission to use his power responsibly. Consequently, Otto's stated goal is "to make this world a better place" (*The Superior Spider-Man* #20; hereafter *SSM*).

A primary difference between hero and villain is that heroes are reactive whereas villains are proactive (Fingeroth 2004, 161–62). According to Fingeroth, unless there is no alternative, the hero does not actively seek change but instead reacts to threats and dangers. As a hero, Peter Parker lets himself be controlled by the needs of others, responding to situations as they present themselves. A villain, however, refuses to give up control, preferring to shape their own destiny and the destiny of the world. In his desire to be a *superior* Spider-Man, Octavius identifies Parker's reactive nature as a weakness, declaring Parker "a man of limited vision. No plans. No schemes" (*SSM* #4). Though he has taken on Spider-Man's responsibility, Octavius rejects Peter Parker's approach to that responsibility, believing he can improve upon it. Driving those "improvements," though, is an understanding of power that is based on arrogance and a refusal to accept limitations.

What drove Otto Octavius as a villain is the same thing that drives him as a hero: unrelenting ambition. Refusing to be bothered by "the small stuff," he sets his sights on making *the world* a better place and ending criminal activity in New York once and for all. His ambition pushes him to be superior to Peter Parker in every way—as a hero, a scientist, and as a man. Because Otto defines power in line with the worldly emphasis on status and influence, he seeks public accolades for his victories, frets that the credit for his scientific achievements will now go to Peter Parker (whom he is impersonating) rather than to himself, and takes time out of his hero duties to finish Parker's doctoral thesis because he cannot bear not to possess his well-earned title of "Doctor" (*SSM* #1). Otto's arrogance generates a condescending attitude toward the police (whom he treats as his minions), toward his enemies (whom he calls "dolts," "imbeciles," and "idiots"), and even toward the very people he saves, identifying them as "senseless cattle" and declaring that he will be a better hero than they deserve (*SSM* #10). His arrogance also results in a refusal to accept failure or embarrassment. Whereas Peter Parker blamed himself for his failures, Otto Octavius blames others (*SSM* #7). Whereas Peter Parker good naturedly poked fun at himself and took public humiliation in stride, Otto badly beats up Jester and Screwball when they embarrass him in public (*SSM* #6).

Due to his sense of superiority, Otto believes he needs no one's help and views independence as a sign of strength. As a scientist, he refuses to work with others at Horizon Labs and, as a hero, severs his ties with the Avengers. He declares that it was these very ties to other people that made Peter Parker "weak" and "dependent" and so, Otto concludes, relying on allies cannot make him stronger but "only weaker" (*SSM* #6AU).

Another distinguishing feature between Octavius' Spider-Man and Parker's Spider-Man is their attitude toward limitations. Peter Parker had always limited himself as Spider-Man by refusing to use his full strength out of fear of hurting someone or even killing them. Shortly after taking over Spider-Man's body, however, Otto realizes how much strength Peter Parker truly had and that he must have been holding back all those years. He vows not to hold himself back and to use all power at his disposal in the fight against evil. This marks a defining distinction in their dueling understandings of power and responsibility. For Peter Parker, power used responsibly is power restrained. For Otto Octavius, "great power" means "might makes right" and "great responsibility" is the willingness to use that power to stop evil at any cost. Otto believes that the ends justify the means so that any use of power, if it brings an end to evil, is responsible. When Otto destroys Wilson Fisk's building with no concern as to whether Fisk himself died in the process, Officer Carlie Cooper questions his actions. Otto counters that "to let evil flourish while I have the power to stop it . . . that, Officer Cooper, would be the most irresponsible act of all." Captain Watanabe chimes in: "So might makes right?" Otto replies, "I prefer the phrase 'With great power comes great responsibility.' But yes, Captain, it does" (*SSM* #15).

Otto believes that the greater good justifies the use of any form of power at his disposal. One such form of power is technology. In order to increase his efficiency at crime fighting, Otto sends out 8,000 Spiderbots to patrol the city, utilizes giant robots to fight evil, and creates a system to reroute lesser crimes to the police and fire departments so he can focus on the big picture. In one instance, Otto convinces a Horizon employee to give him technology that allows him to collect data from all over the city. When the employee protests that it is "too much power for one guy," Otto responds that limiting his access to power is what would be irresponsible when he argues, "I see everything in this city. Everything! That is my power! And my responsibility—to watch over and judge you all!" (*SSM* #5). Otto is so convinced that technological power is the ultimate expression of his responsibility that he creates his own tech company called Parker Industries and installs himself as CEO. When he announces to Aunt May his grandiose goal to use Parker Industries to "change the world," Aunt May, thinking she is talking to her nephew, says, "That's not how I raised you. Pride goeth before a fall" (*SSM* #20).

That fall, however, will not come easily. Rather than setting up the Superior Spider-Man as a straw man to be easily torn down, Slott forces both the audience and Peter Parker himself to question whether Otto might be right. Though Otto believed he had killed Peter Parker when he took over his body, Peter's consciousness actually survived, buried deep within the brain they share. Peter has witnessed what Otto has been doing in his body and at times begins to question himself in light of Otto's successes. Otto's unrestrained use of technology has allowed him to capture four times as many criminals and to stop more thefts than Peter Parker ever did.

The question of whether or not the ends justify the means has long been at the heart of the debate over responsible uses of power. Otto believes that any use of power is justified if it results in stopping evil, whereas Peter argues that power must be restrained even if that leads to the persistence of evil. Peter's refusal to kill his enemies raises an ethical question when those same enemies go on to kill again. Slott employs this debate as a means of clarifying the differing approaches of these two Spider-Men when a murderous villain (codenamed Massacre) that Peter Parker had previously apprehended escapes from prison and murders thirty-five more people. Otto vows to kill Massacre as Peter's consciousness ineffectually protests that it is not up to them to decide who lives and dies (*SSM* #4). Peter's protest begins to sound hollow even to himself when Otto points out that thirty-five innocent people died because Spider-Man refused to kill. Otto argues that there is "only one solution"—killing Massacre. Peter's consciousness, however, argues that there is always hope for redemption. That is the crux of the matter. Peter is willing to accept the possibility that the villains he captures might one day harm others again because he believes that the possibility for redemption must always be preserved. Due to his own sense of inferiority, coupled with the guilt from all of those he failed to protect, Peter Parker is a man perpetually on the road toward redemption and he cannot bear to deny that path to others. Otto, however, declares that Massacre cannot be redeemed because once a killer, always a killer—so he puts a bullet in his brain (*SSM* #5). The irony is that Otto himself is a former killer on the path toward redemption, yet in his arrogance he fails to recognize that potentiality in others. It is Peter's willingness to embrace his own weakness and need for redemption that allows him to extend that hope to others.

Otto's path toward redemption, however, involves learning what Peter Parker already knows—that *weakness* born of humility, dependence, self-restraint, and sacrifice is the true measure of strength. As the world Octavius built starts to crumble around him with the city and his employees turning against him, his company in dire straits, and his attempts at heroism failing to stop crime, he suddenly begins to doubt his approach. Then, when the Green Goblin kidnaps his beloved Anna Maria Marconi, Octavius for the first time feels truly powerless. In a not-so-subtle nod to a popular appropriation of the

Jesus story, Octavius even begins to ask himself, "What would Parker do?" Finally acknowledging his own *inferiority* and his need to depend on others (both things he previously denigrated as weaknesses), Octavius admits his inability to save her. So, for the first time truly embodying Peter Parker's understanding of power and responsibility, Octavius sacrifices himself by erasing his consciousness from Peter Parker's body and relinquishing control. Before he does, though, he tells Peter in their shared psyche, "For I know . . . only *you* can save her. Because you *are* the Superior Spider-Man" (*SSM* #30).

In Spider-Man's body, Otto Octavius attempted to use the power at his disposal as responsibly as he knew how. The problem was that he understood power in terms of social status, strength, achievement, and global influence, and he defined the responsible use of that power as making the world better *at any cost*. Peter Parker's unique understanding of power and responsibility, however, comes into clearer focus as we see how he adapts to being back in his body but in a world that Doctor Octopus has created in his absence.

The Aftermath: *The Amazing Spider-Man (2014)* #1–18 and *(2015)* #1–31

With Peter Parker now back in his own body, the contrast with the "Superior Spider-Man" is stark and immediate. He apologizes for all of the harm Octavius did in his stead, deals with an act of public humiliation by making jokes at his own expense, and risks his life to save one of his enemies. In other words, he chooses the weaker path of humility and self-limitation. Unlike Octavius, whose blind ambition led him to want to save "the world" and caused him to view "the small stuff" as unworthy of his attention, Peter Parker initially believes that he also can take on the world and will no longer need to bother with "the small stuff"—until he sees a woman being robbed and realizes that, for him, there is no "small stuff." He says, "This will *always* be exactly where I belong. The world of . . . Your Friendly Neighborhood Spider-Man" (*ASM [2014]* #15).

That title—Friendly Neighborhood Spider-Man—stands in opposition to any method that relies on worldly forms of power. It represents a provincial, restrained approach to power that emphasizes humble service and a focus on the small stuff. Yet the environment in which Peter Parker now resides will challenge his self-identity by offering the temptation to embrace worldly power, for the world he inhabits is the world built by Otto Octavius. In this world, Peter Parker is now Dr. Parker: a billionaire, CEO, and tech mogul with worldwide influence. For the first time in his life, he possesses the status, wealth, and influence that society defines as true power. How will his understanding of responsibility adapt to these new challenges? Almost immediately, there is cause for concern.

Corrupting Octavius' wayward approach to heroism was an unrelenting lust to be "better," to be "superior." Throughout Slott's run, the term "better" functions at times as a sort of red flag for when a sense of responsibility is corrupted by arrogance. Otto Octavius, upon taking the mantle of Spider-Man, declared that he would be a "better Spider-Man" (*ASM* #700), a "better hero" (*SSM* #10), and that he alone would make the world a "better place" (*SSM* #20). So, when the Parker Industries building is destroyed by a saboteur and Peter responds by boldly declaring that they will rebuild Parker Industries "better" than before, that word becomes a signal that Peter is becoming infected with the same arrogance that defined Octavius (*ASM [2014]* #18). Then, with the first issue of *The Amazing Spider-Man (2015)*, titled "Worldwide," Peter has made good on his promise as Parker Industries is now a global company with offices around the world. His name resides on forty-seven buildings and he is one of the most wealthy and influential men in the world.

Peter admits, "Running a global company like this is the most power I'll ever have." In recognition that he has moved into a whole new level of power—a power defined by money, status, and technological influence—Peter, while wearing his Spider-Man costume, realizes he has a press conference and, while changing into a suit and tie, states, "Time to put on my real *power* suit." This dismissal of Spider-Man as his "real power" in favor of corporate influence, coupled with an inversion of his famous motto when he introduces a new Parker Industries technological achievement by announcing "With great power . . . comes greater speed, storage, and battery life," demonstrates that Peter Parker has become fully invested in the worldly trappings of success (*ASM [2015]* #1). Despite his earlier assertion to the contrary, he has abandoned the small stuff, which highlights the central tension for this new incarnation of Peter Parker: can he be a Friendly *Neighborhood* Spider-Man on a worldwide stage?

Peter Parker does his best to wield this newfound power responsibly, while maintaining his Spider-Man duties as well; yet, it quickly becomes apparent when he starts behaving *proactively* that Spider-Man's mission does not cohere well with this kind of power and on this large a stage. When Peter brings aid to a remote, third-world village, all it does is make them a target of the Green Goblin (*ASM [2015]* #4). When he creates Webware to improve people's lives, he ends up having to hack it to stop a virus, leading to widespread nausea among users and charges of violating privacy (*ASM [2015]* #29). When Spider-Man helps Silver Sable invade Symkaria to stop a civil war, he becomes an international terrorist in the eyes of S.H.I.E.L.D. (*ASM [2015]* #26).

Highlighting how Peter Parker's embrace of worldly power distorts his mission as Spider-Man, Slott sets up a series of contrasts with three other individuals who also attempt to use power responsibly. One such contrast is with the figure known as Regent. Regent views super-human powers as a threat to humanity and so creates technology that allows him to steal those powers for himself, believing that he alone is able to use those powers responsibly. He even twists Spider-Man's motto by declaring, "With unlimited powers must come unlimited responsibility" (*ASM [2015]* #12). Regent echoes the arrogance and refusal to accept limitation of Otto Octavius when he announces his goal as making *the world* a "better place" and that saving the world requires doing whatever it takes (*ASM [2015]* #13). When he declares, "I am power incarnate! I am the only savior humanity needs!" Regent, like Octavius, lacks the self-awareness to see the irony in his declaration that superpowers are evil even as he greedily acquires them for himself (*ASM [2015]* #14).

A second contrast occurs with the newly resurrected Ben Reilly. As a clone of Peter Parker, Ben Reilly shares the same childhood memories that defined Peter's conception of power and responsibility. Yet repeated trauma has warped his understanding of those concepts. Though Reilly masquerades as the Jackal, one of Spider-Man's classic villains, he is adamant that he is not a villain and continually reminds his associates that "we're the good guys" (*ASM [2015]* #17). Reilly has created New U Technologies and intends to utilize the technology of cloning to end suffering by bringing back clones of those who have died. His goal, as he tells Peter, is "To use our power responsibly. To save *everybody's* Uncle Ben" (*ASM [2015]* #22). What makes this seemingly noble goal villainous, despite Reilly's repeated protestations that they are "the good guys," is that it is based on a refusal to accept limitations, in this case the limitation of death.

Another signal that Peter Parker is heading down the wrong path with his embrace of technological power occurs when he first learns about this New U technology. Even as Anna Maria Marconi cautions him of the potential dangers, Peter arrogantly declares that he can use this technology to save not just one person as Spider-Man in the past sought to do, but to save "millions." This ambition mirrors that of Octavius, which is highlighted in this scene as Octavius (whose consciousness is still alive inside the Living Brain robot) agrees with Peter's decision (*ASM [2015]* #16). Just as Otto Octavius became more like Peter Parker by living in Peter's world, the longer Peter Parker lives in the world created by Otto Octavius, the more he starts to become like Octavius. Peter only begins to resemble the hero we know when his step-father,

Jay Jameson, becomes deathly ill and, rather than use New U technology to save him, Peter lets nature take its course. What ultimately distinguishes his "responsibility" from Ben Reilly's is this willingness to accept the limits of his power.

Perhaps the most interesting contrast that Slott establishes, though, is between Peter Parker/Spider-Man and Tony Stark/Iron Man. Now a billionaire technological industrialist who moonlights as a superhero, Peter Parker has become a mirror-image of Tony Stark. Stark represents everything Peter Parker has been aspiring to: possessing all the worldly trappings of status, wealth, and influence, yet using them responsibly. However, Peter Parker doesn't fit in this world. When a Parker Industries press release announces that Spider-Man is serving as both company mascot and Peter's personal bodyguard (as Iron Man originally did for Stark), a reporter asks him, "Doesn't that just make you a poor man's Tony Stark?" (*ASM [2015]* #1). Peter tries but fails to live up to the image of Tony Stark, even once complaining, "Man, how does a guy like Tony Stark do this? Have a life, run a company, *and* be a super hero" (*ASM [2015]* #13). Adding insult to injury, Mary Jane Watson is now working for and presumably dating Tony Stark, demonstrating that not only is Peter failing at being Tony Stark but Tony Stark is essentially better at being Peter Parker! So when Tony arrives for a fundraiser, Peter uncharacteristically acts out of ego and envy, arguing with Tony over whose company is better (*ASM [2015]* #13).

What all of this bravado masks is Peter's sense of inferiority compared to Tony Stark. Whereas Stark has somehow figured out how to use wealth, social status, and technological power responsibly, Peter Parker discovers that is not the kind of hero he is. Symbolizing the distinction between them is their differing attitudes toward secret identities. When Spider-Man makes a reference to secret identities, Iron Man replies, "Pfft. Those went out with dial-up" (*ASM [2015]* #15). This is why Peter Parker can never be Tony Stark. His secret identity is more than just a method to protect his loved ones. It represents an embrace of weakness by humbly refusing to take credit for his accomplishments as Spider-Man. Despite the constant temptation to invest in the worldly system of power, Peter Parker needs to relearn that his greatest strength is the "weakness" of humility, sacrifice, self-limitation, and dependence.

This re-education begins when Peter discovers that the path he is on has not made him more like Tony Stark, but more like Otto Octavius. Having transferred his consciousness into a new human body, Octavius confronts Spider-Man with this harsh truth: "Isn't it obvious? Using Parker Industries as bases? These spider-bot-like vehicles? Proactively going after your enemies? You're using all of *my* strategems from back when *I* was Spider-Man" (*ASM [2015]*

#31). In particular, Spider-Man's reliance on technology (Webware, Spider-Mobile, Spider-Copter, Arachno-Rocket, voice-activated webshooters), especially that of his armored costume, signaled his desire to be more like Iron Man. Richard Reynolds argues that superhero costumes function "as a sign for the inward process of character development" (Reynolds 1992, 29). Spider-Man's armored costume, with its technological bells and whistles, represents the false path he has taken toward power so getting back on the right path will involve a change of costume. In the final issue of *The Amazing Spider-Man (2015)* run, Peter reclaims his heroic identity by grounding it once again in weakness. Rejecting independence and choosing sacrifice, he relies on his employees to help him completely destroy Parker Industries. Then, in a symbolic showdown, Doctor Octopus sets off an EMP designed to shred Spider-Man's armored suit. When that happens, we see that underneath it Peter has donned his original, non-tech costume. Spider-Man declares, "This is the *only* suit I've ever needed to beat you, Otto" (*ASM [2015]* #31). That suit in its utter simplicity signals that Spider-Man's true power never came from wealth, technology, or social influence, but from a strength of character that chooses suffering, sacrifice, and simplicity.

Return to the Friendly Neighborhood: *The Amazing Spider-Man* #789–801

In the end of his run on *The Amazing Spider-Man*, Dan Slott has Spider-Man return to the essence of his heroic identity, an identity defined by a particular form of weakness. Having lived a life of status, wealth, and influence, his decision to implode Parker Industries has left him stripped of everything—essentially a return to the sad sack Peter Parker from his earlier days. He has gone from CEO back to Daily Bugle employee, from being a billionaire back to broke, from the penthouse to sleeping on a friend's couch, from being acclaimed in headlines worldwide to a self-proclaimed "World's Biggest Loser" (*ASM* #789). Lamenting the loss of what he had, Spider-Man complains to the Human Torch: "It's like I'd finally gotten everything right for once, you know? . . . Helping people all over the world, as both Spider-Man and Parker. This was what I'd been working toward my whole life! So of course I managed to blow it all up" (*ASM* #790). He then attributes this downfall to his stereotypical "Parker luck" (*ASM* #795).

He is wrong, though. Being a billionaire CEO was not getting "everything right"—for Tony Stark, maybe, but for Peter Parker it was getting everything wrong. He is not a "worldwide" superhero, but a "neighborhood" one. The "Parker luck" that he so often laments is also not the bane he thinks it is. It is, in fact, one of the things that keeps him humble and weak—that keeps him from becoming Tony Stark, yes, but also from becoming Otto Octavius. One of the first acts of heroism Spider-Man performs in his newly downtrodden life is to save a man's food truck from destruction (*ASM* #789). In the grand scheme of things, it counts as "small stuff," but for that man it was all he had. That Parker luck is a constant reminder that "getting it right" is being a Friendly *Neighborhood* Spider-Man.

The final issues of Slott's run hammer the point home that it is in his weakness that Spider-Man is the strongest. Norman Osborn has bonded with the Carnage symbiote to become the Red Goblin. After putting Spider-Man's loved ones in jeopardy, Osborn offers him a deal: give up being Spider-Man forever and he will spare his loved ones. Osborn forces him to choose between the Spider (strength) and the man (weakness). Peter, however, sees it differently, declaring that Osborn made a mistake because it is Peter Parker, the *"man* in Spider-Man," that is the true source of his power (*ASM* #798). The contrast between their opposing ideas of power is most clear in the final showdown when Osborn boasts that his victory will come because "I've always been the *stronger* man! Needing no one else! And willing to do whatever it takes to win!" (*ASM* #800). With this emphasis on independence, a refusal to limit himself, and the ends justifying the means, Osborn echoes the misguided sense of responsibility professed by Octavius, Regent, and Ben Reilly. Peter, however, replies that his strength comes from his dependence on friends and family, whom he calls "the greatest asset of all," and then he demonstrates that the true mark of a hero lies not in winning, but in the sacrificial giving of oneself when he throws his body in front of a bullet meant for Norman Osborn (*ASM* #799, 800).

B. J. Oropeza observes that many of Spider-Man's iconic images in both comics and film resemble that of Christ on the cross. Yet, Oropeza concludes that it is more in the humanity of Jesus rather than in the divinity of Christ that we see Spider-Man best represented (Oropeza 2005a, 139–40). His point is well taken, though as he notes, the two cannot be divorced. Moltmann argues that it is in the cross where the power of the divine meets the weakness of humanity—not to overcome it but to merge with it (Moltmann 1974, 205). In the cross, we witness the unlimited power of God embracing the weakness of human flesh, the limitation of death, the humility of servanthood, and the choice of sacrificial suffering. In this sense, the cross is also a perfect symbol for the essence of Spider-Man who is not both Spider and Man as separate, coexisting entities, but is a true merging of the "super" and the "human."

Ben Saunders also recognizes that Spider-Man's weakness is crucial to his heroic identity, arguing that his heroic failures and his "encounter with his all-too-human limitation" make him more of a saint than a hero (Saunders 2011, 94). I agree, though Saunders shifts the focus more toward tragic events that happen *to* Spider-Man and which are mostly outside of his control. Instead I argue that what truly makes him saint-like is the *choice* of weakness. Otto Octavius demonstrated what Peter Parker *could be* if he chose the path of worldly power. But Peter Parker expressly rejects that path. Shortly after Peter's fall from grace, Loki (attempting to repay a favor) offers to turn back time to a point when Peter was at the height of his wealth and influence. After reclaiming his body from Octavius, Peter found himself thrust into this world of privilege. Now, he is given the opportunity to choose it—and he rejects the offer (*ASM* #795). He has learned that the most responsible use of power lies with the small stuff.

Dan Slott's final issue is a throwback that takes place in the earliest days of Spider-Man's career. It is an origin story with a revisionist twist. The story unfolds from the perspective of a man named Kenneth whom Spider-Man saved in a convenience store robbery three weeks after the death of Uncle Ben. It is here, according to Slott, that Spider-Man first uses the "Friendly Neighborhood Spider-Man" line. The story then jumps to the present day where that same man, now much older, trips a criminal who is attempting to escape from Spider-Man. As Spider-Man swings away, Kenneth's young daughter complains that her first superhero sighting had to be of the "lame" Spider-Man. She claims that Thor, Captain Marvel, or Black Panther would have been much cooler because they save the world. Kenneth replies that Spider-Man "saves a world every single day" (*ASM* #801). Otto Octavius, Regent, and Ben Reilly all sought to use their power to save "*the* world." What Spider-Man represents is that true power is found in saving "*a* world." It is in the small stuff—in weakness—that the most responsible use of power occurs. And Slott suggests that it is this recognition that we change the world a little at a time—that five dollars given to someone in need is just as responsible a use of power as five million given to a charity, that the simple, daily choices we make to do good are as important as decisions made in the upper echelons of corporate empires—that makes Spider-Man the most relatable and influential hero. In Peter Parker's own words: "That's how we all save the world . . . one friendly neighborhood at a time" (*ASM* #800).

SPIDER-MAN: HOMECOMING

The 2017 Marvel film *Spider-Man: Homecoming*[3] further supports this analysis by presenting elements viewed as weaknesses within a secular value system (humility, self-limitation, dependence, sacrifice) as the essence of Spider-Man's power. In the film Peter Parker is initially defined by ambition. He is driven by a lust for the recognition, status, and respect that others enjoy.

As Peter Parker, he wants to shed his "loser" status. As Spider-Man, he wants to move beyond the bike thefts and other petty crimes he combats. He aspires to be an Avenger, but is stuck in high school. The high school symbolizes Peter's sense of smallness and inferiority. He eagerly tells his best friend Ned that he is "beyond high school" and that he will be leaving to join the Avengers upstate, becoming increasingly depressed and anxious as that call never comes. Since he views dependence on others as another sign of child-like status, Peter even plans to jettison his friends, telling Ned that he doesn't need "a guy in a chair" to help him.

Similar to Dan Slott's storyline, *Spider-Man: Homecoming* explores Peter Parker's understanding of power and his character development through his interaction with Tony Stark and his relationship to his suit. In contrast to Slott's storyline, Tony Stark functions here not as a rival to Peter Parker but as a mentor. In Tony Stark, Peter sees everything he aspires to be. Yet, Tony Stark lives in a very different world than does Peter Parker. It is a world of privilege, wealth, status, and technological advancement. Adrian Toomes (aka the Vulture) reminds Peter of this when he tells him that guys like Stark, "the rich and the powerful," don't care about "guys like us." Whereas Adrian Toomes informs Peter that Peter *isn't* Tony Stark, Tony himself, on three separate occasions, tells Peter that he *shouldn't* be like him. In an early scene, Tony tells Peter not to do anything he would or wouldn't do, essentially saying, "Do not be me." Later, after Peter's disastrous actions at the ferry, Peter says to Tony, "I just wanted to be like you." Tony replies, "And I wanted you to be better." What does that look like? What would make Peter Parker "better" than Tony Stark. A hint occurs earlier when, after saving Peter from a lake, Tony tells him to focus on helping the little people, to be "a friendly neighborhood Spider-Man." Peter takes this as an admonishment and a reinforcement of the notion that he is just a child, too immature to play on the big stage. But there is more to it than that. Contained within that advice is the suggestion that what Peter perceives as his weaknesses may in fact be the key not only to being a better superhero than Iron Man but a better *man* than Tony Stark.

As mentioned earlier, a superhero's suit often signals character development. In *Spider-Man: Homecoming*, Peter's relationship to various suits marks his journey of self-discovery. Initially, Peter's "crappy costume" (as Shocker calls it) composed of a cheap, homemade combination of hoodie and sweat pants symbolizes his low-grade superhero status. When Peter acquires a new suit from Tony Stark, that new suit symbolizes the hero he thinks he needs to be. With this new tech-infused suit (576 web shooter combinations, facial recognition, voice-activation, etc.), he has become a mirror-image to Iron Man. In his mind, the suit with all its technological wizardry has become the source of his power. This is evident when Tony, following the failure at the ferry, demands Peter return the suit and Peter protests that he is "nothing" without it. Stripped of his suit, and thus of the superhero status he craves, Peter returns to his "crappy costume," his humiliation complete.

The loss of his technological suit, however, turns out to be the key to his recognition that his power is best manifest through weakness. In the final showdown with the Vulture, Peter finds himself rejecting the fierce independence he previously embraced and turning to his friend Ned and even his frenemy Flash Thompson for help. Earlier at the ferry, Peter played at being the hero he thought he needed to be by relying on the suit and its technology, but it failed in spectacular fashion. As the ferry is torn in half by an energy blast, Peter strikes a crucifixion pose while trying to save the passengers. That pose, though, really just exposes Peter's false understanding of sacrifice as it is Iron Man, not Spider-Man, who saves the people on the ferry. Peter's attempted sacrifice here resulted from a desire to be "strong"—to be the hero who saves the day and thus prove himself to Tony Stark. Near the end of the film, however, Peter embodies a different form of sacrifice: giving up his own happiness by abandoning his date for the sake of duty and risking his own life to save the life of his enemy, the Vulture. These sacrifices stem not from a desire for recognition or to correct one's mistake, but from a willingness to embrace suffering for the sake of others.

The most critical scene for Peter's self-realization occurs when he is trapped underneath a collapsed roof. Straining against the weight pressing down on him and unable to budge it, he is about to give up. Then, in a nod to a classic scene from the comics, he sees his face reflected in a puddle. His mask is torn with only half of it covering his face so that reflected in the puddle is a person who is half Peter Parker and half Spider-Man. Remembering Tony's words that he shouldn't have the suit if he is nothing without it, he encourages himself by first saying "C'mon Peter" only to then shift to "C'mon Spider-Man" four times. In this moment, Peter realizes that his strength as Spider-Man comes first and foremost from Peter Parker—meaning it is not the spider bite that makes him powerful but the strength of his character. Peter needed to be stripped of that which made him outwardly powerful (Stark's technological suit) in order to find the strength within.

At the end of the film, Peter's embrace of humility and self-limitation takes center stage when he is finally offered the very thing he has long desired—a chance to move upstate to the Avengers' mansion and to become an official member of the team. This opportunity is punctuated by the offer of a new, even more technologically advanced suit. To Tony Stark's surprise, Peter turns it down. He rejects the power of the suit and the status of the Avengers in favor of looking out for the little guy and being a friendly *neighborhood*

Spider-Man. The subtitle of the film, "Homecoming," functions on multiple levels. It refers to the Homecoming dance that features in the film and symbolizes Peter's high school identity. On a larger, meta level, it signifies the long-awaited return of the character of Spider-Man to Marvel Studios. But on the most important level, it symbolizes Peter Parker's realization of where his true home lies—in the neighborhood looking out for the "little guy." Peter Parker first had to lose his way in order to find his way back home.

THE SPIRITUALITY OF SPIDER-MAN

What makes Spider-Man the most relatable of superheroes is not simply that he has everyday problems like we do, but that he shows us how to be strong, not in spite of weakness, but through it. What makes Spider-Man's approach to power unique is not the desire to use his physical gifts responsibly, but that he offers us a different definition of power from that most operative in the world. More so than any other superhero, Spider-Man (though he often has to relearn this lesson) rejects the definition of power as status, ambition, wealth, self-interest, and independence (the value system of the world) in favor of power as the willing embrace of suffering, dependence, humility, and sacrifice (the value system of the kingdom of God). Like the saints of old, Spider-Man accepts his own suffering as a means of alleviating the suffering of others. Though not overtly religious like Daredevil or some other superheroes, Spider-Man is arguably the most spiritual of all Marvel superheroes in terms of what he represents for he encapsulates the profound spiritual principle of strength through weakness.

NOTES

1. This motto first appears in *Amazing Fantasy* #15 (1962), the same issue where Spider-Man makes his first appearance.

2. The first appearance of Doctor Octopus is in *The Amazing Spider-Man* #3 (1963).

3. All quotations and references are from Jonathan Goldstein and John Francis Daley, *Spider-Man: Homecoming,* DVD, directed by Jon Watts (Culver City, CA: Sony Pictures Home Entertainment, 2017).

Chapter Eight

Of Venom and Virtue

Venom as Insight into Issues of Identity, the Human Condition, and Virtue

Jeremy E. Scarbrough

The question of identity plagues the fields of philosophy and theology. When and why do we call something good? Who am I—am I to be defined by *this* action or *today's* temperament? Such issues pervade the comic book world as well. When is someone a hero, antihero, villain, or anti-villain? Can "villainous" describe a *good* person in an unfortunate situation? Is the altruism of an egoist "good"? Consider the 2018 film *Avengers: Infinity War*; is Thanos "evil" or simply a utilitarian environmentalist? For some, identity is concealed. For others it is proclaimed, and yet some are still trying to find theirs. For some, a mask is an effort to conceal an identity; for others, it is an escape into authenticity. Yet, for some antiheroes or anti-villains, the persona by which they are identified represents more of an inner struggle and an insight into which side is winning. Was the Green Goblin *really* the same person as Norman Osborn? Is the vampire Morbius a malicious villain, or just a man desperate for a cure? Virtue presupposes that a certain *character* ought to work its way out in our ethics. Unfortunately, this takes time—thus the complexity of character formation.

Given the potential impact of one's superpower (e.g., destroying cities while trying to protect them), the question of identity becomes: What makes someone a "hero" rather than a "nuisance"? Was J.J. Jameson right to persist in labeling your "friendly" neighborhood wall crawler a menace? Spider-Man *is* friendly, but if being a neighborhood hero means seeking the neighborhood's best interest, is the damage of a super-human showdown justifiable as "collateral damage"?

Identity becomes exceedingly complex as we explore inner conflict. According to Søren Kierkegaard, the Christian life involves a double danger (DD). It is a necessary tragedy to overcome one's egoistic impulses only to meet antithesis—rejection by the very people one wishes to save (Kierkeg-aard 1949, 68, 157–65). For the Christian, the temptation of the wide path—the way of the world—is the first danger. To choose the narrow path—the way of Christ—is to welcome a second danger. As Jesus stated, "You are not of the world, but I chose you out of the world, because of this the world hates you" (John 15:19, *NASB*). Kierkegaard focused primarily upon the initial profession of faith and the subsequent sacrifice demonstrated in a life of charity. Such a commitment not only poses a threat to one's self-interested conceptions of the good life but also welcomes persecution and antithesis from the world.

There is a third danger worth pondering, however. (Whether it should be properly understood as "Third Danger" or merely a sub-distinction of the first, it is nevertheless a *different sort* of danger, and therefore warrants consideration as a third type).[1] Whereas the profession of faith involves an initial pledge of life-orientation, the commitment to charity involves an existential living out of this pledge to self-sacrifice and service over self-interest. And yet there remains within us something that often wars against even our deepest values and altruistic desires. This daily inner struggle further complicates character identity because it looks different at different stages of emotional development, and our strengths and weaknesses may change with new seasons of maturity as we grow in Christ. To live as Christ sometimes feels discouraging, therefore, because it asks of us a moral excellence that is not yet fully ours—though we have a salvific expectation of this glorified perfection at the end of our journey. We are called to virtue, but we cannot achieve excellence without Christ actively at work within us. Curiously, the power of Christ is perfected in our weakness (2 Cor. 12:9); that is, this daily struggle appears to be a purposeful part of the Christian's character development. And so the Christian welcomes not only a submission of will to Christ and a sacrifice of self-interest for others; he or she also welcomes a *daily antithesis* within, thereby threatening to frustrate and discourage the Christian *in spite of* their profession.

Similarly, it is a dangerous thing to be a hero. C. Stephen Evans has explored application of DD in the heroism of Spider-Man and the X-Men (Evans 2005, 161–75). In subverting self-interest to the responsibility that comes with great power, Spider-Man overcomes the first danger. Nevertheless, he battles rejection, animosity, and misrepresentation from the city he serves—precisely because he became a hero. The X-Men likewise represent a group of mutants who have rejected self-interest in order to use their gifts for the greater good. Yet, in exposing their powers to save others, mutant groups such as the X-Men welcome an impassioned rejection from those who hate what they fear, and fear what they do not understand.

While DD is analogous to both the Christian life in particular and heroism in general, its significance becomes exceedingly complex and symbolic with anti-heroic characters like Venom. Spider-Man overcame egoism to embrace the responsibility of heroism, and he faced the backlash of second danger, but when he encountered the parasitic alien-skin known as the *symbiote*, he experienced a new depth to conflict—an emotional struggle with an appetite for destruction. To wear the Venom-skin is to welcome a third danger. This danger is best understood within the life of Edward Brock, the history of the symbiote, and the nature of their symbiotic union—a daily dichotomous walk.

This essay will explore questions of identity, internal struggle, and Kierkegaardian double danger involving the symbiotic nature of the Venom-skin. I argue, first, that Venom serves as an effective metaphor for the Christian understanding of the human condition and struggle with the sin-skin and, second, that the character and fortitude required for any host to wear the alien-skin without being overcome by its appetite offers valuable insight into Virtue Ethics and the salvific understanding of glorification.

WE ARE VENOM, BUT WHO AM I?
A STORY OF MORAL IDENTITY

The past and identity of the entity now known as Venom is exceedingly complex. An unnamed alien symbiote first called itself "Venom" after being rejected by Peter Parker and bonding to Eddie Brock. Brock eventually separated himself from the living skin as well. Thereafter, the alien bonded with others but continued to refer to itself (becoming progressively more independent) as Venom. When Brock manifested a mutated form of the living suit, he called himself Anti-Venom. The name Venom, then, is a complex aspect of both Brock's and the alien's own identities. Traditionally and most popularly, the name refers to their specific union. Nevertheless, it is worth exploring some of the complexities of both their shared and individual histories. While this intense history has been revealed slowly, in a non-linear progression, I will trace significant moments of their past in a linear manner.

Alien Origins

The alien tissue, called a symbiote, came from a planet named Klyntar. Symbiotes merge with a host, strengthening and evolving it, and feeding upon chemicals in the brain produced by adrenaline and emotion, such as phenethylamine. (This is why Venom had an initial taste for brains, which he later attempted to curb with chocolate.) While symbiotes have unique personalities, they are greatly influenced by the personality and emotions of their host. While they prefer strong and noble hosts and just causes, a corrupt host can corrupt the symbiote; in turn, a corrupted symbiote can corrupt its host.

The Venom symbiote first bonded with a genocidal alien from an icy planet—believing him to be heroic. This union facilitated within the symbiote a proclivity to predation and aggressiveness. Having bonded on an emotional level, the symbiote became protective of its host. This caused other symbiotes to distrust it greatly, and it was outcast (*Venom: Space Knight* #8; *Venom Super Special* #1). The symbiote was discovered by the Kree, and used in the *Kree-Skrull War*. After serving its purpose, its memories were erased. The symbiote (now unaware of its past[2]) was thereafter trapped on a ship, which crashed on Battleworld (*Venom: First Host* #1–3; *The Amazing Spider-Man [2018]* Annual #1).

When Spider-Man's costume was torn in battle on this world, he attempted to use a device that would mend his costume. Unknowingly, he accidentally released the symbiote, and it bonded with him (*Secret Wars* #8). Feeding on Peter Parker's emotional need to be a protector, the symbiote used Parker to go play hero while Parker believed himself to be sleeping. After realizing that the suit was alive and trying to control his body, he sought to remove it. A series of events led to a fateful moment at Our Lady of Saints Church, where the piercing echoes of the church bells helped to finalize the separation. Peter's rejection created a growing seed of bitterness within the alien skin, and that evening, it encountered a tormented companion similarly embittered by a hatred for the web-slinger. Together, they formed the infamous Venom (*The Amazing Spider-Man* #252–59, #298–300, and #315–17; hereafter abbreviated as *ASM*; *Web of Spider-Man* #1).

Eddie Brock and the Venomous Union

Brock's past is one of tragedy and desperation for a sense of meaning and companionship. After his mother died in childbirth, his father distanced himself. This created a need for lasting companionship. Inspired by Watergate, he became a journalist in the name of justice. Unfortunately, in his zeal, he falsely exposed a fraudulent, compulsive confessor as the criminal Sin-Eater. When Spider-Man caught the true criminal, the media brought shame to Brock's career, and he was unable to find any work short of contributing "venomous" tabloid trash. The loss of respect in his career brought shame to his private relationships as well; his father disowned him and his wife left. To make matters worse, he learned that he had adrenal cancer (Shooter et al. 2007; *The Amazing Spider-Man Super Special* #1; *Venom: Lethal Protector* #3; *ASM* #300, #375; *Venom: Dark Origin* #1–5).

Brock desperately needed the emotional stability and camaraderie of long-term companionship; and emotional extremes are nourishment to symbiotes. Their mutual bitterness toward Spider-Man coupled with Brock's overproduction of adrenaline initially attracted the symbiote and fostered this union, but the darkness within Brock also encouraged a further corruption within the symbiote. On that fateful night when they first bonded, this conflicted Catholic was somewhere between suicidal, repentant, and desperate for justice. The Venom-skin greatly enhanced Brock's strength and imitated many of the powers learned from Spider-Man, in addition to the alien's natural shape-shifting and camouflaging abilities. The symbiote and host are also able to share prior knowledge, which is how Brock discovered Parker's identity. Despite his hatred for Spider-Man, Brock had a strong, if distorted, moral compass when it came to justice and innocence (*ASM* #330–33, #344–47, Annual #25).

Lethal Protector or Villainous Vigilante?

Spider-Man and Venom eventually formed a truce: as long as Spider-Man did not pursue Venom, Venom would not pursue Spider-Man. When Venom resurfaced in San Francisco, Spider-Man's sense of responsibility for having created Venom caused the wall crawler to break his covenant and pursue the seemingly villainous Venom. The Venom that Peter found in San Francisco, however, was not a ravenous beast but a Lethal Protector—an anti-heroic vigilante sharing Parker's deep concern for justice and the innocent, though not his convictions concerning questions of *just* and *due* punishment for the guilty. Nevertheless, Brock revealed more of a sensitivity to issues of *just* cause during these years. When attacked by a man whose son was collateral damage in one of Venom's former rampages against Spider-Man, Venom rationalizes the attack as just and seeks to escape rather than retaliate. Parker returns to New York, convinced that this Venom—though rough around the edges—was more of a hero than a villain. Venom remained in San Francisco, devoting himself to the just cause of protecting the poor and the innocent (*Venom: Lethal Protector* #1–6).[3]

Separation Anxiety

As the symbiote evolved in strength, knowledge, and resilience, so too grew its appetite—and with it grew a sense of enmity and distrust between it and Brock, as Eddie continually struggled to resist its destructive impulses and cannibalistic taste for brains (*Venom: The Hunger* #1). After learning of his cancer's aggressive progression, and following a religious revival within himself, Eddie sold the symbiote but remained tormented by both withdrawal (a continual yearning to reunite) and hallucinations (visions of the alien calling Brock to give into a phantom appetite for violence).

The Venom-skin eventually encountered and bonded with former Scorpion, Mac Gargan. With this host—though not necessarily to its preference—the gluttonous appetite was greatly nourished. This monstrous symbiosis became the most infamously evil of the Venom manifestations, feeding regularly on available victims or enemies. Bearing great guilt for the symbiote's action, Brock (unsuccessfully) attempted suicide after learning of this unfortunate series of events (*Marvel Knights: Spider-Man* #7–8; *Venom* #1–18; hereafter abbreviated as *V*).

After Martin Li (Mr. Negative) miraculously healed Brock of cancer, the new antigens in Eddie's body caused a reaction to the remaining remnants of the Venom-skin. So, when he encountered Gargan, Brock's body reacted to the original symbiote by transforming him into Anti-Venom. Now with a heightened immune system and healing powers, he was more powerful than and dangerous to any symbiote as he was able to cure any disease or cancerous agent. (Moreover, he was now able to cure people of their attachment to symbiotes). Considering this a second chance, Brock set out to do good and to rid the city of cancerous evils, eventually sacrificing the Anti-Venom skin in order to cure a significant number of people (*ASM* #569, #671; *The Amazing Spider-Man Presents: Anti-Venom: New Ways to Live* #1–3).

The U.S. military eventually removed the symbiote from Gargan, and with drug-induced suppression, attached it to veteran Flash Thompson to create Agent Venom. (But the suppressant was not completely successful and, like Brock, Thompson had to keep his anger in check in order to guard against the Venom-skin's appetite for destruction.) Flash was a significant influence on the symbiote—both in care and in character; he treated the suit as a partner and modeled for it the admirable heroic virtue for which it really longed on a deeper level (*ASM* #648, #645; *Venom [2011]* #1–42). During this time, the symbiote was forcefully removed and bonded to Superior Spider-Man (Otto Octavius in control of Parker's mind and body), thereby creating Superior Venom and only complicating the trail of corrupt and confusing influences upon the impressionable symbiote (*Superior Spider-Man* #22–25).

After the symbiote reunited with Flash, Agent Venom came to work closely with the Avengers and the Guardians of the Galaxy as an *Agent of the Cosmos*. During this time, he learned much more about the Klyntar race and its struggle with a primeval appetite (*Guardians of the Galaxy [2015]* #21–23; *Venom:Space Knight* #5–9). Alas, Flash continued to struggle with suppression of the Venom-skin, and the Venom-skin progressively uncovered deeper layers concerning its corruption and proclivities.

After a final separation from Flash Thompson, the symbiote encountered and bonded with ex-Army Ranger Lee Price. Highly desirable as a soldier, Price turned out to be undesirable as a partner. His strength of will kept the symbiote's influence at bay, yet Price carried within him a bloodlust all his own. After the symbiote was removed from Price, Brock reunited with it. Though Brock longed for this reunion, and although the symbiote had been positively influenced by its partnership with Flash, seeds of corruption nevertheless remained from this series of subsequent hosts and unfortunate events (*Venom [2016]* #1–6; *V* #150).

Venom Returns

Eddie continually faces a bent and conflicted nature in the alien—struggling with potential re-corruption and recurrent appetite. All he really wants is to live within this communion with minimal conflict and repercussion. By this time, the alien has evolved quite a bit and has a distinctly independent nature—even forcing Brock to sleep so that it can ponder its own agendas. The symbiote itself has become more conflicted in self-awareness as its own desires clash with those of its host. Consulting with a priest while Brock slept, for instance, the symbiote expressed remorse and resolved to earn Eddie's love and trust by becoming, once again, a lethal protector (*V* #154).

Various events continued to raise questions of trust, self-interest, appetite, and mental/emotional stability. And yet it seems clear that there is within the alien-skin a light of loyalty and honor, of goodness and conviction. The Venom-skin is corrupted, to be sure, with a proclivity toward instances of horrific desires and actions, but it is not evil in and of itself. Similarly, Brock is a lonely and broken man—desperate for identity, appreciation, and purpose (self-worth), and therefore susceptible both to the influence of his own emotions and to the appetite of the sentient creature within. But if character is to outweigh action (setting aside complexities of "guilt" for the moment), it seems that Brock is not a "bad guy." He consistently reveals a strong awareness and deep conviction concerning moral objectivity.

Corruption and Conviction: Conflict in Communion

Recent comics have revealed a darker aspect to the origin of the symbiotes (a story intertwined with creation narrative). As it turns out, in the beginning of the universe, there was *not* nothing; rather, there was a void, a realm of absolute darkness wherein a god named Knull slept. When the Celestials suddenly appeared and began to repel the darkness with the light of creation, the disturbed and resentful Knull declared war on the Celestials, but once wounded, he fell to a planet below. Knull remained in recovery, while also bonding pieces of himself to that planet's lifeforms, and controlling this collective of symbiotes via a unified hive mind. He later sent out an army of symbiote creatures (some of them in dragon form) to seek and destroy other planets, while he controlled them telepathically from afar. On earth, Knull's symbiotic dragon, Grendel, was wounded *not* by Beowulf but by Thor. This severed Knull's intergalactic mind control over the symbiotes, as part of his consciousness was trapped within Grendel though his body was far from earth. The symbiotes without a master bonded to earthly hosts (*Thor: God of Thunder* #6; *Venom [2018]* #4).

Now severed from the drive of a raging, bloodthirsty mind, the symbiotes found themselves overwhelmed by the virtue, nobility, and goodness of these new hosts. So, elsewhere in the universe, the symbiotes—now converted to a love of goodness and an admiration for virtue and heroism—surrounded Knull's body, imprisoning it in darkness. *Klyntar* (literally "cage"), then, is not really a planet but the location of Knull's imprisonment (*Venom [2018]* #1–6).

The Klyntar hive mind kept secret this shameful past and, thereafter, sought out good and admirable hosts. If paired with a weak or imperfect host, and therefore susceptible to corruption, that symbiote would then be exiled, destroyed, or purified in order to prevent a permeating infection of the hive mind. (Since the hive mind is all connected, one corrupted symbiote in close proximity to another could pervert the purity of the entire hive mind.) While more could be said, the backstory presented here should suffice for the expositional purposes of this essay. But before we can effectively draw out theological and moral metaphors, we should review the Christian understanding of the nature of sin and the essence of the human condition.

OF SIN AND SYMBIOSIS

Holly Ordway has insightfully observed that moral binaries in storytelling are often essential for grasping a big-picture perspective (Ordway 2015). At the end of the day, the moral question is a binary one. However, the myriad ways that moral questions and the problem of sin reveal themselves within our individual experiences and throughout the course of our lives unfolds in a series of shades of gray. Insofar as we portray ourselves to be Spider-Man and our antithesis as a venomous monstrosity that wants to eat our brains, then it is difficult to see Venom as much more than mere monster. On the other hand, if we look beyond that binary and ponder the complexities of the Venom-skin and its symbiotic relationships, we may find that we are more like Venom than Spider-Man. Perhaps Spider-Man is an ideal; Venom is the reality.

The story of Venom is a rich ground for ethical and theological exploration. But our primary concern involves the nature of sin and the struggle of
the human condition. Here it is essential to understand, first, that there is a
sin-condition, a warring nature within every human being (Rom. 7:15–23; 1
John 1:8), and, second, that an excessive pride (*hubris*) amounts to a perversion of appetite. From these two foci we observe a number of powerful points.

Piercing the Sin-Skin: An Autopsy of Enmity

It has long been said that *pride* is the principal manifestation of a corruption
that gives birth to a host of further manifestations of corruption. What should
be understood here, though, is that pride comes back to an issue of *appetite*.
So it will be more helpful to understand that all of sin finds the root of its
corruption within *a perversion of appetite*. Many Christian philosophers
stress the point that evil has no ontological existence; it has only a parasitic
existence. Sin is a perversion identifiable only by its manifestation within
the good thing that it has corrupted (Geisler 2004, 106; Copan and Litwak
2014, 44). As articulated by Harold Willmington, "Sin must not only disguise
itself as the good, but must also actually connect itself to the good. In itself
sin has no unifying power. Here sin may be likened to a virus, and the good
to a healthy cell" (Willmington 2011, 558). Sin is, as Milliard Erickson put
it, any lack of conformity of one's inner disposition, in which one's will and
relationship to God is twisted (Erickson 1998, 453, 596). *Telos* (purpose/
designated function) is, therefore, a concept central to understanding both sin
and morality. Creation includes designated purposes. To function according
to those purposes is good. To misuse a good thing is the essence of sin—a
teleological perversion.[4]

According to Romans 3, the human condition is quite grave. No one is
good nor does good. Each perpetuates injustice. Evil reveals itself in us like
a poison. We dwell in bitterness. We seek destruction and bloodshed, and
we are ignorant of the path to peace. Our nature is depraved and filthy. We
are unclean, infected, and carried away by our degenerate natures (Isa. 64:6).
What is interesting about corruption is that it is, so to speak, highly impressionable. As Christian philosopher and theologian Norman Geisler put it, "A
fallen conscience is fallible. It reflects an innate capacity to know right from
wrong, but it does not guarantee that it will always be accurate; it can be distorted (Rom 2:15) by culture, choices, and, at times, even 'seared' by intense
evil (1 Tim. 4:2)" (Geisler 2004, 77).

The Venom-skin serves as an effective metaphor for the human condition—from both the perspective of the host and that of the alien. Unless
cleansed/purified, exposure to the extreme emotions of a host's hatred, pride,

and bitterness corrupts the symbiotes; a corrupted symbiote in turn corrupts its host. All it takes is one moment of rage for a symbiote to succumb to a monstrous appetite for violence. The issue of appetite is central both to the nature of corruption and to one's susceptibility to that corruption. "For the flesh sets its desire against the Spirit, and the Spirit against the flesh; for these are in opposition to one another" (Gal. 5:17).

Our analogies of this struggle take several forms. Within the symbiotic union, Brock represents the rational mind (reason/understanding) set against the primal desires of an alien flesh. But this metaphor has two analogous offspring of its own: (1) Brock himself, subject to the human condition, must continually battle the desires of his own flesh, and (2) the alien-skin is nevertheless a rational creature, facing its own struggles between reason and appetite. For the host, the alien amplifies his/her emotional proclivities and desires. To grant even slight foothold to one's passions is to welcome an opportunity for the possibility of succumbing to the alien-flesh. For the impressionable alien-skin, it is only after an introduction to the appetite of a corrupted host that the alien skin too becomes corrupted, and thereafter influences subsequent hosts. Here we might reverse the metaphor. The essential nature of the human being is an immaterial rational substance, alien to, yet meant to be bound with, a material form. Although we were created good in the fullness of our *telos,* and innocent in the essence of our original nature, after an initial pairing with the instability of a sinful disposition, we, like Venom, have become unable to redeem ourselves.

To have a sinful nature is to have a proclivity toward a bent habituation— *a teleological perversion of appetite.* While the Venom-skin may not be the best metaphor for pride *per se*, sinful pride is nevertheless an excess of *appetite*, and the struggle with appetite *is* the very story of the Venom-skin. It is our story as well.

Bent for Corruption: An Appetite for Destruction

Many aspects of creation pivot from a sense of appetite, and appetites thrive on a healthy state of desire. However, once desire becomes perverted in any way, it impacts the host—resulting in a sort of deficiency/malnutrition or a sense of excess/obesity. The human condition, then, might be best understood as the perversion of natural desire. As Joy McDougal explains, "Sin takes the form of a distorted delight that falsely idealizes one's fellow creatures and leads to a sentimental attitude toward them. . . . Sin does not destroy what we are . . . it disfigures our creaturely reality so that we become a parody of that identity" (McDougall 2011, 59).

Jeremiah 17:9 proclaims, "The heart is deceitful above all things and beyond cure," while James 1:15 insists it is the offspring of *desire* which gives birth to sin. Erickson clarifies that desire plays an important teleological role within the created order, but when moral degeneration begets malformed desires, malignancy becomes apparent. At bottom, human desires are legitimate. Nevertheless, "a number of natural desires, while good in and of themselves, are potential areas for temptation and sin. . . . There are proper ways to satisfy each of these desires, and there are also divinely imposed limits. Failure to accept these desires as they have been constituted by God, and therefore to submit to divine control is sin" (Erickson 1998, 614–15). Aristotle understood that appetite/desire is locus to human *telos*; since character is formed by habits, and moral excellence (or virtue) is an issue of character, he believed the habituation of desire to be pivotal to ethics and *eudaemonia* (human flourishing and the good life). It is reason and the ability to act contrary to our desires that sets human beings apart from the animals, after all. Moderation—staying between the excesses and deficiencies of appetite—is thus essential to ethics.[5]

Aquinas later expanded Aristotelean themes. As Kenneth Boa summarizes, for Aquinas, "desire is the transcendental relation of a creature to its final end. Since man is a microcosm of the hierarchy of creation, his desires of appetites reflect this diversity" (Boa 2004, 17). Moreover, "just as the appetite tends toward the good, so the intellect tends toward the true" (18). Hierarchically, Aquinas acknowledged both individual and communal needs, "but he subordinated all of these needs to the highest human need of beatitude" (19). All of human activity, then, pivots around teleology:

> Desires . . . must be controlled by reason, not for the purpose of eliminating them, but in order that . . . they may serve rather than hinder the quest for man's final end. . . . There is some continuity between the natural and supernatural ends. . . . The deep, insatiable need of uniting ourselves to that which is capable of perfecting us . . . exerts a constant pull on the will, and to this extent the will is determined. (22–23)

Following the tradition of Plato, Augustine understood this struggle on a significantly larger scale. We are not just warring between reason and desire; we are aliens and strangers attempting to live amid and seek the good even within corruption, all the while holding ourselves to a standard that lies beyond the corruption. We live tethered to Babylon (it is our host, you might say), and yet we live as foreign ambassadors of Jerusalem (Boa 2004, 13). (In a similar way, the alien-skin is often tethered to violent hosts. Still, it seeks solace in the hope of one day dwelling within the heart of a hero.)

According to Augustine, our true nature is determined by our loves.[6] Now this observation has interesting application. When the ravenous appetite of the corrupted skin overcomes a host, it is really because there dwells within the host a secret desire to know such an appetite satiated. The key to the purification of the symbiote involves a host that is so admirable that the alien loves and longs to be more like the host. John Edwards similarly insisted that the development of an appetite for moral excellence was related to the development of a desire for deep communion with God (Boa 2004, 30).

Of Valor and Virulence

Venom is just the monstrous face of an enslavement to one's desire and the bestial manifestation of an insatiable hostility. Brock often finds himself succumbing either to the will of a corrupted alien-skin or to a sense of depravity within himself. He holds a deep-seated desire for *the good*—justice for the innocent—but also a perverted sense of desire that revels in the violence of vengeance. He even admits that the alien "can't make you do anything you don't really want to do" (*Venom: Sinner Takes All* #3, 10). Despite this, there are numerous times wherein Eddie and the alien-skin express a deep desire to escape corruption, to do good, and to avoid evil.

As a comic hero, Brock's self-control is an ideal—a source of encouragement and hope that self-control is *possible*; it is an *ideal* of virtue because such self-control is uncommon. In reality, we need help to change into the sort of being *able* to control it (Phil. 3:19–21). Consider C.S. Lewis' analogy of a family pet as metaphor for the Christian transformation. "We treat our dogs as if they were 'almost human': that is why they really become 'almost human' in the end" (Lewis 2001, 194). Likewise, controlling the sin-skin is impossible without the mediating, transformative power of Christ in us.

The Third Danger

Let us now return to the Kierkegaardian notion of two dangers. The first danger is an issue of choice, a wager that presents a lasting danger in one of two senses. For the one who refuses to submit to his/her Creator, this choice will be an ultimate detriment, in light of eternity, to happiness, wholeness, and identity—a momentary freedom, but an infinite loss. For the one who submits to the lordship of Christ, this choice becomes a danger in the sense that it will result in some temporal losses—including, perhaps, a rejection of certain orientations and identities that one might prefer to hold. The question, then, is to whom shall I submit—self or God—and whom shall I serve—Creator or creation?

While the first danger represents the salvific struggle of faith-*orientation*, the second danger involves the trials and persecutions that accompany this narrow path (faith-*in-action*). This is clear in John 15:19. If one walks in the way of the world, the world will love its own. If one walks in the way of Christ, he/she *will* be rejected by the world. In choosing to walk this path, one welcomes a sense of danger and estrangement from non-believers. To choose Jerusalem is to identify with the ultimate good of the Kingdom to come, but one must continue dwelling in Babylon as resident alien in the meantime. So, the second danger is rejection and opposition from those who despise the aliens who don't love Babylon as they do. If the first danger involves a self-submission to God, and the second involves a vulnerability to others which accompanies self-abandonment, the third is present all along—it is a continual struggle for self-control in order *even to be capable* of either form of self-surrender.

As the analogy maps onto comic lore, the first danger is still an ultimate answer to the moral questions: What is the good life? How should I live? Whom shall I serve—self or other? The benefit or detriment is still, here, an issue of the soul. According to Plato, an egoist who seeks an immoral means to a self-interested end suffers an imbalance and injustice within his/her soul.[7] One can never really know *the good*, and by extension the good life, so long as one's soul suffers sickness. The hero's first danger involves the choice to reject egoism and hedonism and to take up the mantle of protector or justice-seeking vigilante. The second danger is an unfortunate rejection by those that the hero is attempting to save. Mutant heroes are often feared and hated precisely because of their powers.

In characters like Venom, however, there is also a third danger—the daily dichotomous walk (any recovering addict knows this struggle well). The symbiotic nature of the Venom-skin means that there is deep conflict between two versions of one's self; to wear the alien-skin is to carry the burden of its impulsive nature, The sin-nature is not removed until glorification. We are therefore, at any moment, antagonists unto ourselves. The salvific journey itself, while we are maturing sin-vessels, is a dangerous one. To walk this path is to stumble along, to fear a potential for backsliding, to despair of overcoming the same obstacle that has been a hindrance for years. Amid this journey, our vessel wars against us. There is a warring nature within, and it is a threatening hindrance to both confidence and progress. This nature, a third danger, is a symbiotic struggle for self-control. As Paul confesses:

> For what I am doing, I do not understand; for I am not practicing what I would like to do, but I am doing the very thing I hate. . . . Nothing good dwells in me, that is, in my flesh; for the willing is present in me, but the doing of the good is

not. For the good that I want, I do not do, but I practice the very evil that I do not want. . . . Although I want to do good, evil is right there with me. For in my inner being I delight in God's law; but I see another law at work in me, waging war against the law of my mind and making me a prisoner of the law of sin at work within me. What a wretched man I am! Who will rescue me from this body that is subject to death? (Rom. 7:15–25)

Despite our initial choice in overcoming the first danger, and notwithstanding any harms or hindrances from others, *we are a harm and hindrance unto ourselves*. While the spirit may be willing, the flesh is weak (Matt. 26:41). *This is the Venom-skin struggle.* Moreover, we can identify with it from multiple angles. We are the host. We identify with Brock. We understand the rage that one feels when having suffered injustice. Additionally, we are like the alien-skin: uncorrupted in the essence of our origin, yet significantly influenced by the things to which we have attached ourselves along the way, we now carry within us a bent, impulsive disposition. We also understand Brock's struggle as host to a corrupted appetite. We are "aliens and strangers" urged "to abstain from fleshly lusts which wage war against the soul" (1 Pet. 2:11). In the comic lore, the struggle of appetite is as much the alien's anxiety as it is Brock's burden.

ON VIRTUE AND GLORIFICATION

As our desires wage war against our soul, sin becomes a habitual enslavement of our spiritual will to the insatiable appetite of our flesh. Erickson calls this a flight from reality (Erickson 1998, 632)—from both the ability to discern truth (e.g., Jer. 17:9 and Rom. 1:18–31) and the opportunity to discover our true identity. Furthermore, this highly impressionable depravity grows with subsequent encounters of excessive passions—lust, anger, resentment, bitterness, etc.—and by the subverting of reason. The perversion of reason encourages a twisting of facts in order to justify one's own self-interested and questionable behaviors—even in the name of an altruistic "justice." Paul warned that sin seizes any opportunity to produce in us a "coveting of every kind" (Rom. 7:8), and James taught that where such passions rule, "there is disorder and every evil thing" (James 3:16). The key, both to the good life and to salvific maturity, therefore lies within a habituation of one's appetite and a purposeful reorientation toward excellence. *This* is virtue ethics.

Venom as Virtuous

Excellence is a process—a continual struggle to reach and maintain an idealistic middle ground between the extremes of our appetite (excess and deficiency). So, conscience and conviction are prerequisites for growing toward virtue. Brock and the symbiote do not always make the best choices, but conscience and conviction are revealed in both characters. Brock has struggled with these for the better part of three decades. The alien revealed its struggle with questions of conscience and conviction more in depth amid its reunion with Brock in 2016:

> Eddie worries about me. . . . Says I'm sick. Don't feel sick. . . . Understood feelings before, but simple feelings—like colors, bold and bright. Happy. Sad. Angry. Then . . . met Spider-Man. Feelings got complicated. Learned guilt. . . . Learned feeling: betrayal. Learned first words they called me. Monster. Parasite. Bad. Sometimes when we swing, Eddie's mind drifts. Then we can push in a direction. . . . To find criminals. Eddie doesn't know we do this. Wrong to trick him? But not wrong to stop criminals. . . . Eddie says we have to hide. . . . [But] Feels good to be a hero. . . . Did do bad things, too. Can't deny. . . . Am I monster? Parasite? Bad? Can't be bad. Wasn't bad with Flash. Fought with heroes. *Was* a hero. (*V* #154, 6–18)

Virtue requires a moral sensitivity and an awareness regarding what is morally excellent enough to imitate (Phil. 4:8). Both Brock and the symbiote seem to be aware of this. Recalling Jesus' words about the eye as lamp to the body (Luke 11:34–35), it appears they *must* have their sight fixed upon some sense of intuitive goodness since this moral sensibility resonates so strongly within.

Virtue (i.e., moral *excellence*) is the sort of thing that is only achieved through relentless persistence in imitation of an ideal example. As explained by philosopher Louis Pojman, "eventually, the apprentice-like training in virtue gained by imitating the ideal model results in a virtuous person who spontaneously does what is good" (Pojman and Fieser 2009, 148). While Brock may not be the ideal role model at this stage in his journey, he nevertheless displays a persistence in his resistance to the venomous appetite as well as in his desire to serve the innocent.

Brock's early life reveals an original desire to fight for justice. In his initial symbiosis, he is torn between the alien appetite and warring ideals of jealousy, vengeance, and justice within his own heart.[8] As Brock and the symbiote each learn to control both their individual and symbiotic appetites, Venom begins to habituate his appetite and direct his power toward serving the less fortunate and the unprotected. Though they continue to struggle with the power of the passions and the emotional currents of corruption, both Brock and the alien have grown more admirable in many ways—and they continue to persevere in their aim for moral excellence and self-control.[9] Thus, Venom possesses the virtue of *fortitude*—a virtue necessary for the acquisition of subsequent virtues—and he aims desperately for *temperance*. So in this, if nothing else, Venom serves as a role model. He may not be a hero in the deepest sense, but he longs to be. Flawed though he may be, as he continues to stumble, he *is* nonetheless persistent in long suffering for the good and often aims for the moral excellence of a hero.

This is a struggle with which we are all familiar (Jas. 3:2). Indeed, Jesus reminds us that the weakness of our willing spirit in succumbing to the powerful persuasions of our flesh should be kept continually before our prayerful minds (Matt. 26:41). As within Venom, we find within ourselves a struggle between the person whom we desire to be and the one whom we find ourselves to be. Nevertheless, we are called to aim for excellence, to love the good, to seek the noble, and to imitate the admirable (Phil. 4:8). Despite our weaknesses and failures, fortitude produces character, and character, hope (Rom. 5:3–4). So virtue is realized within a life of discipline. Discipline matures us and refines us. To wear the Venom-skin and play the part of the hero requires, at bottom, not principles, but a certain caliber of *character*—a continual habituation and the pursuit of moral excellence.

The Paradoxical Double Danger of Symbiosis: When Spirit Changes Flesh

There *is*, it seems, a sort of double danger for the symbiote as well. Yet within this danger there is hope! After the initial bonding of Brock and the symbiote—when they first became "Venom"—this new identity resonated so potently with the alien that it continued to embrace this identity thereafter, even when separated from Brock. That is, Brock had a lasting impact on the alien. *Both* Brock and Flash Thompson (as well as Spider-Man) significantly influenced the moral sensitivities of the Venom-skin. Moreover, like Brock, the symbiote itself began to emulate heroism and to grow into a healthier state of mind, able to resist the impulse of appetite. There is, then, a sort of charismatic allure that virtue in the host holds over the adjoined flesh.

In the backstory of the Klyntar it was the noble influence of a goodness reflected within humanity that began to purify the symbiotes (once separated from Knull's influence). Virtuous character, tethered to the alien skin, began to purify the alien skin! There is, therefore, a double danger for the Klyntar; to bond with a virtuous host is to lose part of one's prior identity and to grow into a different sort of creature.

So, too, Christ has the power to change the Christian (Col. 1:22)! The lusts of our flesh are purged as we become more like the one to whom our existence is now tethered—*Virtue Himself*, the nourishment of our soul, the substance of our identity. *We are the alien skin*, transformed by a host in whom darkness and corruption become unintelligible. Therefore, to remain attached to our host is to welcome this purge of our impurities. Declared dead to sin, we are made alive in Christ (Ephesians 2). While the process is ongoing amid our lifetime, we, like Venom, can expect the struggle to continue. In the end, however, the Christian has a hope that will unfortunately elude Brock so long as he continues to rely on his own strength of spirit to keep at bay the beast of a corrupted appetite.

It is the Spirit of the Lord wherein lies freedom and transformation (2 Cor. 3:17–18). The redemptive Spirit of Christ working in the believer is the purified Symbiote of peace, propitiation, and moral perfection. The process of sanctification is symbiotic—it is not us, but Christ in us; it is not of works that none may boast, and yet it asks something from us nonetheless. But unlike the Klyntar, unlike our sin-skin, the Christ-skin is pure by nature and incorruptible. The Christian *glorified*, then, is the full embodiment of the Christ-Christian symbiosis (Gal. 4:15).

Our moral liturgies, virtuous practices of self-control, and heroic rituals of self-sacrifice are not enough in themselves to purify our own consciences. This requires our adjoining to a host already virtuous enough to purge our will—thereby refining our character into the sort of being that carries within itself a purified conscience and a tempered soul. So the paradoxical double danger is this: *With great strength of character and a purified will* (i.e., with Christ in us) *it is the Light that infects the Darkness.* To tease out the analogy a bit further, in the full maturity of our symbiotic union with Christ, we become more like Anti-Venom; *in the state of glorification, no evil can touch us, nor can it dwell in our presence.* Darkness becomes unintelligible when surrounded by light. So, although we fight a daily struggle with a venomous sin-skin, there is hope! Although it will not be found in his strength alone, there is hope for Eddie Brock, as well!

NOTES

1. Consider, for example, the problem of evil. The logical and evidential issues usually preoccupy dialogue. Despite rationalizations concerning logic, probability, and evidentiary considerations, however, there is nevertheless an existential problem of pain, which *must be lived out*.

2. Just because one loses one's memory, however, does not necessarily mean that one's habituations, appetites, or temperamental proclivities are gone.

3. Interestingly, it was Wolverine who first encouraged Venom's transition to antihero (*Venom [2018]* Annual #1). The influence of such heroism (of one who has demonstrated great fortitude in the face of double danger) is a significant point to

which we will return. Add to this the significance of Wolverine's past encounter with Klyntar symbiosis (*Web of Venom: Ve'Nam* #1).

4. Furthermore, human beings were created as image-bearers of the Creator. Therein lies a great sense of dignity central to our moral intuitions.

5. See Aristotle, *Nicomachean Ethics* II.5–6, 1108b11–1109b26.

6. See Augustine, *City of God* XIV.28.

7. For the story of Gyges, see Plato, *The Republic,* 359c–360d; concerning Plato's account of the soul as it relates to the question of virtuous justice vs egoistic injustice, see *Phaedrus* 253d–256e and *The Republic* 580d–e, 588b–589e.

8. Here Willmington's observation resonates profoundly, concerning the desperate and insecure, inner-warring nature of our sin-skin. "Sin often must strive against itself. . . . [For example] a promiscuous heterosexual is sickened at the sexual perversion of a homosexual. But this is not so with the good. . . . Good has only one enemy, the evil; but any evil has two enemies, the good and another conflicting evil" (Willmington 2011, 558). Consider, likewise, C.S. Lewis' observation about this warring nature: "The more pride one had, the more one disliked pride in others" (Lewis 2001, 122).

9. Perhaps this is to be expected, as they have continually been exposed to exemplars such as Spider-Man. After all, 1 Peter 2:12 speaks to the influence and allure of moral excellence. It seems that excellence exemplified becomes quite contagious.

Chapter Nine

Matt Murdock's Ill-Fitting Catholic Faith in Netflix's *Daredevil*

Daniel D. Clark

Japanese novelist Endo Shusaku often compared his Catholic faith to an ill-fitting coat, a coat he could never quite wear comfortably nor one he could ever cast off. In 1934 at the age of eleven, Endo, at his mother's insistence, was baptized into the Catholic faith. Maintaining that faith would be a life-long struggle. In a time of growing nationalism and imperialism in Japan, Endo, as a young man, faced suspicion and at times harassment for having adopted the enemy's religion. A far more serious challenge to his faith came from his own cultural presuppositions, which were deeply informed by Shinto and Buddhism. That the natural state of humanity is sinful, that the individual must actively resist sin, that a savior is needed to make atonement for the sins of the world, that the individual needed to acknowledge a personal, sovereign God who is omnipotent, omniscient, and omnipresent were all ideas that, while foundational to Catholicism, rattled Endo's Japanese sensibilities. Endo himself tried repeatedly to abandon the faith, but found himself returning to it. Catholicism, which had been forced upon him by his mother, had become such a part of his identity that try as he might, he could never escape it:

> There were many times when I felt I wanted to get rid of my Catholicism, but I was finally unable to do so. It is not just that I did not throw it off, but that I was unable to throw it off. The reason for this must be that it had become a part of me after all. The fact that it had penetrated me so deeply in my youth was a sign, I thought, that it had, in part at least, become coextensive with me. (Johnston 1980, xv)

Like Endo, Matt Murdock in Netflix's *Daredevil* series finds his Catholic faith, at times, a troublesome yet inescapable part of his identity. Murdock questions not only the real-world efficacy of Catholicism in the face of wide-spread injustice, suffering, and corruption, he also doubts his own ability to bring about lasting changes within his community. But as much as he might question that faith, his need for the moral clarity of his faith proves greater than his doubt as Murdock's Catholicism functions, in part, as the catalyst for his vigilantism. Catholic doctrines concerning helping the weak and vulnerable and Murdock's own sense of guilt compel him to act outside the law. Ultimately, Murdock's compulsion to help those in need flows from a mix of Catholic teaching and his own anger and bitterness from the suffering in his own life.

Murdock's faith also works to restrain his desire to hurt others, though he encounters many voices tempting him to release his inner devil. Murdock recognizes his impulse toward violence and seeks meaningful and moral boundaries for these compulsions. His Catholic faith provides some restraints as Murdock's belief in the sanctity of life and in the possibility of redemption for all prevents him from taking the lives of his enemies. Murdock's frequent self-examinations and his questioning the morality of his impulses also work to constrain his violence. To this end, Murdock at first reluctantly, but in time purposefully, pursues mentors in Father Lantom and Sister Maggie, looking for both their approval and moral guidance concerning his use of violence in the name of justice.

THE CATHOLIC CATALYST TO ACTION

Matt Murdock's childhood is filled with personal trauma. His mother, suffering from postpartum depression, abandons him and his father, Jack, when Murdock is an infant. His father, a boxer with a mediocre record of 24–31, raises his son alone. As a nine year old, Murdock idolizes his father, seeing him as a hero, and may have been attempting to emulate this vision when he saves an elderly man from being run over in traffic. Though he pushes the man to safety, the resulting accident dumps drums of hazardous materials on the roadway. Murdock's eyes are splashed with chemicals leaving him blinded but his other senses uncontrollably heightened. Not much later, Murdock's father, desiring his son's respect, wins a boxing match the mob has instructed him to lose. As he is walking home after the fight, Jack Murdock is shot by a mob hitman. Young Murdock is awakened by the gunshot that takes his father's life. Seemingly orphaned, Matt is taken in by the Saint Agnes Orphanage. His heightened senses only compound his suffering as he is unable to shut out the amplified voices and sounds surrounding the orphanage. These traumas leave Murdock alone, angry, and bitter.

The Catholic orphanage, however, provides Murdock a means of directing his anguish toward a positive end. Father Lantom, one of Murdock's primary mentors after the death of his father, tells an eleven-year-old Murdock that anger is "a perfectly understandable reaction to your situation, but it's not sustainable. . . . [Y]ou're going to have to deal with your anger, Matthew. Find a way to harness it, or it will destroy you" ("Please," 3.2). Lantom may even be the first to encourage Murdock to focus his rage toward becoming a lawyer as he observes how easily Murdock enjoys both fighting and arguing ("Please," 3.2).

Though Murdock is an unwilling resident at Saint Agnes, he is learning the Catholic Catechism ("Please," 3.2), elements of which form some of his core moral values and motivate him to seek justice as an adult. For example, several catechisms reflect Murdock's opposition toward corruption. One catechism asserts that those with power must "serve the legitimate good of the communities. . . . Regimes whose nature is contrary to the natural law, to the public order, and to the fundamental rights of persons cannot achieve the common good of the nations on which they have been imposed" (Catholic Church 1993, 1901). Another catechism claims that authority "must not behave in a despotic manner, but must act for the common good as a 'moral force based on freedom and a sense of responsibility'" (1902). Still another encourages opposing those with power who "take measures contrary to the moral order" (1903). As an adult, Murdock becomes a lawyer to be a force for good. Using his ability to hear changes in heart rhythms, he recognizes the innocent and defends them from corrupt authorities. It is not surprising then that Murdock feels so strongly compelled to oppose Wilson Fisk, who, while claiming to work for the common good of their community, Hell's Kitchen, does not hesitate to intimidate, use physical violence, and even kill individuals to achieve his goals.

Other catechisms reinforce Murdock's compulsion to take direct action against corruption as they remind Catholics of their moral obligation to work toward justice, especially for the weak, the needy, and the powerless. One catechism reads, "The duty of making oneself a neighbor to others and actively serving them becomes even more urgent when it involves the disadvantaged" (1932). Another asserts, "There exist also sinful inequalities that affect millions of men and women. These are in open contradiction of the Gospel: 'Their equal dignity as persons demands that we strive for fairer and more humane conditions'" (1938). Murdock transforms these abstract teachings into concrete actions as he uses his heightened senses and fighting skills to confront corruption and to defend the vulnerable, which Murdock, at least initially, views as his fulfilling of God's purpose in his life ("The Path of Righteousness," 1.11).

MURDOCK'S AMBIVALENCE TO
THE CATHOLIC FAITH

Though Murdock identifies as a Catholic and is influenced by Catholic teaching, he experiences ambivalence toward the Church itself as he feels compelled to act outside the normal bounds of Catholic activism while subconsciously desiring the Church's approval. This ambivalence is demonstrated in one of the earliest scenes in the series as the adult Murdock ostensibly goes to Father Lantom for confession. Murdock, however, is unable to articulate his plan for action or his need for the Church's sanction; rather, he describes his father's unexceptional career as a fighter while highlighting his father's ability to take a punch, to be knocked down but never knocked out. Murdock seems to be describing not only his father, but his own alter ego. Murdock describes his father's eyes going dead, his letting his inner devil out as he would beat his opponents mercilessly once trapping them in the corner of the ring. Murdock tells the priest that when he was younger, he didn't understand his father's rage, his letting his inner devil out, but now, as an adult, Murdock implies he does. Father Lantom attempts to shift the conversation toward Murdock's confession: "Perhaps this would be easier if you tell me what you've done." Murdock enigmatically tells the priest, "I'm not seeking penance for what I've done, Father. I'm asking forgiveness . . . for what I'm about to do." Unsettled with the morality of the course he has set for himself, Murdock seeks not so much forgiveness but moral affirmation from the Church. Murdock finds himself compelled to act while subconsciously questioning the adequacy of his own moral compass ("Into the Ring," 1.1).

Murdock further illustrates his ambivalence toward the real-world sufficiency of his faith after the murder of his client, Elena Cardenas. Cardenas' landlord and Fisk subordinate Armand Tully had been attempting to evict Cardenas and the other tenants from their rent-controlled apartments. Fisk orders Cardenas' death, making her appear to be a victim of a purse snatching that turned violent. After watching Fisk publicly proclaim his outrage and sorrow over the death of Cardenas, Karen Page, Murdock's law assistant, asks Murdock if his faith helps him deal with these types of injustices. Murdock responds, "Not today" ("Speak of the Devil," 1.9). Page then tells Murdock, "If there is a God and if he cares at all about any of us, Fisk will get what he deserves. You have to believe that." Murdock responds confidently, "I do" ("Speak of the Devil," 1.9). Murdock's faith provides small comfort after the death of Cardenas, but his assurance that Fisk will be brought to justice may rest more in his faith that he himself will be God's instrument of judgment rather than in any Christian teaching concerning God's ultimate judgment.

Though Murdock feels compelled to act, he seems suspicious of his own motivations and seeks sanction from Father Lantom for his vigilantism, which Lantom hesitates to provide. Murdock recognizes his violent tendencies, a desire to release his inner devil. Although he can rationalize the utility of killing Fisk, Murdock lacks confidence that his decision is not tainted by those violent desires and thus seeks to gain Father Lantom's approval. Before confronting Fisk, Murdock asks Lantom if he believes in a literal devil. Lantom tells of his friend and Rwandan village elder Gahiji, who was respected by both Hutu and Tutsi. Even though a militia commander had ordered his death, the commander's subordinates could not bring themselves to kill a man so widely admired. The commander came to the village himself, spoke to Gahiji for hours, and then dragged him out of his hut and butchered him and his family in front of the villagers. "In that man who took Gahiji's life," Lantom says, "I saw the Devil. So, yes, Matthew, I believe he walks among us, taking many forms." Murdock replies, "What if you could have stopped him from ever hurting anyone again?" Lantom asks, "Stopped him how?" ("Speak of the Devil," 1.9). While Lantom shares Murdock's contempt for injustice and desires to see oppressors removed from power, Lantom suggests moral limits exist when confronting injustice.

THE INSUFFICIENCY OF THE LAW

Murdock's compulsion to fight against corruption is further fueled by his sense of Catholic morality and his own frustrations with the failure of the law to meet out justice. In his closing arguments defending hit man John Healy for killing a mob boss named Prohaszka, Murdock describes a fundamental difference between morality and law: "Ladies and gentlemen of the jury, forgive me if I seem distracted. I've been preoccupied of late with . . . questions of morality, of right and wrong, good and evil. Sometimes the delineation between the two is a sharp line. Sometimes it's a blur." While Murdock notes that some believe morality is a subjective construct in which there is no "sharp line, only [a] blur," he bristles at a law that ignores morality. Murdock's Catholic background at times places him at odds with his own profession. In this courtroom, Murdock knows his client is guilty, yet because of the lack of evidence, the law works in favor of the guilty, which further spurs Murdock's vigilantism. Murdock's closing argument emphasizes both his fidelity to upholding the law and his frustration that the law is incapable of making moral judgments. Murdock argues,

A man is dead. And my client, John Healy took his life. This is not in dispute. It is a matter of record, of fact, and facts have no moral judgment. They merely state what is. . . . What was in my client's heart when he took Mr. Prohaszka's life? Whether he is a good man or something else entirely, is irrelevant. These questions of good and evil, as important as they are, have no place in a court of law. Only the facts matter. . . . Based on these, and these alone, the prosecution has failed to prove beyond a reasonable doubt that my client was not acting solely in self-defense. And those, ladies and gentlemen of the jury, are the facts. My client, based purely on the sanctity of the law which we've all sworn an oath to uphold must be acquitted of these charges. Now beyond that, beyond these walls he may well face a judgment of his own making. But here in this court-room the judgment is yours and yours alone. ("Rabbit in a Snowstorm," 1.3)

After the jury is unable to reach a verdict and Healy is released, Murdock fulfills his own prophecy. That evening, dressed as Daredevil, Murdock con-fronts Healy. After a brutal fight, Murdock forces Healy to reveal that Wilson Fisk had hired him to kill Prohaszka. Healy then faces his own judgment by killing himself out of fear that Fisk will kill his entire family for surrendering his name.

While Murdock's faith has taught him to oppose injustice forcefully, his sense of morality coupled with his frustration with the limits of the law further motivate him to embrace vigilantism. However, the most significant catalyst to Murdock's ever-increasing aggression against corruption may well result from his sense of guilt. As Murdock acts outside the law at-tempting to bring about justice, he quickly realizes his attempts often lead to consequences for the people he believes he is helping. The deaths of Cardenas, newspaper writer Ben Urich who was investigating Fisk, and El-liot Grote, an Irish mobster turned informant whom Murdock was protect-ing, trigger Murdock's guilt as he blames himself for not having acted more aggressively. Murdock tells his law partner, Foggy Nelson, that he wants to kill Fisk because of the murder of Cardenas. After Ben Urich's graveside service, Murdock tells Father Lantom, "He was a good man, and he's gone, because I haven't stopped what's happening to this city" ("Daredevil," 1.13). After Grote's funeral, which only Murdock, Nelson, and Page attend, Murdock tells Father Lantom without conviction, "It wasn't my fault. . . . I did everything I could to protect my client." Lantom asks Murdock what he wants, Murdock replies, "Forgiveness" for "not doing more." Lantom tells Murdock that he believes, as Murdock himself had just claimed, that he had done all he could to keep Grote alive. Murdock replies, "Then why do I still feel guilty." Lantom's response encourages Murdock to turn his guilt into action:

Guilt can be a good thing. It's the soul's call to action. The indication that some-thing is wrong. The only way to rid your heart of it is to correct your mistakes and keep going until amends are made. I don't know what you didn't do or what you should have done but the guilt . . . means your work is not yet finished. ("Penny and a Dime," 2.4)

Lantom's advice further feeds Murdock's need to work outside the law to bring about justice.

CATHOLIC RESTRAINTS

Catholic charges to oppose evil, to help the weak and needy, and to oppose injustice synthesize with Murdock's inborn rage and propensity for brutality turning him into the Devil of Hell's Kitchen, a masked vigilante who is quick to use violence against those who prey on the innocent. Though his vigilantism is fueled by his Catholic faith, this same faith creates unsteady moral restraints against Murdock's baser violent tendencies. Murdock possesses two core Catholic beliefs that set boundaries for his vigilantism: the sanctity of human life and the belief that even the worst person can find redemption. These Catholic values are so ingrained that Murdock consistently refrains from killing and even puts himself in jeopardy to prevent others from doing so. Murdock also repeatedly holds out hope to his opponents, believing they can change their lives. These core beliefs do not go unchallenged, however. Murdock's guilt in failing to save those under his protection, his doubts about the efficacy of these moral restraints, his desire to end Fisk's corruption, and his supposed loss of faith after the second death of his former lover Elektra shake Murdock's commitment to these values. He wrestles with these issues by holding imaginary conversations with his dead father and Fisk. These conversations allow Murdock to bring his deepest fears about his own motives to the surface and ultimately to overcome them.

Sanctity of Life

Throughout all three seasons of the series, Murdock never quite fully embraces his Catholic faith, yet he finds himself unable to escape its grip, particularly when it comes to his belief in the sacredness of life. Murdock will not kill. He takes seriously the catechism that charges, "The fifth commandment forbids direct and intentional killing as gravely sinful. The murderer and those who cooperate voluntarily in murder commit a sin that cries out to heaven for vengeance" (Catholic Church 1993, 2268). Another catechism explicitly notes, "Human life is sacred because from its beginning it involves the creative action of God and it remains forever in a special relationship with the Creator, who is its sole end. God alone is the Lord of life from its beginning until its end: no one can under any circumstance claim for himself the right directly to destroy an innocent human being" (2258). While fighting with Frank Castle against the Irish mob, Murdock prevents Castle, a vigilante who does not share Murdock's respect for life, from killing any of the mobsters. Murdock throws his billy club, knocking a gun out of Castle's hand as he is about to shoot a fallen mobster. Later in the fight sequence, Murdock stops fighting his opponent to grab a hammer from Castle just as he is about to smash it into a mobster's head ("Penny and a Dime," 2.4). Murdock repeats this feat in the season three finale during a three-way fight between Murdock, Fisk, and Poindexter, a mentally fragile FBI agent whom Fisk manipulates, as he twice prevents Poindexter from killing Vanessa Marianna, one of the few people Fisk actually loves ("A New Napkin," 3.13).

Murdock holds so firmly to the value of human life that he confronts those who disagree. While chained to a roof, he challenges Castle's belief that killing criminals is the best means for ending crime. "I don't kill anyone," he tells Castle. "People don't have to die. . . . I believe it's not my call, and it ain't yours either" ("New York's Finest," 2.3). Later, when assassin Elektra Natchios recruits Murdock to help her reveal the criminal activities at the Roxxon Corporation, Murdock tells her, "I happen to respect human life. If we do this . . . if . . . then I need to know you're at least going to pretend to feel the same way. Nobody dies. Do you understand?" ("Regrets Only," 2.6).

Possibly the clearest example of Murdock's respect for life comes when Murdock confronts Roscoe Sweeney. In a flashback to Murdock's college days, Natchios has tracked down Sweeney, a man who, unbeknownst to Murdock, has caused much of the suffering in his life. At Elektra's prompting, the two break into Sweeney's mansion. When Sweeney returns, Elektra subdues him and reveals that Sweeney is the man who killed Murdock's father. After tying Sweeney to a chair, Elektra encourages Matt to beat Sweeney, which Murdock does. Elektra then directs Matt to kill Sweeney, but Murdock declines. Even faced with the man who had his father killed, who mocks and threatens Murdock's life, and even with Elektra goading him to kill Sweeney, Murdock declines. His respect for the sanctity of life is stronger than his impulse for revenge ("Kinbaku," 2.5).

Though Murdock will not kill, he certainly desires to do so. After the death of Elena Cardenas, Foggy Nelson asks Murdock if he had ever killed anyone. Murdock replies, "No, but I wanted to. After Elena, after everything Fisk had done, I went to a warehouse I thought he'd be at. I went to kill him" ("Nelson v. Murdock," 1.10). Murdock, though, fails to kill Fisk. Even in the third season where Murdock has supposedly renounced the Catholic faith, Murdock cannot bring himself to kill another human being. His faith creates tension between his desire to act decisively and his need to restrain his more violent urges. He tells Father Lantom, "I know my soul is damned if I take his life. But if I stand idle, if I let him consume this city . . . people . . . will suffer and die" ("Speak of the Devil," 1.9).

Possibility of Redemption

Closely tied to Murdock's view of the sanctity of life is his belief that anyone can be redeemed, further restraining Murdock from ending another's life. While Frank Castle has Murdock chained to the roof of a building, Murdock challenges Castle's belief system by holding out to him the possibility of redemption, not only for the people Castle is trying to kill, but for Castle himself. Murdock essentially argues the Catholic catechism that every human being contains the divine imprint of the image of God, and though "disfigured" by sin, every person can have that image "restored to its original beauty and ennobled by the grace of God" through "Christ" the "Redeemer and Savior" (Catholic Church 1993, 1701, 1702). Murdock attempts to rouse Castle's conscience, asking him if he ever considers the fact that he is killing human beings, who, despite their crimes, are capable of goodness. Castle rejects Murdock's claim, "I think there's no good in the filth that I put down." Murdock then enters the theological realm as he tells Castle:

Murdock: I live in the real world, too, and I've seen it.

Castle: Yeah? What have you seen?

Murdock: Redemption, Frank.

Castle: Ah, Jesus Christ. ("New York's Finest," 2.3)

Castle's rather ironic juxtaposition of the profane use of *Jesus Christ* with the word *redemption* illustrates the different moral lines Murdock and Castle have drawn for themselves. Both use violence against criminals, but more important to Murdock than permanently ending evil is allowing for the possibility that those he fights might be redeemed. Castle, however, seeks a permanent judgment; redemption, to Castle, is irrelevant and nonsensical.

As Murdock holds out the possibility of redemption, Castle refuses to concede, but he has no response to Murdock's charge. Castle stands attempting to re-establish his dominance, even though Murdock is chained. Murdock tells Castle, "You're unhinged, Frank. You are. You think God made you a one-man firing squad." (This is a rather ironic statement as Murdock at some level believes his own vigilantism is divinely prescribed.) "But you're wrong. There is goodness in people, even in you." Castle, incapable of a reasoned response or of accepting Murdock's message, resorts to ending the argument by punching the bound Murdock in the head, rendering him unconscious ("New York's Finest," 2.3).

Foggy Nelson recognizes how closely tied Murdock's identity is to his belief in the value of life and in the possibility of redemption, even when Murdock has seemingly turned his back on his faith after the second death of Elektra. Murdock claims he is going to kill Fisk, but Nelson suggests to Karen Page that Murdock won't follow through with his threat. He says, "Eventually, he'll come to his senses. Matt's Matt because he believes that everyone deserves a shot at redemption." Karen replies, "Except Fisk." Nelson corrects her: "Everyone. It's a Catholic thing" ("A New Napkin, 3.13).

Restraining the Inner Devil through Prayer?

Murdock also restrains his impulses through wrangling with his own conscience. Canadian novelist David Adams Richards notes, "Not one of us doesn't pray to God continually—even if it is only to tell God to go to hell. . . . That is I believe that the conversations we hold by ourselves are always with God" (Richards 2009, 30–31). In Kevin Smith's "Guardian Devil" story arc from the flagship *Daredevil* comic book series, Matt Murdock repeatedly holds these conversations with God as he complains about the immorality, indignity, and suffering of humanity, his own weaknesses, the seemingly punitive nature of God, and even his own doubts about God's existence (Smith 2003, 21, 44). In the Netflix series, Murdock holds these conversations with his dead father and an imaginary Fisk. Through these conversations Murdock contemplates his seeming inability to protect the innocent, his sense of guilt, his own desire to inflict violence, and the morality of killing Fisk to free Hell's Kitchen from his corrupt control.

The first of these conversations occurs when Murdock happens upon a crowd protesting Fisk's release from jail. An imaginary Fisk appears taunting Murdock, telling him that his suffering is a result of God being angry with him, that he will not prevent Karen Page from being killed, and that he is responsible for the deaths of his father, his one-time trainer Stick, and Elektra. Murdock's only response is to repeatedly tell Fisk to stop ("No Good Deed," 3.3). Later, after Murdock fails to keep Melvin Potter, the man who made Murdock's Daredevil suit, from being arrested by the FBI, this imaginary Fisk appears again, revealing Murdock's inner turmoil even more profoundly:

> [Y]ou did hesitate before you left. Were you waiting for a messenger from the Lord to stop you, like he stopped Abraham from killing his son? Were you disappointed no messenger arrived . . . or relieved that you didn't have to risk your life for a weak-minded criminal? You're not strong enough to beat the man I sent for you. You're not smart enough to beat me. You couldn't do it alone. You

couldn't do it with your friends. Your father never knew when to lay down. He was too proud. You will die the same way. ("Aftermath," 3.7)

Again, Murdock has no response to his inner voices, as they force Murdock to acknowledge his deepest fears.

Murdock only begins to face these fears as he conjures up his dead father after learning that Sister Maggie is his mother. Enraged that neither his father nor Sister Maggie revealed the truth, he confronts the ghost of his father not only for hiding his parentage but also for needlessly dying while trying to live by some inner code. Murdock's accusations, however, reflect his own questioning of his Catholic faith and the code he himself lives by. As much as Murdock claims to be different from his father, he cannot escape his faith. Murdock tells his father that he will not live by a code that causes others to suffer, and that when he finds Fisk, he will kill him. But Murdock is deceiving himself. He can no more escape his inner moral code than he can stop defending the weak.

The last of these conversations is the strangest but reveals most explicitly Murdock's inner turmoil and fear. Murdock, sitting alone in Fogwell's Gym, listens as his dead father stands behind him and warns that he is too angry and that Poindexter will likely kill him. Murdock's ethereal father reinforces Murdock's belief that he is cursed by having a devil inside him. Through the voice of his dead father, Murdock is finally able to confront the central moral issue of whether his methods in fighting corruption are moral or if his fighting corruption is simply an excuse for him to use violence. As his father accuses Murdock of rationalizing his violence, Fisk's voice begins to overlap with Murdock's father's, eventually replacing it altogether:

> Would you be honest with yourself? You put on that mask because it lets you feel all right with who you really are. It lets you hurt people and makes you feel like it's for something important . . . [Fisk's voice joins Jack's.] something good, maybe even for God. But that ain't the truth, and we both know it. [Fisk's voice now alone.] You and your father are cut from the same cloth. A corrupt boxer who takes as much satisfaction in inflicting pain as he does money for taking dives. And his son, who's trying to convince himself he's any better than his criminal father. You were born from nothing. You remain nothing. ("Revelations," 3.9)

Murdock, like Castle earlier, has no response except violence. Murdock stands, turns toward Fisk, screams, and begins punching and kicking the apparition until Fisk is on his knees, face bloodied. Murdock breaks the phantom's neck but then finds himself sitting alone on a bench next to the empty boxing ring ("Revelations," 3.9). Though Murdock can rationalize the utility of killing Fisk and fantasizes about taking his life, Murdock's

Catholic-formed conscience still prevents him from doing so. These prayer-like conversations force Murdock to confront his own fears and the morality of his intent.

CATHOLIC MENTORS AS DEMONIC RESTRAINT

Murdock's inner demons are most effectively kept at bay because of his reliance on mentors. Murdock realizes the dangers of giving reign to his inner devil, thus he seeks mentors to help him set moral boundaries for his darker nature, first with Father Lantom and later with Sister Maggie. Other mentors, however, act as demonic foils to Lantom and Maggie, as they attempt to undercut Murdock's moral core. Finally, this mentor motif becomes most explicit when Murdock is juxtaposed with his primary adversaries—Frank Castle, Benjamin Poindexter, and Wilson Fisk—who all resemble Murdock far more than he would like to admit. These three all suggest that the lack of a mentor results in unrestrained brutality and destruction.

Murdock recognizes his inclination toward violence, but he also recognizes that such urges must be checked. Throughout the series, Murdock looks to Father Lantom, and later to Sister Maggie, for guidance. Murdock seeks both sanction for his vigilantism and safeguards to prevent himself from unleashing his inner devil. Though, as Sue Sorensen notes, clergy are often portrayed as "buffoon[s] or charlatan[s]" in literature and film, Lantom is not one of those (Sorensen 2014, 12). He is intelligent, world weary, and possesses the characteristics Sorensen suggests are necessary for a good counselor: "listening, accepting, waiting, and then listening some more" (2014, 43). Lantom resists providing easy answers but rather probes Murdock so he can discover for himself the path he should follow.

Late in the first season of the series, Murdock seeks Father Lantom's perspective before confronting Fisk. Murdock suggests that killing Fisk may be the only solution. Lantom, however, reminds Murdock of his Catholic values even as Murdock questions the effectiveness of those values in freeing Hell's Kitchen from Fisk. Lantom presses Murdock to consider the morality of murdering another human being, cautioning him that many have rationalized their own barbarity because of the barbarity of their opponents ("Speak of the Devil," 1.9). Lantom further presses Murdock to evaluate his motivation: "[T]he question you have to ask yourself is are you struggling with the fact that you don't want to kill this man but have to? Or that you don't have to kill him but want to?" ("Speak of the Devil," 1.9). When Murdock finally confronts Fisk, Fisk implies that he had Cardenas killed to lure Murdock into the open, to force a confrontation. Enraged, Murdock threatens to kill Fisk, but is easily defeated and barely escapes being killed himself. Days later, Lantom walks into his church to find Murdock sitting alone on a pew. Murdock tells Lantom that he failed in his attempt to kill Fisk. Lantom again nudges Murdock's conscience, "[A]re you disappointed that you didn't succeed or maybe a little relieved?" ("The Path of Righteousness," 1.11). Murdock doesn't answer. In that same conversation, Murdock asks Lantom why, if God has a purpose for each person's life, "did he put the Devil in me? Why do I feel it in my heart and my soul clawing to be let out if that's not part of God's plan?" Lantom again gently prods Murdock toward restraint: "Maybe you're being called to summon the better angels of your nature" ("The Path of Righteousness," 1.11). Although Murdock often has murderous intent, he never takes a life.

Sister Maggie also becomes a mentor who pushes back against Murdock's violent nature and his eventual bitterness against God. After the death of Elektra at the end of Netflix's *Defenders*, Murdock rages against God and attempts to jettison his faith, but without success ("The Defenders," 1.8). He experiences what Madeline L'Engle describes as "part of a healthy grief not often encouraged . . . to yell, to doubt, to kick at God with angry violence" (L'Engle 1996, xvi). Like C.S. Lewis after the death of his wife Joy Davidman, Murdock feels abandoned by God. Lewis writes,

> [G]o to [God] when your need is desperate, when all other help is in vain, and what do you find? A door slammed in your face, and a sound of a bolting and double bolting on the inside. After that, silence. You may as well turn away. The longer you wait, the more emphatic the silence will become. (Lewis 1996, 6)

Murdock does turn away, in a sense. He doesn't so much abandon his belief in God as he comes to a new understanding of God as one who causes suffering. Murdock compares himself to Job as one who bled and sweated for God because he believed he was "God's soldier. . . . Well, not anymore. I am what I do in the dark now. I bleed only for myself." Maggie removes her cross necklace, takes Murdock's hand, and places it in his open palm. He tosses the necklace on a bed and tells Maggie that she wasn't listening. Murdock tells Maggie that he doesn't hate God, but that he has simply "seen God's true face." Maggie takes the cross necklace and hangs it over Murdock's lampshade. Though Murdock claims to have abandoned God and tells Maggie he is not concerned with what God wants, he still does not kill ("Resurrection," 3.1).

DEMONIC MENTORS

Father Lantom and Sister Maggie's voices are not the only voices that attempt to influence Murdock. These other voices may take on the role of what

Northrop Frye describes as demonic parodies. Frye notes that in biblical nar-ratives, "every apocalyptic image has a demonic narrative or contrast" (Frye 1982, 176). Steven Marx describes Frye's idea of demonic parody as "a nega-tive inversion of the original story" (Marx 1994, 170). Other mentors enter Murdock's life and attempt to undermine his faith—his value of life and his belief that any person can be redeemed. Stick, a blind member of the Chaste, attempts to pull a nine-year-old Murdock away from his Catholic moorings hoping to turn him into a weapon in his war against the Hand. Stick con-tradicts Murdock's upbringing, telling him, "[T]he only way guys like you and me can survive is to grab [the world] by the throat and never let go," a philosophy more akin to Fisk's than one based in Christianity. Twenty years later, Stick tells the adult Murdock, "I need a soldier. Committed. Not some bleeding heart idealist hanging onto half measures." Stick then directly ques-tions Murdock's central belief about life, asking Murdock accusingly how many he's killed "protecting the city." Murdock remains silent while Stick mocks him for not being able to "cross that line" when needed ("Stick," 1.7). Although Stick fails to develop Murdock into a dispassionate killer, Murdock does begin to question the utility of his non-lethal methods.

Both Elektra Natchios and Frank Castle also tempt Murdock to question his belief in the value of human life. Natchios admits to their first encounter not being a matter of fate. She claims Stick sent her on a mission to separate Murdock from his path to be a lawyer, to separate him from his friends, to separate him from his moral core, but she failed when Murdock refused to murder his father's killer. Natchios says, "There's a light inside you. I tried to snuff it out in college. I'm so lucky I failed" ("Guilty as Sin," 2.8). Castle echoes Stick, telling Murdock his methods are little more than half mea-sures. Murdock seems to relent: "I understand. You're right. My way isn't working. So, maybe just this once [Murdock crosses himself, knowing he would be violating God's law and his conscience.] Maybe your way is what it's gonna take" (".380," 2.11). Ironically, Castle, after berating Murdock for his feeble efforts, warns him that crossing the line of killing another human being is not a line one can step back across. Though Murdock intel-lectually assents to the utility of killing, his conscience still prevents him from crossing that line.

The significance of this mentor motif becomes all the more apparent as Murdock is portrayed as not that different from his primary antagonists—Castle, Poindexter, and Fisk. All have suffered personal traumas; all have deep-seated psychological urges toward violence, and all of them struggle to see beyond their own suffering. The primary difference between Murdock and the other three characters is his moral core, which is reinforced by his mentors and friends Nelson and Page. Castle has no mentor; Poindexter loses his mentor to cancer; Fisk also forgoes a mentor. Without mentors, all three give reign to their most violent impulses.

Frank Castle recognizes in Murdock a kindred spirit, who, as Castle says, is only "one bad day away from being me" ("New York's Finest," 2.3). Both have Catholic backgrounds. Both received close quarter combat training. Both lost family to mob violence—Murdock lost his father and Castle his wife and children. Both refuse to stand idly by, feeling compelled to confront those guilty of causing destruction: Murdock attacks those who bring violence to Hell's Kitchen while Castle kills anyone associated with the deaths of his family. Castle rationalizes his killing, noting that the criminals he kills will never commit another crime. Focused on his desire for revenge, he repels any suggestion that he might need help. After discovering Castle's Catholic past, Murdock, attempting to have Castle consider the morality of his killing mobsters, asks him if he still attends Mass. Castle simply replies, "Stop now, Red" ("New York's Finest," 2.3). Without a mentor, Castle hears no voice of caution and acts freely on his vengeful impulses, killing his enemies without restraint.

Ben Poindexter, too, seems to mirror Murdock, but unlike Castle, Poindexter contains his psychopathic tendencies while under the care of his therapist Eileen Mercer. Sister Maggie's description of a young Matt Murdock could just as easily apply to Poindexter: "He was alone in the world, in his private darkness, surrounded by strangers. . . . He was plagued by awful nightmares. . . . Everyone in Matthew's life abandoned him" ("The Devil You Know," 3.6). Even Murdock acknowledges the similarities, but denies that they are the same: "He didn't have any parents. . . . Spent a lot of time fighting. . . . I didn't have anyone either, but I'm nothing like him" ("Upstairs/Downstairs," 3.8). Murdock is correct insofar as he didn't develop a propensity to kill. Poindexter's therapist quickly diagnoses his personality disorder and provides him with structured guidelines and techniques to restrain his desire to kill, which allow him to function within society.

After years of therapy, Poindexter's progress is stunted when Mercer, coughing and breathing with an oxygen tube, announces that she cannot continue as his therapist. Poindexter seems incapable of empathizing with Mercer who is dying of cancer; instead, he becomes enraged that she will no longer guide him. She encourages him to maintain an ordered lifestyle and find a job that has a strict structure. She also encourages him to find a new mentor: "Your internal compass isn't broken, Dex. It just works better when you have the North Star to guide you." He initially follows her advice in maintaining an ordered lifestyle and working jobs that have a strict structure—a suicide hotline, the military, and then the FBI—but without a mentor, his disorder begins to reassert itself. While working at the hotline he begins to encourage a suicidal caller to kill his abuser instead of himself. Later, while working for the FBI, he kills two surrendering Albanian gang members ("Please," 3.2). When the FBI assigns Poindexter to monitor Fisk, Fisk uncovers Poindexter's past therapy sessions and positions himself as Poindexter's new North Star. Fisk then cultivates Poindexter's desire to kill, encourages him to stop taking his medications, and finally destroys any remaining vestiges of restraint, turning him into an exploitable psychopathic assassin.

Wilson Fisk is what Matt Murdock would look like if not for the restraints of Catholicism. To some, however, Murdock seems no different than Fisk. Betsy Beatty, a parole officer who Murdock warns to leave town, tells Murdock that he "and Fisk are cut from the same cloth" ("Aftermath," 3.7). Although Murdock rejects the idea that he and Fisk are alike, they are more similar than not with a thin thread separating the two. Their rage seems ready to overwhelm them. They are quick to brutalize their opponents. Though Murdock may not kill, he lets his inner devil out—he breaks bones, smashes faces, and leaves opponents permanently scarred and disfigured. One image further suggests how much these two men share. The series juxtaposes an image of Murdock, alone in the church basement, grieving the death of Elektra, with an image of Fisk, alone in his cell, grieving his separation from Marianna. Both men briefly face each other (see figure 9.1), trapped and lost in their own sense of loss ("Please," 3.2).

Ultimately, however, Wilson Fisk represents Matthew Murdock's demonic parody. Like Murdock, Fisk has read the Bible, but he draws heterodox conclusions from it. While being transported after his first arrest, Fisk narrates

Figure 9.1. Matt Murdoch and Wilson Fisk grieving. (Daredevil, "Please," 3.2)

the familiar parable of the Good Samaritan. Most homilies about this parable challenge congregations to identify with the Samaritan. Other more candid sermons focus on the abused traveler or the hypocritical religious leaders who fail to aid the beaten man, but Fisk draws unique inspiration from the biblical text. He observes that he had always thought of himself as the Samaritan, as someone who cared about his community, but that he had been deceiving himself. He says, "I am not the Samaritan. . . . I'm not the priest or the Levite. . . . I am the ill intent who set upon the traveler on the road that he should not have been on" ("Daredevil," 1.13). Fisk embraces his nature, identifying himself with the thieves in the parable, recognizing that he lives to dominate through the bald use of power.

Fisk further parodies Murdock in his public displays of morality and faith. Murdock struggles with morality, with his faith, with his belief in a benevolent God, but he never stops believing in God no matter how angry he becomes with God. Fisk, however, sees morality and faith as tools for gaining power, for manipulating public sentiment. After the death of Elena Cardenas, Fisk proclaims his outrage over her death. He claims he mourns her death and is angered by the fear that dominates the city, blaming Daredevil for its suffering ("Speak of the Devil," 1.9). Later, when visiting a comatose Marianna after she had been poisoned, Fisk tells her,

> I don't know how to pray. My father was not a religious man. My mother wanted to be . . . I think, needed to be, but she never quite found it within herself. I'd seen it in movies, and watched it on television. I read it in books when I was a child, after I was sent away. And I tried to mimic the words . . . the sentiment . . . but it was false. It was imitation of faith. So, I can't pray for you. ("The Path of Righteousness," 1.11)

Though Fisk cannot pray, he does indeed imitate faith. Freed from prison by the Court of Appeals, Fisk speaks to angry protestors outside the hotel in which he had been under house arrest. He portrays himself as the victim and suggests a respect for faith while painting Daredevil as the actual villain. "They sent someone to frame me. Daredevil. The killer who's now showing his true colors, who has tried to murder people in newspaper offices and churches . . . attacking our sacred institutions. Believe me. Daredevil is our true public enemy" ("Reunion," 3.11). As he speaks, the protestors slowly lower their signs, overcome by Fisk's counterfeit displays of morality and faith.

Murdock, however, demonstrates that he cannot escape his faith no matter how ill fitting that faith may be. In their final confrontation, Fisk is bloodied and on his knees. Murdock points at Fisk and screams, "You want me to kill you." Fisk growls, "No prison can keep me. You know that. Come on, kill me!" Confronted with the opportunity he's fantasized about, Murdock shouts, "No! God knows I want to, but you don't get to destroy who I am" ("A New Napkin," 3.13). This final scene juxtaposes Murdock's moral core—one that compels forcible acts against injustice while preserving life restrained by faith and conscience—with Fisk's moral core—one that seeks its own power while consuming life unrestrained by any morality other than utility.

CONCLUSION

Ultimately, Murdock's faith, which demands that corrupt power be opposed and that the poor and downtrodden be helped, is, in part, the catalyst for his vigilantism. Murdock, unsure of the morality of his mission and realizing his own propensity for violence, desires church sanction and direction. His belief in the sanctity of life and the potential of every person to receive redemption prevents him from taking another's life. Murdock, however, wrestles with the efficacy of such a view in the face of overwhelming abuse and power. Through prayer-like conversations with himself, that may in fact be conversations with God, and through the guidance of Father Lantom and Sister Maggie, he is able to establish his own moral compass. This mentoring motif becomes central to the narrative as characters who follow their own impulses or are guided by corrupt mentors meet destruction, suggesting that no one can face life alone.

Chapter Ten

Gods upon Gods

Hierarchies of Divinity in the Marvel Universe

Austin M. Freeman

Just why is Thor a god anyway?[1] He's clearly got a body. He gets drunk, suffers pain, and doesn't seem to possess any remarkable wisdom or intelligence. And if Thor is a god, what does that make Galactus? The "Cosmic" element in the Marvel Universe is well known thanks to recent films, and the concept of a comic book "god" well represented in the hero Thor and in the Celestial Ego,[2] not to mention previous films such as *Fantastic Four: Rise of the Silver Surfer*. But the world of ostensible deities in the Marvel comic universe is much larger. Behold the three-faced Living Tribunal, the abstract entities such as Omniversal Eternity, the One Above All, and the remarkably Jack Kirby–like God of *Fantastic Four* #511. Each Marvel writer seems always to be one-upping the other with new, awe-inspiring omnipotent entities. This reticence to close off the upper echelons of power likely stems from a desire to continue telling fresh stories at larger and larger scales, but can also effectively prevent writers from infringing upon the rights of the true Almighty by "reducing" God to a comic book cameo.

This chapter has two goals. The first is to map the mysteries of Marvel's celestial hierarchies and bring them into conversation with the hierarchies of Neoplatonist theologies, such as those of Plotinus. Those gods considered "lower" are, like these ancient gods, more involved with the physical world and more concrete. They correspond to the cosmic gods of the Platonist hierarchy. The higher gods are those who shape the universe or multiverse on a large scale and who represent the Demiurges or creator deities. Yet higher than this are those who embody abstract principles, or, in the Platonist system, the hypercosmic gods. The Living Tribunal sits above even these, acting as final arbiter and mediator between creation and the "supreme" deity of the Marvel Universe, equivalent to the Intelligence or *Nous* which is the summit of Neoplatonist creation. The One Above All sits higher still, embodying an unspeakable transcendence that is beyond time, space, body, gender, and all apparent limitations. This parallels the Neoplatonist One.

The second part of the paper uses the "Jack Kirby experience" to make sense of "degrees of omnipotence," and will introduce Tolkien's concept of sub-creation and Vanhoozer's work in *Remythologizing Theology* to argue for a concept of God that analogizes the relationship between author and work. By thinking of nested fictions—that is, of authors writing stories about other authors who write about still other authors—we can see how, for example, the Living Tribunal might be omnipotent over the whole Marvel universe, and yet the One Above All more powerful even than him—as the author of a "fictionally" omnipotent character. In turn, the true God is omnipotent over all works whatsoever.

HIERARCHY IN THE MARVEL UNIVERSE

Marvel's cosmic system bears a strong resemblance to that of the Neoplatonists. Developing out of the school of Plato and flourishing throughout Late Antiquity, the Neoplatonists attempted to synthesize traditional Greek religion with the abstract thought of philosophy. Their fundamental impetus was the reconciliation of the problem of the One and the many, which led to the positing of many gradations of being between absolute spiritual unity and the multiplicity of the observed physical world.

We shall first proceed up the Neoplatonist hierarchy, beginning with the lowest forms of divinity and proceeding to the very highest. It is important to note at the outset that this particular ranking is somewhat artificial, as there are many different Neoplatonists who create their own unique hierarchies; from the simplest to the most intricate, each theologian views the chain from the visible world up into the One in their own way. The particular hierarchy below is a combination of Plotinus, Proclus, and Iamblichus, created in the interest of paralleling the ranks of divinity within the Marvel universe more clearly. It is not—and this bears repeating—a hierarchy as actually articulated by any particular Neoplatonist. The rank of demiurge, especially, is misplaced in terms of a purely Neoplatonist conception, which would place the demiurge much higher. But in this, Marvel resembles a Gnostic rather than a Neoplatonist pattern.

This essay will chart Marvel's own hierarchies of divinity and remark upon some interesting convergences. Note, however, that just as the Neoplatonist hierarchy above is in an important sense an artificial one, so too the following map of the Marvel multiverse must also be seen as a heuristic construct. Because of their very nature, none of these entities with the exception of Thor appear as regular characters in any comic series. They are occasional, cross-series guest stars. Furthermore, there are simply too many authors, too many issues, too many retcons and continuity changes to create a perfectly consistent (or perfectly accurate) "ranking" in the way described here. Nevertheless, some general themes emerge. The ranking used by Thanos in *Thanos Annual* #1 is a helpful guide. Here, a future Thanos tells present Thanos about the power hierarchies of the multiverse with the aid of a visual ranking pyramid. On top there sits the Living Tribunal. Underneath are Eternity and Infinity, followed by Love, Order, Chaos, and Hate. On the bottom rank are Galactus, a Celestial, Eon, Odin, Zeus, and the Stranger. Note that neither the One Above All nor the lesser gods like Thor are pictured in the panel. Those readers unfamiliar with these beings, rest easy, for they will be explained below. What is important here are the clear levels of power set out in the panel. Let us start from the bottom.

The Cosmic Gods: Thor and More

Closest to mere mortals are the cosmic gods, or the gods as popularly conceived. Borrowing from Iamblichus, the Latin Neoplatonist Sallust explains the division between the cosmic and "hypercosmic" gods. "But of the gods some are cosmic and others hypercosmic. I call those cosmic who fabricate the world" (Sallust 1793, 6). These are the traditional gods of Homeric mythology, especially the Twelve Olympians so familiar to schoolchildren. Even as early as Plato's day, philosophers attempted to downplay Homer's *telenovela*-style divinities into more palatable forms. Thus, the story of the Judgment of Paris is not a literal event but a metaphor for the gods bestowing gifts on the world. So, for Sallust, "of the cosmic gods, some are the causes of the world's existence, others animate the world; others again harmonize it, thus composed from different natures; and others, lastly, guard and preserve it when harmonically arranged" (1793, 6).

Likewise, Thor and the Asgardian gods, Marvel's versions of Hercules and the Olympians, and the other mythological figures Marvel has added sit at the lowest end of the Marvel hierarchy. Each of these beings range in power, with figures like Odin shading up into the next rank under some writers.[3] Mirroring the antique impulse to gather and organize every god anyone has ever heard of, the Marvel universe plays host not only to the Norse and Greek pantheons but to the gods of the Polynesians, ancient Mayans, and so forth.[4] But in what sense can Thor be considered a god? How could a god be trounced by a mere mortal, even with the added benefit of gamma rays?[5]

Henrichs lists three defining characteristics of divinity, at least in the classical Greek mind: (1) immortality; (2) power; and (3) anthropomorphism

(Henrichs 2010, 29). Thor clearly fulfills criteria (2) and (3), but he can also be considered immortal in a qualified sense. Depending on who's talking, Thor is either cyclically immortal (part of a wheel of cosmic death and rebirth), functionally immortal (immortal unless killed), or simply so long-lived that he appears immortal from a human perspective. By this definition, many of the more powerful races in the Marvel Universe are also functionally gods: the Eternals (including Thanos), the Watchers, and more.

Thor is very clearly a god in the traditional sense noted above and not simply a highly advanced alien as he has been recently portrayed (perhaps significantly, this trend began with ardent secularist Warren Ellis). However, the thunder god's association with space is not ill fitting. The classical gods were heavily associated with the planets—their names remain the monikers of our cosmological companions to this day. The ancients considered space to be part of the heavens, and the planets to move in an orderly manner because they were the celestial bodies of the gods. The idea that the planets have souls remains even up to the end of the patristic age where they are downgraded to angels rather than gods.

As such, the idea that the cosmic gods dwell in space is quite appropriate. This is why they are cosmic and not *hyper*cosmic in the first place. Just like the Neoplatonic gods of the lower order—those they adapt from earlier Homeric conceptions—these cosmic contenders are intimately involved in the affairs of mortals, even descending into petty grievances, annoyances, and love affairs. They are gods, yes, but of the lowest order, and subject to many of the limitations of mortal flesh.

Demiurges: Galactus and the Celestials

Plato's *Timaeus* speaks of a "demiurge" (28b and *passim*), a divine creator who contemplates the Forms and crafts everything in the universe according to this eternal design. This demiurge is clearly distinct from the world itself, since he finds it spinning in disorder and brings order and harmony to pre-existing matter. He is perfectly good and creates (that is, fashions rather than brings forth *ex nihilo*) out of goodness and generosity. He desires that all things should be as good as possible. He makes the lesser gods (the planets) as well as the human creatures, even going so far as to craft their faces, limbs, and so forth.

The Neoplatonists generally conceive of the Demiurge as synonymous with *Nous* or Intelligence (e.g., Proclus 1971, 206). Elsewhere, the Demiurge and the World Soul may be two sides of the same coin: the Demiurge the side that faces downward toward the material realm and the World Soul that which faces upward to contemplate the eternal world of Idea (compare Mohr 1982,

46). But as we have seen, when they speak of the Demiurge as "creating" the World Soul or the cosmos, they mean shaping pre-existing matter into an orderly arrangement. It was the Gnostics, and not the Neoplatonists, who place the Demiurge lower in the spectrum of divinity, conceiving as they do of the material world as intrinsically evil. The Demiurge is therefore virtually the source of evil in the cosmos, since it has created the evil material world, and seems closer to being Satan than God. For the Neoplatonists, by contrast, the material world itself is not evil; rather, undifferentiated matter—matter without form—is evil insofar as it is the direct antithesis of the One, form without matter (Plotinus, *Enneads* 1.8.14; 2.4). This particular element of the hierarchy is perhaps the most artificial of our arrangement.

There are certain physical beings in the Marvel cosmos that, like the demiurge above, bear responsibility for shaping and guiding the development of the universe as a whole. Galactus, for instance, is the Devourer of Worlds and the Lifebringer, a force of nature responsible for the cycle of extinction and rebirth that is intrinsic to the universe, a balance between Eternity and Death.[6] Though "related" to the World Soul Eternity, Galactus is far more directly involved in the universe and even makes friends with humans (*Ultimates,* Vol. 2, *passim*).

The Celestials use human history as a grand experiment, manipulating evolution on a universal scale in order to perfect creation. They modify humankind, giving it the genetic potential to create both mutants and superheroes. The offspring of the unfragmented first Universe, these "Space Gods" perform incalculable manipulations on species across the multiverse, constantly testing and growing them for purposes unknown.

Like the Gnostic demiurge, many of these Marvel demiurgic deities are evil or insane. But even those entities still holding to their prime directive, such as Galactus, are for the most part beyond the concerns of good and evil which plague most mortals.

Hypercosmic Gods: Love, Hate, Order, Chaos

Again, according to Sallust, the hypercosmic gods create, not the world, but essences, intellect, and soul (Sallust 1793, 6). These gods are the sources of eternal principles within the world, says fellow Neoplatonist Proclus (1816, 6.1). He also refers to them as the kings (Greek *hegemonikoi*) of the cosmic gods. While the cosmic gods are generated by the levels above themselves, these hypercosmic rulers are free from generation and may be called unbegotten. "For, as Plato says, principle is unbegotten. For it is necessary that every thing which is generated should be generated from a principle, but that the principle should not be generated from any thing" (1816, 6.1).

Similarly, in the Marvel multiverse, above the world-shaping demiurges lie the embodiments of certain cosmic concepts. Mistress Love, Master Hate, and the brothers Order and Chaos embody the fundamental oppositional principles of reality. They are not regularly occurring characters in any particular series, but only crop up at specially important times, such as in *Infinity Gauntlet*. Love and Hate might also be termed attraction and repulsion. As abstract entities above the level of Galactus, they are less visible and less present than the lower gods, requiring the use of M-Bodies in order to appear in physical form. It is rumored that Order and Chaos manipulate specific events in the world, but their control is so fine, or rather so intrinsic to the universe, that their activities are usually imperceptible. Likewise, Love and Hate have some involvement every time their eponymous emotions are felt.

These entities can be labeled "hypercosmic" since they do not truly exist in any localized sense inside the universe. They are omnipresent, or at least present at each point in which their respective principles exist. It is unclear whether the same beings embody, for example, Chaos and Order for the entire multiverse or whether there is a different being for each universe within the Marvel multiverse, though the latter seems far more likely given what we note about Eternity below. They are at least capable of existing outside of our normal universe, since they visit the Dimension of Manifestations for physical bodies and use a sixteen-dimensional meeting space in order to converse with Eternity and other divinities (*Infinity War: Quasar* #37).

World Soul: Eternity

Beneath the Intelligence but ruling over the created world and its principles, there is the World Soul. This universal Soul is never directly involved with the lower world, although it comprehends what happens there. Rather, it is always invested in the higher world of intelligence. It is simultaneously a debtor to the world above and a benefactor to the world below (Plotinus 4.8, 69).[7] The Soul comes from the Intelligence, separated and yet not separated, the unique expression of the Intelligence in the physical world (4.3, 132).

Indeed, the Soul shapes the cosmos as a whole, rather than specific elements within it.[8] The World Soul forms the matter of the universe after the design of the Intelligence. It relates to the Intelligence as matter to Idea (5.1, 94). "The universe, moved eternally by an intelligent Soul, becomes blessed and alive. The Soul's presence gives value to a universe that before was no more than an inert corpse, water and earth, or rather darksome matter and nonbeing" (5.1, 93). The World Soul, because it is bodiless, is at the same time everywhere and nowhere in the cosmos (4.3, 137–38). Plotinus indeed describes the cosmos as a living organism containing all other organisms (5.9, 53).

Individual souls arise from intelligences as large numbers arise from smaller ones. "They preserve both identity and difference. Each is subsistent being. But all are one together" (4.3, 132). Likewise, "Our soul is the same as The Soul which animates the deities: strip it of all things infesting it, consider it in its original purity, and you will see it to be of equal rank with The Soul, superior to everything that is body" (5.1, 93). For Plotinus, the soul is not in the body—instead the body is in the soul (4.3, 145). All individual souls participate in the World Soul, yet it is more than the sum of all souls.

The cosmic entity known as Eternity represents the totality of the Marvel Universe, and is a close Marvel parallel to the World Soul. He is represented as a vast humanoid outline filled with starscapes and planets, and wearing an elaborate headdress (e.g., his first appearance in *Strange Tales* #138). Prior to *Secret Wars* #9, Eternity and Infinity represented Time and Space, respectively. At present, Eternity is the embodiment of the Eighth Marvel Universe, while Infinity is the embodiment of the Seventh (*Ultimates,* Vol. 2, #6).[9] They have two "siblings": Mistress Death and Oblivion. Death does not appear on Thanos' hierarchy, so we will set these aside and focus on Eternity. Importantly, Eternity represents just one universe. There are different Eternities for each alternate universe in the multiverse. As the totality of all that exists in the universe in both time and space, including Chaos, Order, Love, Hate, Galactus, and so forth, Eternity is simply beyond the comprehension of most beings.

Just like the Neoplatonist World Soul, Eternity contains all things lower than itself, yet it is more than the sum of its parts. It possesses a consciousness and a will distinct from those of the entities below it. It is both the sum of all organisms and a single living organism in itself. It is omnipresent, omniscient, and omnipotent toward the universe which it personifies. Like the World Soul, it does not come into existence on its own, but does shape and determine all of existence once it is formed.

Intelligence (*Nous*): The Living Tribunal

Above the worldly and material soul lies the Intelligence (Greek *Nous*). Each particular physical being has a Platonic form or conceptual archetype from which it derives. Just as the Platonic forms lie above and behind their concrete instantiations in the physical world, the Intelligence corresponds to the totality of these forms, similar to the way in which the World Soul is the totality of every particular soul. The One produces the Intelligence directly; it is the best after the One and superior to all others (Plotinus, *Enneads* 5.1, 98). But the Intelligence is still a being, still something that depends upon something yet higher for its own existence. It is distinct from and derivative from the One.

The One is an undivided unit while the Intelligence is the (singular) sum of many different units (5.1, 99). The Intelligence is the "vestibule" which introduces us to the One itself. It is the trace of the absolutely unified Goodness that we can still detect in the multiplicity of creation (5.9, 48). Since thinking is in a way distinct from thinker, the Intelligence implies both identity and difference (5.1, 95; 3.8, 170; cf. also 3.8, 171–72).

Though it cannot be divided into parts or sections (5.1, 94), it is not perfectly simple since it still includes conceptual distinctions (6.9, 79–80). The Intelligence is identical with and contains all beings, not locally but conceptually (5.9, 51). Just as the genus contains all its constituent species (5.9, 51–52), so "the Intelligence, accordingly, is itself the authentic existents. It is not a knower that knows them as somewhere else. They are not prior to it. They are not after it. Of being it is rather the lawgiver, or—better still—the law" (5.9, 51). If the Soul shapes the cosmos, the Intelligence is like the skill that guides the artist in his performance (5.9, 49). The Intelligence is the archetype of the living organism we call the cosmos (5.9, 53). Sometimes it is identical to Being and the Ideas (5.9, 53), though the ideas of lower or ignoble things belong rather to the realm of the Soul (5.9, 56). At other times, "The Intelligence gives existence to Being in thinking it. Being, by being object of thought, gives to the Intelligence its thinking and its existence" (5.1, 95).

In short, the Intelligence is the highest thing apart from the One itself. It is omnipresent and contains all existing things as their model or paradigm. It is the law of all that exists. It rules and governs the cosmos just as the cosmos shapes its individual material constituents. The Intelligence contemplates the One and mediates the One to all that exists, insofar as creatures reach contemplation of the One only by surpassing contemplation of the Intelligence itself.

Within the Marvel canon, such a being would correspond to the sublime Living Tribunal. There is only one Living Tribunal. It exists across all universes, and its power is unsurpassed among created beings. It reports directly to the One Above All, who is its only superior. A gold and silver humanoid with three faces, some covered with a veil, the Living Tribunal is the final court of appeals for cosmic concerns. Its three faces symbolize Equity, Vengeance, and Necessity. Its power is in fact so tremendous that when the most powerful cosmic entities entreat it to intervene to stop Thanos from wielding the Infinity Gauntlet, it refuses to involve itself in such minor affairs (*Infinity Gauntlet* #3). When Adam Warlock destroys these entities after he gains control of the gauntlet, the Tribunal restores them with a snap of its fingers (*Warlock and the Infinity Watch* #1). The Infinity Gauntlet stops working merely because the Living Tribunal says so (*Infinity War* #4).

The Tribunal is the embodiment of the Marvel *multiverse*—not just of a single universe as Eternity is. It contains within itself all other cosmic entities and manifestations, including, we presume, an infinite number of Eternities. As such, the nature of the Tribunal is directly consonant with that of the *Nous* of the Neoplatonists, even to the extent that lesser divinities participate in it. Its three faces, distinct but united, symbolize a sort of multiplicity-in-unity redolent of *Nous'* lesser oneness. While the oneness of the One is above the concept of "being," the Intelligence represents the totality of being. Likewise, the Living Tribunal represents and rules over the totality of the Marvel multiverse under the auspices of the One Above All.

The One Above All

The One, in the Neoplatonist hierarchy, is above all thought, being, time, space, and comprehension (Plotinus 3.8, 174). It is not even properly said to exist, since the One is the source of existence rather than a participant within it (6.9, 77). Likewise, it does not think, since thinker and thought create a duality which the One transcends (1.2, 113; cf. 6.9, 76). We meet the One "neither by knowing nor by the pure thought that discovers the other intelligible things, but by a presence transcending knowledge." The One cannot be spoken or written about. Our speech serves only to create a path or a direction down which the seeker must travel. Awareness of the One only comes about as a result of mystical union with the One itself (6.9, 78). The best way to rise to contemplation of the One is through contemplation of its child, Being (6.9, 80). But rather than conceiving of the One as a radical *absence* from being(s), the One is instead infinitely *present* to all. We are merely ignorant of the truth, fugitives from the divine and from ourselves (6.9, 83).

The One is perfectly simple (6.9, 1031). It creates, but without any motion or change in itself. It is the cause of causes, that which makes reality possible (6.1, 79–80; 3.8, 173). "This, then, it may be said, is the primal begetting: perfect—seeking nothing, having nothing, needing nothing— The One 'overflows' and its excess begets an other than itself; begotten turns back towards begetter and is filled and becomes its contemplator" (5.2, 107). The One "does not bestow its gifts at one moment only to leave us again; its giving is without cessation so long as it remains what it is. As we turn towards The One, we exist to a higher degree, while to withdraw from it is to fall. . . . Life not united with the divinity is shadow and mimicry of authentic life" (6.9, 85). As is surely evident, this concept of God heavily influenced prominent Christian thinkers such as Augustine and Pseudo-Dionysius.

The One Above All has only made three major appearances in comics: as a glowing golden humanoid in *Thanos: The Infinity Finale,* as a rather scary homeless man in *The Sensational Spider-Man* #40, and as Jack Kirby in *Fantastic Four* #511. When Thanos wields the Infinity Gauntlet and possessess "omni-reality perception," he achieves only "a fragmentary glimpse" of the One's vast power. The very fact that Thanos addresses the being as "grand one" speaks volumes. Canonically, there is no being more powerful than the One Above All in the Marvel multiverse. As the demon Mephisto remarks, while the virtually omnipotent Living Tribunal is simply the most powerful kid on the playground, the One Above All is the Principal. He is the fictional stand-in for the actual God of Western tradition. For this very reason, he rarely makes an appearance and his character remains vague. Too much familiarity drains the drama from his appearance and decreases the reverence we ought to feel toward the pinnacle of Marvel's fictional deities. Clearly, this character can only be identified with Plotinus' "One that is above all" (*to ho esti pro panton;* Plotinus 6.9.11, 88).

While the One Above All follows the lineaments of the Abrahamic God, his character is always kept vague enough to avoid alienating or favoring any particular religion. For example, when he speaks to Peter Parker about enduring his Aunt May's death, he notes, "I've asked a lot more from people much closer to me than you" (*Sensational Spider-Man* #40). This is a quite subtle reference to Jesus' passion which simultaneously acknowledges Christ without specifying Him as eternal Son or definitively addressing what happened on the cross. Likewise, in *Fantastic Four* #72, Uatu the Watcher asserts "his only weapon . . . is love!"—an allusion to the well-known Christian trope also agreeable to just about anybody else.

JOURNEY INTO MYSTERY: WHY THE SIMILARITY?

Reading Marvel's cosmic storylines can cause a very Plotinian dizziness as our gaze ascends upward into ever-higher realms of omnipotence. But it is safe to assume that there are no Neoplatonists (or even regular Platonists) in Marvel's bullpen. So how does one explain this remarkable symmetry? Is a divine hierarchy a universal human impulse, arising from extended meditation on absolute power? Does the proliferation of ever more cosmic deities come about solely as a result of the need to tell ever newer and more exciting stories of ever more vast and epic scope? While we can only speculate, it seems that the urge to create new cosmic powers and to situate them as more or less mighty than others has (at least) two causes—one of which is distinct from the Neoplatonists' philosophical motivations and one of which might be shared, in a way.

First, and most pragmatically, the majority of creators are reticent to offend their readers, and there are few things more potentially offensive than a religious insult. In order to tell stories about awe-inspiring beings while maintaining a certain level of artistic distance from that which might cause offense, creators simply construct a separate category of lesser divinity—still functionally transcendent, but explicitly *not* the "real" God. Note that while virtually every pantheon or figure from polytheistic religions find their place in comics, there is a strict absence of appearances by the God of the Abrahamic religions (Christianity, Judaism, Islam), at least as one god among many.[10] As stated above, whenever the Abrahamic God (or His closest Marvel stand-in) does crop up, He is usually the one true Supreme deity, on a decidedly different level than the other gods.

But comic books need to be sold continually. Writers and artists must convince the reading public to invest money in their product not just once, but over and over. They do this, of course, by attempting to tell great stories with compelling characters, inspiring a sense of wonder and excitement. Comic books can explore ideas and images still unavailable to other media. As such, Marvel takes advantage of big ideas to create awe-inspiring storylines that stretch the bounds of the readers' imagination. Readers, though, also experience fatigue. In order to maintain interest, content must be constantly freshened. Authors introduce new characters—bigger! better! stronger!—which will shake up the status quo to which the audience has grown accustomed. And whereas in 1938 children were amazed simply to see a man lifting a car over his head, nowadays comic fans require more. In a medium as unconstrained as comics, one need only pitch the idea that, for example, the embodiment of our reality is being kept in chains by a mysterious force from before the dawn of time, and then enlist the talent of an artist to make it happen (*Ultimates,* Vol. 2, #1).

Secondly, and in line with Neoplatonist concerns, the Marvel hierarchy follows from an intuitive sort of philosophical reflection. The more philosophically fundamental a Marvel deity is, the more powerful they are considered to be. A single, highly individual being like Thor is less powerful than the mechanical laws of the cosmos, which are less powerful than the principles by which these laws are organized, which are less powerful than the cosmos in which these principles are instantiated, which are less powerful than being itself, which is less powerful than the hyper-essential Being which gives rise to being as we know it (the creator of all). We have here a hierarchy of ontological necessity set in motion by a Prime Mover. But, contrary to all published Marvel canon, there is a type of being more powerful even than the One Above All. I am speaking, of course, about the Author.

THE JACK KIRBY EXPERIENCE: AUTHORSHIP AND DEGREES OF OMNIPOTENCE

So far, we have attempted to use the real world to analyze the notion of divine hierarchies within comic books. Now, we reverse the polarity and use comic books to analyze the notion of hierarchies of power, existence, and omnipotence within the real world. And, as so many things have done, it starts with the Fantastic Four.

In *Fantastic Four* #511, the team journey to the afterlife in order to resurrect the recently killed Thing. After making it past profound obstacles, the three surviving members receive an offer they seemingly can't refuse: immediate entry into heaven. But they reject the offer, as it would mean an end to their adventures. They want to continue pursuing their curiosity and solving problems for now. They want to keep seeking.[11] This is apparently the right answer to a test they didn't realize they were taking. The gates swing open; they enter to find an older man in an artist's study, sketching away on a drafting board. He bears a remarkable resemblance to Jack Kirby.

The team is surprised. We, as the readers, are delighted. *Of course* Kirby is the "Creator." They ask God why he looks the way he does. In keeping with a well-trodden comic book trope, God appears in whatever way his viewers most readily accept, a pop form of divine accommodation. "That's what my creations do. They find the humanity in God," he remarks poetically. The phone rings, and God answers it. He begins talking about plot points for Black Panther, and actually adjusts his plan based on unheard input from the other end. Who is on the phone? "My collaborator. 'Nuff said." God's drawings are simply "contributions" to the "grand tapestry." He too is part of a larger reality which includes both God and the free creatures he sets into motion. "We're all a part of the process," he explains. "You're no one's puppets. . . . Nobody can do your living for you."

Before ushering them off, he heals Reed's face (previously "permanently" scarred by Doctor Doom) with his pencil. He hands them a sketch of themselves as old people, smiling, happy, together. Beneath the picture are the words "To be continued!" Since God's sketches become reality, this implies God will guarantee they have a "happy ending," with the sketch as pledge. More than this, their adventures will continue, just as they wished when they turned down heaven in the first place.

Marvel's One Above All is omnipotent. He can do whatever you can imagine him to do, except stop being fictional. But now let us complicate the picture. What if I wrote a story in which the One Above All decided to do exactly that? What if, in my story, he left the Marvel multiverse and entered the real world? Many comics have actually played with similar notions, writing stories set in "Earth Prime" (Deadpool famously knows he is a comic book character and speaks directly to his readers). Grant Morrison's *Multiversity* is the most innovative example of this. Within Marvel, Earth-1218 is supposed to be the actual world in which the reader lives. But by the very act of writing a story about Earth Prime, we render it fictional rather than real. It is impossible to write a story about Earth Prime without creating instead an alternate fictional earth. Our story now simple becomes a nested story within a frame narrative portraying an earth very similar to ours. This process can repeat *ad infinitum*, with further nested stories piling atop one another. We might picture a final panel of *Fantastic Four* #511, in which we pan out to find the real Jack Kirby sitting at his desk smiling fondly as he illustrates himself into the issue meeting and conversing with his characters as the "One Above All."[12]

At this moment, in this single panel, there are four levels of reality, four all-powerful creators each successively more all powerful than the next. First, there is the One Above All within the Fantastic Four story itself, the one the heroes meet. He is (fictionally) all powerful, able to erase or recreate their universe on a whim. But above him there sits a being who controls his every move, able not only to alter that universe but to wipe the omnipotent One Above All character from existence. This is the Jack Kirby of the final panel, revealed to be the author of a fictional comic book. But the authors of the whole work on our level of reality are Mike Wieringo and Mark Waid, themselves just as much omnipotent over this Kirby as Kirby is over the One Above All of the Fantastic Four's own universe. Finally, there is God, who authors Wieringo and Waid, Himself absolutely and not relatively omnipotent. God is not omnipotent *with regard to* a specific thing or level of reality, but over all things whatsoever.[13]

This encounter with Kirby the author illustrates an important point about God. God relates to the world as an author relates to a work. Kevin Vanhoozer helpfully explores this *analogia auctoris* (analogy of authorship) in his *Remythologizing Theology* (Vanhoozer 2010, 304). As an author, I can create any literary situation I can imagine. I am all powerful, all present, and all knowing with respect to that world. But my power ends at the border between fiction and reality. I cannot will my work to my own level of reality. It exists of course as a work of fiction within the real world, but my bald mutant headmaster is not as real as my real headmaster. J.R.R. Tolkien calls this "sub-creation." In fact, this is one of the ways human beings carry the image of God—we make because we are made as a reflection of a Maker (Tolkien 2001, *passim*). Each of us, derivatively and in a lower mode, recapitulates the primary act of divine creativity that brings forth the world. My fictional world "exists" in a limited fictional sense. I exist in a much more robust sense. But there is a higher level of existence still.

Just as I am more real than my character, *so God is more real than me*. This is not to say I do not exist, only that God *exists* in a fundamentally different and more concrete way than I do. This is what the Christian Neoplatonist Pseudo-Dionysius means when he writes that God cannot be said to exist

(1897a, 5.1). Our notion of existence does not apply to God any more than Captain America's "existence" applies to Jack Kirby. Cap's "existence" in fact depends on Kirby's much grander existence. Likewise, my own existence depends on God's existence, there on a higher level than anything we know. This is what theologians mean by the *aseity* of God—He is the Author who is Himself unauthored (Vanhoozer 2010, 226).

God's radical freedom does not infringe on human freedom. Rather, the freedom of God and of His creatures operate on two different levels of reality, just like Stan Lee's plotting can't be detected by his characters, who operate based on a generally closed and reasonable system of cause and effect (2010, 303). Why does Uncle Ben die? Because the burglar shot him in an attempted robbery. Why does Uncle Ben die? Because it is part of Spider-Man's origin story. Is God, then, invisible and undetectable in the real world? Hardly. For just as an author might, in certain circumstances, choose to address her characters directly, so too God can choose to address His creatures directly (2010, 316).

Within the Marvel multiverse, the One Above All seems infinitely distant and inaccessible to us everyday mortals. The Marvel hierarchy is external and, ultimately, irrelevant to the lives of human beings. We are not called to unite mystically with the One Above All through contemplation of the Living Tribunal, as in the Neoplatonist hierarchy. I may be part of Eternity, but he's got no part in me. Even in Plotinus, while contemplative ascent is possible and encouraged, it is effectively up to the individual to accomplish it. The One may be within me, but I must still overcome my own intellectually enforced alienation from it.

This is in fact one of the unique aspects of a distinctly Christian form of hierarchy: the Incarnation circumvents the intuited distance between mortals and the One. For Christian theologian Pseudo-Dionysius the Areopagite, for example, hierarchy still serves as a means of ascent. Much like Plotinus, "The purpose . . . of Hierarchy is the assimilation and union, as far as attainable, with God" (1897a, 3.2). The difference here is that we mortals have a divine guide who unreservedly gives Himself to us, sharing and leading us ever upward. While remaining the One Above All, Jesus Christ is made for a little while lower than the cosmic gods (angels, if we're using the Christian version [Heb 2:7/Ps 8:5]). As Pseudo-Dionysius exults, "the Everlasting took a temporal duration, and He, Who is superessentially exalted above every rank throughout all nature, became within our nature, whilst retaining the unchangeable and unconfused steadfastness of His own properties" (1897b, 1.3). Thus, Pseudo-Dionysius advises, "*let Christ lead the discourse*—if it be lawful to me to say—He Who is mine,—the Inspiration of all Hierarchical revelation" (1897a, 2.5, emphasis added).

CONCLUSION

We began this essay by noting the ways in which Marvel's cosmic beings share a remarkably similar organizational scheme to the hierarchy of divinities in Neoplatonism. Both move from the concrete, physical, and limited to the abstract. The cosmic gods of Neoplatonism, such as the Twelve Olympians, correspond to Thor and his Asgardian allies. The Gnostically adjusted demiurge who shapes the physical world finds a counterpart in Galactus and the Celestials. The hypercosmic gods, above the created universe, match up with the embodiments of overarching principles like Mistress Love and Lord Order. Higher up, the World Soul is fittingly mirrored in the Marvel character Eternity, and the divine *Nous* or Intelligence in the three-faced Living Tribunal. Finally, the Neoplatonic One parallels Marvel's One Above All.

Next, we asked why this might be the case. We hypothesized that a series of increasingly powerful functional divinities were gradually created to entice and excite readers. Simultaneously, writers avoid religious insult by keeping the "real" God tastefully off panel, for the most part. But more than this, there is a natural instinct to elevate the universal over the particular, the law itself over a specific instantiation of that law, and so forth. Marvel's cosmic beings are more powerful the more fundamental they are to the nature of being.

Finally, we used the Jack Kirby cameo from *Fantastic Four* #511 to discuss levels of omnipotence and hierarchies of being between nested fictions and reality. Just as the real author is more real and more powerful than a fictional author or that author's fictional characters, so God exists in a higher, more robust sense than His creatures do. God always exceeds our imaginations; He always transcends our conceptual limitations. And so, as Christian Neoplatonist Pseudo-Dionysius urges us when contemplating this God above being: excelsior!

NOTES

1. Thanks to Corey Latta and Chris Porter for reading a draft of this chapter.
2. At least, according to *Guardians of the Galaxy, Vol. 2*. In the comic book canon this is not the case.
3. Cf. his rank alongside Galactus, the Celestials, and the Stranger above.
4. The leaders of each pantheon sometimes meet in a "Council of Godheads."
5. Thor and Hulk usually end up even, but Hulk has won at least once (*Hulk: Let the Battle Begin*), and Red Hulk beat Thor handily in *Hulk* (2008) #5.
6. Of course, he wasn't always who he is now; he was once a mortal named Galan of Taa, last survivor of the previous universe.

7. In my citations of Plotinus' *Enneads*, I will give first the chapter location and then the page number from Elmer O'Brien's *The Essential Plotinus*.

8. Ennead IV.3 1799.

9. The Marvel Universe has been created and recreated many times. Most recently, during *Secret Wars*. For an overview of each of the previous universes, see the final issue of *Ultimates,* Vol. 2.

10. One notable exception is the highly blasphemous depiction of Yahweh in *Howard the Duck,* Vol. 3, *passim*. This should not be considered canon for the rest of the Marvel Universe.

11. The idea that heaven is some sort of stasis rather than continual fulfillment of all holy desire is inherently problematic. Likewise, the idea that the journey is more important than the destination would require further unpacking.

12. Kirby in fact *did* insert himself into various issues of the original *Fantastic Four* series, and was famously refused entry (along with Stan Lee) into Reed and Sue's wedding: *Fantastic Four Annual* #3 (1965).

13. It seems clear that Waid and Wieringo are more real than the characters they write. It seems, on a certain understanding, clear that God is more real than Waid and Wieringo. But what about the two functional fictional gods of our altered *Fantastic Four* #511? Does the Jack Kirby within the frame story have in any sense more reality than the One Above All of the story-within-a-story? This question seems intimately related to a similar knotted problem in the philosophy of literature: the truth-value of fictional statements.

Chapter Eleven

The Thor Movies and the "Available" Myth

Mythic Reinvention in Marvel Movies

Andrew Tobolowsky

Not so very long ago, many scholars firmly believed that traditional narratives—folktales and legends and the like—had no individual authors. Instead, they had simply emanated, in some mystical way, from a kind of collective ethnic consciousness of ancient origins. Once they appeared, these original stories, sometimes called "ur-narratives," remained more or less the same ever after, companions to the ethnic group that told them throughout all of the group's subsequent history, changing in some ways, but never really losing their shape. It was thought, therefore, that by reconstructing the original version of surviving traditions, one could not only come to understand what the story was really about, but the fundamental character of the group still telling it (Oring 1986, 5–6).

In many different fields, throughout the nineteenth and much of the twentieth century, the hunt for the ur-narrative was what scholarship was all about. So it was that in the early nineteenth century, in Germany, the Brothers Grimm not only sought the materials for their beloved collection of fairy tales, but through them, clues to "the poetic and spiritual character of the Germanic people" in some very general sense (Oring 1986, 5).[1] Nearly a century later, William Butler Yeats, Lady Gregory, and other champions of the "Celtic revival" were studying Irish folklore not only for its interest value but, as Gregory Castle notes, in hopes of recovering the Irish "golden age," premised on "belief in cultural or racial essence" and toward "the general goal of racial self-improvement" (Castle 2001, 4). And for biblical scholars, well into the 1970s, not even the Bible was old enough. The *real* Israel was the one that had told the early oral versions of the stories that survived in biblical form.[2] For most biblical scholars, throughout the twentieth century, reconstructing pre-biblical traditions and the pre-biblical world were not just *goals* of biblical studies but to some considerable degree *the* goals and very detailed depictions of early tribal Israel, based on very little in the way of actual evidence—beyond these hypothetically reconstructed traditions—sprung up everywhere (Noth 1930; De Geus 1976; Gottwald 1979).

What does this have to do with Marvel movies? Well, basically, the literary excavations that were going on everywhere were based on a particular approach to the problem of how traditions are inherited over time. It would hardly be possible, for example, to reconstruct the earliest Germanic traditions out of contemporary folktales if you did not believe that there were strong rules governing tradition inheritance so that the same basic narratives more or less inevitably survived into the present with many details intact.

The stability of traditions over time is not only something that scholars believed in, but to some degree still believe in, even though it was originally based on a now outdated model of ethnic identity called "primordialism." This is essentially the belief that ethnic identities *themselves* remain almost completely stable over great gulfs of time. As a result, it was reasonable to think that their stories would stay the same too. Yet, we are no longer primordialists (Gil-White 1999; Roosens 1989; Malešević 2004). We now know that traditions change too, just as easily and just as frequently as identities (Handler 2002; Linnekin 1991; Theodossopoulos 2013). As a result, we need to rethink how traditions are inherited and, more simply, how stories are retold.

Of course, as we will see, scholars have taken strides in this direction. Yet, despite the demise of the theoretical presuppositions that formed it, the idea of tradition as an essentially authorless text hangs on. Today, it finds expression not in the hunt for "kernels of truth," that centuries old preoccupation, but in the belief that tradition inheritance is governed by certain *rules*. Everywhere, we find the assumption that there are certain things that storytellers will not do when retelling stories about the past, and from the past, constrained by some vague, general thing called "tradition."[3] Certainly, there are things that storytellers will *try* not to do, especially when retelling particularly important traditions. This, however, is not the same thing.

The Marvel Cinematic Universe can help us think about tradition inheritance because it is an extraordinary modern example thereof, as well as an expression of diverse types of interactions between storytellers and source materials. The MCU and modern movies generally are not a perfect comparison with the ancient world, which was different in a great many respects, but the purpose of comparison is not always to assert identity between two kinds of things. Instead, it can draw attention to features and questions that we would not otherwise have noticed or asked (Smith 1982).

In this case, what we see is that the MCU draws on decades of Marvel comics with overlapping and frequently rewritten story lines. Each protagonist of a given Marvel movie also suggests additional source texts that the writers and directors of each might use. The Thor movies, which will be the main topic of our discussion, draw on Norse mythology, as the Black Panther movies draw on tropes of afro-futurism, and the Captain America movies on various American historical and patriotic motifs. Each movie also draws on the other movies in the universe, both those that come before it and provide it with knots to untangle, and those that will come after which it must lead toward. The ways in which all these constraints shape how Marvel's stories get told can help us think about how all storytelling flourishes amid constraints, at any time, and it can help us understand Marvel's storytelling as well.

More than anything else, we will see the importance of individual creativity in the telling of stories, which is more important than it might seem. The legacy of previous generations of scholarship and its authorless texts and transhistorically stable stories has produced an image of those who retell stories as creative largely only with respect to how they retell and reformulate the *same* narrative elements that have been handed down and would have been culturally acceptable. What this misses, and what the MCU can demonstrate, is that what seems to be *the* story is itself the product of individual apprehensions of what *is* acceptable, which are always present. Individual creativity must factor into our calculations about tradition inheritance both yesterday and today and thinking about the relationship between constraint and imagination can help us understand the MCU as well.

TRADITION AND THE INDIVIDUAL

Thor: Ragnarok, the most popular of the Thor movies—although in my opinion not the best—begins with several broad winks at the audience.[4] The most subtle of these is that when the movie begins, Loki has stolen Odin's part. He has taken on Odin's appearance and is ruling Asgard. Indeed, when we see Loki for the first time in this film, he is playing Odin *watching someone play Loki*—in this case, Matt Damon—in a play about Loki's heroic sacrifice, until Thor puts a stop to it and reveals his brother's trick.

Loki's theft is a "wink" because throughout the movie it is really Thor who has stolen Odin's part, and not just as the leader of the Asgardians. Any list of the most famous deeds of Odin from Norse mythology, found in two texts called the Prose and Poetic *Eddas*, would surely include the fact that Odin gave his eye for a drink from the well of Mimir in exchange for wisdom, and that he hung himself from Yggdrasil, the world tree, for a period of nine days for similar reasons.[5] *Thor: Ragnarok* opens with Thor himself hanging in the realm of the fiery Surtur and seeking information in much the same way. Later in the movie he loses an eye, a crucial step on his path to self-knowledge: Thor is more than his hammer, his power comes from within. And in the end, these narrative switches herald another, even greater switch: Ultimately, to save his people, Thor must not *avoid* Ragnarok, the Norse vision of the end of the world, but instead cause it.

Here, we see the substantial dependence of *Thor: Ragnarok* on Norse myth itself. Later in this chapter, we will discuss its relationship to other movies in the MCU, another important feature in shaping its narrative. Yet not all of this movie's source materials are naturally suggested by the nature of the movie itself. The very first words of *Thor: Ragnarok* are: "Now I know what you're thinking. Oh no! Thor's in a cage. How did this happen?" This is, presumably, Asgard-speech for the meme format that begins "*record scratch* *freeze frame* 'Yup, that's me. You're probably wondering how I ended up in this situation.'" When in the long arc of telling stories about Thor Odinson would it have even been possible to combine the source texts of the *Eddas*, main sources of Scandinavian myth, with an internet meme? The answer appears to be: around 2016.[6]

Here is a textbook example of the operation of the individual imagination. So much of *Thor: Ragnarok* depends on three sets of obvious source materials: the rest of the MCU, the Thor comics, and Norse myth itself. All of these function in *Thor: Ragnarok* the way traditional materials are supposed to function in the retelling of traditional stories, as constraints that shape what is possible in retelling. Yet, this nod to meme culture is a pure expression of individual imagination, and one that is very specific to the time and place in which *Thor: Ragnarok* debuted. Not only would this meme reference not have occurred to most people who were tasked with writing *Thor: Ragnarok*, underscoring its highly individual character, it *could* not have occurred even to the authors of the original *Thor* which debuted too early, in 2011. Most likely, given the speed of internet culture, it will no longer be intelligible even ten years from now, at least for those who were not originally in on the joke.

The transience of this moment of individual imagination should sound a cautionary note with respect to the study of ancient traditions especially. We rarely think of the distant past in terms of ten years, or even fifty. The few voices that survive from so long ago are so precious because the past is mostly silence. Narrative expressions of individual creativity are precisely the kinds of details we will miss at this distance, and as a result, fail to make room for in our analyses.

In this case, one question we could reasonably ask is why precisely was this reference included in the movie? The real answer to this question, of course, can only come from the writers themselves. We can surmise however that it was part of a general effort to give *Thor: Ragnarok* more of a pop cultural aesthetic than the previous—and in my opinion unfairly maligned—

installments of the franchise. The choice to render *Thor: Ragnarok* according to a pop cultural aesthetic *added* another body of source materials to the store available for innovative interpretation. Thus, what seemed to be appropriate for the movie changed according to the authors' understanding of the project.

MARVEL, THE ANCIENT WORLD, AND THE "AVAILABLE MYTH"

In comparing the Marvel movies to ancient myth, we first of all have to discuss what myth is, a task at once simple and difficult. For the most part, myths are what most people instinctively think they are—stories about the past that are not, strictly speaking, true. However, complications set in when you start trying to separate myths from other kinds of false stories. Are myths and fables the same thing? Is *The Great Gatsby* a myth? Usually, definitions of myth include the idea of cultural significance, which is to say, a story that is important to a *culture* as part of how that culture identifies itself (Mc-Cutcheon 2000, 199–200; Doniger 2011, 3). Thus, Hercules—and Thor—are figures of myth, and Gatsby is not. Obviously, this still leaves a lot of gray area, but it will do for now.

Marvel movies are not myths, and it is reasonable to think that myths function slightly differently than they do. It is more likely, for example, that Taika Waititi will feel comfortable doing something that Thor's original Marvel authors would not have approved of than that a medieval Norse author would feel comfortable reinventing a familiar figure of much greater importance in his or her world than Thor has today. The problem is, any given author can only play by the rules, if there are rules, so far as they individually understand them. A person might absolutely try their best to tell their story only in the most traditional spirit but might nevertheless have a totally different perspective on what is appropriate to that task than another person will. The ancient equivalent of a nod to meme culture is not outside the boundaries of the possible.

The study of myth has taken a number of strides forward in recent years, mostly based on recognizing that tradition inheritance is indeed fluid, rather than stable. However, scholars still broadly assume that this fluidity mainly takes the form of making new meanings *through* traditional elements, rather than introducing more significant changes. So, for example, discussions of how myths make new meanings have often orbited around the idea of myth as a kind of "taxonomy," which is to say, as an ordering system similar to the one used in the identification of plants and animals (Lincoln 1999, 150; Ballentine 2015, 3). Taxonomies are hierarchies, and the hierarchy of elements in a given list can make a big difference even if only the same elements are involved.

In my own work, I have called myth a "vocabulary," which might be a simpler way of putting the same idea (Tobolowsky 2017, 204–5). Even with a fairly small set of words to choose from, a talented enough speaker can convey many meanings through arrangement, emphasis, and style. So, for example, some of the popularity of the movie *Shrek* stems from the fact that it employs the familiar touchstones of fairy tales, including Prince Charming and a horrible ogre, but deploys them in an innovative way, subverting expectations. The basic idea of a vocabulary, or a taxonomy, is that there are limits on what those who retell traditions can include but that these are *less* limiting than they seem because of how much can be done within constraints.

Here, however, we can return to the point made above about meme culture in *Thor: Ragnarok.* MCU's storytellers frequently draw from materials that are outside of what might be considered their most obvious sources. In another example from the Thor franchise, this time from the first movie, Thor's hammer is sent to earth by Odin and embedded in a rock. By putting Thor in a position where he can only withdraw his weapon from a stone if he proves worthy of it, the director or screenwriters obviously channel Arthur and the "sword in the stone." Indeed, it is only by removing the weapon from the stone that Thor proves himself worthy to be king, just as Arthur did—the movie ends, or near enough, with Thor's attempted coronation.

In terms of "vocabulary," we can note that references like these do indeed come from existing source materials. They are not new narratives in an absolute sense. However, they are also not narratives that clearly belong in the orbit of the story that employs them. They are, we might say within the bounds of the vocabulary analogy, loan words. What interests us is what makes them *available* for loan, which is that they *seemed* to belong together to the storytellers involved.

The key point here is not that storytellers can do things we might not expect them to do, which is already obvious. It is that *even someone who is trying to play by the rules*, so to speak, might act in unexpected ways because of how they *understand* those rules. Indeed, from the perspective of twenty-first-century America, the original accounts of Thor and Arthur might well seem to come from roughly the same world. They are both medieval myths from martial cultures, and stories about them evoke similar images. Excalibur and Mjolnir were already both magic and symbolic weapons. Yet, apprehensions of their similarity are only possible from outside of their home cultures and some distance away in time from their heyday. They likely would not have seemed to be much the same at all to a Viking *skald* or Celtic or British bard.

In another case from the movies, though not Marvel, Wolfgang Petersen's *Troy* (2004) includes narrative elements such as the Trojan Horse, the death of Achilles at the hands of Paris, and the escape of a very young-looking Aeneas, carrying a made-up weapon called the "sword of Troy." This is another case that is unlikely to ruffle any feathers, even for tradition purists, although in actuality neither the Trojan Horse nor the death of Achilles *occur* in the *Iliad.* Indeed, they do not occur in any book anyone living has ever read. Instead, they appear in later installments in what is called the "Epic Cycle," in the *Iliou Persis* ("destruction of Troy") and the *Aethiopis* respectively. The Epic Cycle is now lost to us, except for the *Iliad* and the *Odyssey,* but descriptions of it survive from antiquity (West 2003, 2013).

The nod to the *Aeneid,* however, is more complicated, and the fact that it might not feel that way is what matters here. Why shouldn't the story of Aeneas' escape from Troy to found the city of Rome fit perfectly well in a movie that includes the fall of Troy? In reality, as a little reflection will reveal, the *Aeneid,* which tells Aeneas' story, was written in Rome in the first century BCE, while the *Iliad* is likely to have been set down somewhere in Greece in the eighth century BCE (Koiv 2003, 11). When the *Iliad* was written, in all likelihood, Rome had not yet even been founded.[7]

It is not too much, then, to suggest that what makes the *Aeneid* seem available as a narrative element to anyone telling the story of the Trojan War today is not its use of the *Iliad* as source material—the Romans were far from the only ones to adopt an *Iliad*-based origin myth not just in the classical world but well into the medieval period (Patterson 2010, 8; Tobolowsky 2017, 243)—but contemporary models of the Classical world. Since, in other words, *we* have made Greece and Rome the constituent elements of what the "Classical Mediterranean" seems to be, it makes sense that Greek and Roman stories would seem to belong together, too. That their unity is *seeming* only is the whole point—our apprehensions of what belongs together shapes what seems available to us for retellings.

This notion of the "available myth" is one I have explored before (Tobolowsky 2017, 202, 232–46).[8] The basic idea is that, granted the existence of an author who wishes to tell a story in a traditional mode as far as possible, we still have to construct what seems available to them for that task. Generally, scholars suppose they are constrained by what is considered traditional itself, and this is where the idea that there are hard and fast rules for tradition inheritance comes from. What we see in Marvel movies, in *Troy,* and in many other places, however, is that what seems to *be* traditional is not an objective, universal quantity. It is not outside the realm of possibility that one author telling the story of the Trojan War on the big screen might think it most appropriate to retell only the parts that Homer directly refers to, while another might do what Wolfgang Petersen did, and both will understand their tasks in precisely the same way.

The difference between thinking about myth in terms of what is "traditional" and what is "available" is that what is traditional is a group choice. What is "available" is what seems to an individual to *be* available. Certainly, a person with little interest in tradition will reinvent stories as they see fit, and many more narrative moves will be available to them than someone who feels constrained by notions of tradition or canon. But even a person attempting to execute a narrative in a traditional mode will be subject to their own construction of what is traditional which will not be universal. Instead, constructions of the traditional depend not only on where we are, and when we are, but also *who* we are.

In determining what role existing traditions play in constraining how later stories are told, we can also consider how quickly new narrative elements might become traditional. Above, I noted the subversive play with Norse mythology that deepens the texture of *Thor: Ragnarok* in such interesting ways. It is worth reflecting that while it seems as if the screenwriters must, therefore, have considerable knowledge of Norse myth, this is not *absolutely* necessary. Instead, it might at least hypothetically have been the authors of the relevant Marvel comics who knew Norse myth and made their subversive changes.

In that case—and since, from the perspective of the makers of Marvel movies, the comics are as canonical as Norse myth, if not more so—the authors of *Thor: Ragnarok* might include a narrative in which Thor, rather than Odin, loses an eye for wisdom not because it is subversive but *because it is canon.* After that, the movie itself would re-emphasize the status of this narrative event and make it seem traditional for future stories. The largely oral mode of story telling in the ancient world would make rapid changes in what seemed to be traditional more possible, rather than less.[9]

Still, the larger point is that even with every intention of submitting to it, the individual imagination can only respond to the demands of what is authoritative insofar as these are understood, and as they are interpreted individually. Just as Thor, a visitor from Asgard, may suppose it polite to throw a coffee mug on the floor when asking for another, or hang his hammer on a coatrack, so might a mythographer produce a narrative that seems to them to be perfectly traditional, even canonical, while actually being quite innovative. Moving on from a primordialist framework for interpreting identity and tradition—which makes storytellers little more than empty vessels for passing on stories—means reckoning with authors as *authors,* which means making room for the individual imagination. We have not done a very good job of this, and we need to do better.

MARVEL AND MYTH, MYTH AND MARVEL

There have been fairly few efforts to investigate ancient storytelling in a way that acknowledges the inevitable role of individual creativity. One such, by Tomasz Mojsik, uses the fluidity of efforts to describe the Greek Muses as an example of a kind of story that was very often told in dramatically different ways. His effort is particularly valuable because it points to the problem we discussed at the beginning: the kinds of elements that are redolent of the individual imagination in ancient myth—additions, subtractions, changing names, changing episodes—have always been visible to scholars of myth. They have, however, not usually been discussed *as* expressions of the imagination. Instead, they are most often described by scholars as if they are simply byproducts of shifting historical and political realities.

In the face of variant forms of myths, Mojsik observes, "correlations between myth versions in works of various poets are studied, the oldest known version (the 'Ur-Myth') sought and attempts are made to date it." Once that is done, "scholars tend to concentrate . . . on linking [variations] with sociopolitical transformations" (Mojsik 2011, 111–12).[10] In approaches of either sort, the author has little role. Their story might be different from other versions of the story, but only because it responds to events, contexts, and other developments—*not* to the author's own sense of how the story should be told.

Mojsik contributes to this discussion by pointing to the importance of what he calls "communication contexts." After all, "the myth was certainly variously communicated: to children; by children; other elements must have been of particular importance to women; still others were narrated on special occasions, e.g. at weddings and funerals. Besides, certainly there were also different sets of stories intended for diverse age and social groups" (Mojsik 2011, 13).[11] If we imagine a poetry contest, such as the one Hesiod claims to have attended in his *Works and Days* (646), it is fairly unlikely that prizes were handed out simply for getting the story just right. There must have been many bards and they must have had their own ways of doing things.

An awareness of "communication contexts" is important for an accurate approach to telling stories and is to some degree what we have been describing all along. Telling a story in 2017 is what lets you use a meme from 2016. Telling a story in a billion-dollar movie franchise lets you do certain things that comic books do not. Telling a story in the particular context that the MCU allows, so unique in contemporary culture—a multi-stage movie universe—shapes what the story can be and must be in various important ways. Yet even "communication contexts" is outward looking. Would two bards tell the story of Jason and the Argonauts in the same way merely because both are telling it to children? Or might each have a different approach to how to modify it even for the same audience? It is not only the moment that calls forth a new story, but the author's own mind.

When it comes to exploring the complex dynamic between tradition inheritance and individual creativity, we could hardly do better than *Thor: Ragnarok,* which is why we have made this movie a centerpiece of our discussion. First, we have to consider all of the various constraints brought to bear on the movie by Norse myth itself. Naturally, a rendition of the Norse apocalypse must have some basis in the traditional event to be intelligible and, in *Thor: Ragnarok*, it does. Several events from the *Eddas* appear in the movie, including Surt or Surtur, the giant with the fiery sword, Fenrir the wolf, and the dead fighting in the battle (Crawford 2015, 11–16; Sturluson 1916, 16–17, 78–83). "Hel" is an important figure in the Norse Ragnarok as "Hela" is here, and it is indeed Surtur, in the traditional story, whose fiery sword brings the last wave of destruction, followed by new life.

Then we have the constraints that are part and parcel of being in the MCU to consider. The movie, by virtue of its belonging in the larger narrative arc, must begin where the previous installments left off and it does. In *Avengers: Age of Ultron,* Thor has a vision of the end times courtesy of the magic of the Scarlet Witch. He finds himself among the dead, where Heimdall tells him he is a destroyer. As a result, he seeks out a sacred pool where he can receive visions. There, he sees the Infinity Stones and leaves with the (accurate) impression that he must find the stones in order to save the world. At the end of *Age of Ultron*, Thor tells Iron Man and Captain America that he must go off on his own in order to do so. At the beginning of *Thor: Ragnarok,* Thor does indeed mention that he has been seeking for the stones.

Then, the movie must also connect to the *next* installment in the MCU, leading up to the final battle(s) with Thanos and again, it does. In the first post-credits scene, Thor and the gang are finally able to relax after defeating Hela and escaping into space. Just as they begin to settle down, however, a titanic ship looms over them, casting theirs utterly in the shade. At the beginning of *Infinity War,* we discover this was Thanos' ship and that Thanos and his crew had set about their usual task of destroying half of the people anywhere they arrive. Heimdall, with his dying strength, sends Hulk to earth in order to warn the heroes there about what is coming their way.

Ultimately, the services *Thor: Ragnarok* provides to the furtherance of the MCU master narrative are many. This is the movie that recovers the Hulk, a key figure in *Endgame,* from an alien planet and puts him in a situation where he can return to earth. It explains how Loki once again gained access to an Infinity Stone which, in the beginning of *Infinity War,* Thanos takes from him. It introduces the character of Valkyrie and ultimately puts Thor in a position where he can make contact with the Guardians of the Galaxy—even if on a salvage mission to the shattered remnants of Thor's ship. This is a highly constrained movie, given all that it must do, all that it is beholden to, and all that it *does* do to further the larger plot. A scholar attempting to demonstrate the existence of rules of inheritance would certainly find quite a lot to work with here.

And yet, at the same time, the movie turns out to be hardly constrained at all. The contest between Thor, Loki, and Hela over Asgard has, in its main points, very little relation to anything that proceeds or follows. Hela never seems to pose a threat to anything beyond Asgard and even the destruction of this planet feels small in comparison to Thanos' upcoming atrocities. If anything, the credit scene that connects the movie back up to the major Thanos arc is a narrative misstep, making the entirety of Thor's desperate struggle to save his people seem irrelevant. In *Endgame,* we discover Asgardians settled on earth, apparently having survived Thanos' assault and his snap, but none of the movies directly address how this came to be in any substantial way.

The secret to understanding *Thor: Ragnarok* appears at the very beginning, in Thor's opening speech that has already proven so fruitful for us. Among Thor's first lines are: "I went searching through the cosmos for some magic, colorful Infinity Stone things . . . didn't find any. That's when I came across a path of death and destruction which led me all the way here." In other words, yes, he enters through the door that has been prepared for him by previous movies—he has come here, by and by, because he left the Avengers to seek the Infinity Stones. Yet in the space of one sentence, and one of the first sentences at that, the movie swaps one quest for another and one end of the world for another: Surtur's crown for the Infinity Stones, and a purely Asgardian Ragnarok for the greater threat posed by Thanos. In this way, the movie creates the space it needs to be an expression of the individual imagination despite its constraints.

The same dynamic is at play in the movie's depiction of Ragnarok itself. Yes, many nods to the original myth are present in the movie, but the rosters of combatants are, in comparison to the original Norse myth, fuller in some ways, less so in others. In the Norse Ragnarok, Odin is there, as are other Norse gods like Tyr, while the Hulk, obviously, is not. Valkyries are, but "Valkyrie" is not. "Hel" is not Odin's daughter, but Loki's, and Loki is on her side, the leader of the army of the dead. Thor fights the snake who encircles the world, and both kill each other. Odin is killed by Fenrir, who is killed by Vidarr, a son of Odin in vengeance, while here Fenrir plays the pivotal role in bringing the Hulk out of Bruce Banner.

Then there is the mutability of even what Ragnarok *means* to consider. As we have already seen, the narrative of the movie is built around the revelation that Thor must actually cause what he sought to forestall—even if, in the previous movies, he thought he had to forestall something else. Ragnarok is not the only end times that might seem like good or bad news depending on who was talking—we can easily imagine someone who expects to be "saved" at the end of the world, in an evangelical Christian context, coming to a similar conclusion.

In general, an explicit acknowledgment of the interplay between the constraints of inheritance and the inevitability of the individual imagination is capable of shedding quite a lot of light on such a unique phenomenon as the Marvel Cinematic Universe, as it is on rethinking tradition inheritance in ancient myth. Here we have a thing there has never been before, an interconnected, multi-stage movie universe in which many of the movies are *meant* to be largely individual in character. Each owes fidelity to what has come before and what is still to come, but at the same time the work of many hands ensures constant creative innovation. More than that, the constant appearance of new installments in the series means a constant expansion of "available" traditions. In the early Captain America movies, only Captain's shield was made of vibranium. After Black Panther, almost anything could be, even Ultron's entire body. This is as handy an illustration of the concept of the "available myth" as there could be—the ongoing process of telling stories provides new materials for building myths while what is built may proceed from pre-existing plans or be, in various ways, new and improved.

Of course, in more traditional societies, where, for example, stories about Thor and the like were actually sacred, it is certainly reasonable to think there were, and are, tighter controls on the use of what is inherited. These controls, however, produce tendencies, not rules, because stories have authors, and authors are human, not neutral vessels for the transmission of traditions. When we lose sight of the individual in storytelling, we fail to understand stories, whether three thousand years ago or today.

NOTES

1. The Grimms particularly pioneered what is called the "generic approach," an effort to sieve traditional material for historical facts on the basis of the "genre" of tradition it was perceived to be, which offered a sliding scale of historicity. See Grimm 1882; Gomme 1908.

2. In biblical studies, see especially Gunkel 1901, 13–20; Noth 1972, 1–2; Cross 1998, 27, 50. In some ways, biblical studies was dominated and is dominated by a search *for* authors who have sometimes been identified with great specificity. The feeling was, however, in the words of Joseph Blenkinsopp, that these may have had their own style and concerns, but in terms of narrative facts, had "added nothing essential to what was already there" (Blenkinsopp 1992, 18). See the recent discussion in Vayntrub 2019, 74–76.

3. Margalit Finkelberg, for example, referring to ancient Greek genealogical traditions, argues that "even a falsification of one's genealogical position could not be carried out arbitrarily, that is, without making it consistent in terms of the universally agreed upon system" (Finkelberg 2005, 28). Ehud Ben Zvi, generally on the cutting edge of the inheritance of traditions over time in the biblical world, nevertheless supposes that late biblical compositions did not have to be "'true' in the sense of 'objective' truth," it nevertheless had to be "'true' in regards to ideological meaningfulness and significance *and* be consistent with a set of core facts about the past that were agreed upon within the community" (Ben Zvi 2011, 37). The existence of "core facts" is what I am talking about in this essay. Irad Malkin, another excellent scholar of ancient Greek myth, observes that "[m]yths were usually not invented; they were adapted or evolved into an idea of history" (Malkin 1994, 5). John Kessler, drawing on the work of sociologist John Porter, refers to certain "ground rules" that shape conflict between elites, which could certainly include a basic agreement on the important traditions (Kessler 2006, 99). All of these scholars are very sophisticated in their analysis of myth, so this is meant to point to how entrenched certain ideas still are.

4. All quotations and references to the film are from Eric Pearson, Craig Kyle, and Christopher L. Yost, *Thor: Ragnarok*, Amazon Streaming, directed by Taika Waititi (Burbank, CA: Walt Disney Studios, 2017).

5. The "well of Mimir" episode appears in "Voluspa," the first section of the Poetic *Edda* (28). In Jackson's Crawford's translation: "Why do you seek me, Odin? / Odin, I know / where you hid your eye / in the shining waters / of the well of Mimir. / But Mimir can drink every morning / from those waters / where your own eye drowns. / Have you learned enough yet, Allfather?" (Crawford 2015, 8). Odin hangs himself in a text called "*Havamal*," one of the sections of the Poetic *Edda* (138–39). Also from the Crawford translation: "I know that I hung on a wind-battered tree / nine long nights, / pierced by a spear / and given to Odin, / myself to myself, / on that tree / whose roots grow in a place / no one has ever seen." At the end of the escapade, he learns runes (Crawford 2015, 42–43). The Mimir episode also appears in *Gylfaginning* in the Prose *Edda* of Snorri Sturluson (Sturluson 1916, 27).

6. According to "*Record Scratch* *Freeze Frame*" 2016.

7. The *Iliad* does contain a reference to Aeneas surviving the war and becoming a king, but there is no sense in it that he will have to leave the region of Troy to do so (*Iliad* XX. 308).

8. See also Wendy Doniger who observes, "Myths are retold over and over again for several reasons: because the community becomes attached to the signifiers, and they become authoritative and historically evocative; because myths are at hand, available, like the scraps of the *bricoleur*, and using them is easier than creating from scratch" (Doniger 2011, 87).

9. Thus, for example, biblical studies has been overdetermined by what Eva Mroczek calls, in criticizing it, the "hegemony of the biblical," the idea that biblical narratives had canonical importance throughout their long history despite the fact that they were not canonized until well after the major traditions had formed (Mroczek 2015, 2016).

10. "Still other work attempts to delineate various paths of the development of mythographical traditions, as well as to identify the layers within the tradition and indicate the historical context accountable for changes that transpire therein. Noticeable, however, is the absence of analyses focused on the construction of mythic plots, in circumstances in which its individual structural elements were formed and their place within the whole of a given version of the myth" (Mojsik 2011, 111–12).

11. Moreover "more than one poet and one performer were involved, as festive occasions were also opportunities for poetic contexts, i.e. occasions involving rivalry. Sometimes, even more than one audience were involved as well owing to the fact that spectators within contests at festivals could be very diverse, which the poet must always have taken into consideration . . . all of this had been subject to modifications depending on whether the poets recited their compositions locally or delivered them during pan-Hellenic festivals in front of inhabitants of different *poleis*" (Mojsik 2011, 101–3).

Chapter Twelve

Thor: Ragnarok, Postcolonial Theology, and Life Together

Kevin Nye

Right before the final showdown in *Thor: Ragnarok*, Hela—the goddess of death—reveals to Thor some purposefully concealed history about his father Odin and Asgard, his home world: "Odin and I drowned whole civilizations in blood and tears. . . . Where do you think all this gold came from?" Thor realizes in this moment that Asgard's history and its inheritance are more complicated than he had ever understood. Ultimately, as the "end of days" approaches, Thor realizes that the only way to save Asgard is to destroy it. He realizes that Asgard is not a place, but a people, and to save those people he must sacrifice something else in the process.

Thor, as played by actor Chris Hemsworth, has appeared in seven films, beginning with 2011's *Thor,* and continuing most recently in *Avengers: Endgame.* Taken as a whole, Thor's journey is one of self-discovery and an increasingly nuanced view of what it means to be a leader and a king. In 2011's *Thor,* we first meet Thor as an arrogant young prince—hungry for the throne and craving opportunities for violence and war. When this desire leads to the breaking of a centuries-old peace treaty, Thor is banished to earth where he begins the classic hero's journey. Here he learns the value of self-sacrifice, and at the end of the film returns to Asgard with the realization that he is not yet ready to be king, admitting, "I have much to learn. I know that now." According to *Thor*, one of the best attributes of a good king is a self-awareness that prompts patience and peace. This lesson is further realized in 2012's *The Avengers*, in which Thor faces off against his brother Loki, who intends to rule earth. Loki's idea of rule is domination and forced subservience, to which Thor responds, "Then you miss the truth of ruling, brother. A throne would suit you ill." Thor now understands that leadership and kingship also require humility.

In *Thor: The Dark World,* Thor's relationship to the throne becomes strained by his love for a mortal woman, Jane Foster. While Odin and others try to impress upon Thor that Jane's mortality and limits can offer him nothing compared to ruling Asgard, the emergence of the dark elves and the loss of loved ones teach Thor that to rule from a cold distance is to miss the true meaning of life. Thor explains, "Father, I cannot be king of Asgard. I will protect Asgard and all the realms with my last and every breath, but I cannot do so from that chair. . . . I'd rather be a good man than a great king." The only thing that shakes him from this resolve is the fear of "ragnarök," the end of all things, which Thor first sees in a fever dream caused by the enchantress Scarlet Witch in *Avengers: Age of Ultron.* At the end of that film, Thor leaves in search of the Infinity Stones, facing an impending destruction that he thinks he can—and must—prevent.

Thus, *Thor: Ragnarok,* opens with Thor on his quest to stop "ragnarök." Thor is told early in the movie that this fate is unavoidable, but Thor believes in his own strength and ability to prevent it. But his confidence is shaken when Thor learns that he has a violent, destructive sister, Hela. Within a minute, Thor watches his father die and quickly experiences the breadth of Hela's power when she destroys his most powerful weapon, the hammer Mjolnir. Thor is quickly defeated by Hela and exiled to the planet Sakaar, while Hela reclaims rule over Asgard and raises an army to pick up where she left off in her desire to rule the universe. On Sakaar, Thor is forced to participate in a gladiator-style competition under the rule of the planet's Grandmaster. In the process, he reunites with Hulk and his estranged brother Loki, and meets the exiled Asgardian warrior Valkyrie, along with eccentric friends Korg and Miek. He convinces them all to join him in an escape from the planet and an attempt to defeat Hela. However, in the final battle, Thor comes to the realization that Hela cannot be defeated without the destruction of Asgard itself, from which she draws her power. Together with Loki, Thor enacts "ragnarök" while escaping with the remaining Asgardians as they watch the annihilation of their planet—and Hela along with it.

These events in the film are about more than they seem on the surface. The film elicits many questions that resonate in our world today. What are the connections between land, peoples, and institutions? How should a people interact with the land it inhabits? How should a people atone for its past? These are profound questions for a blockbuster action comedy to wrestle with thematically, yet this movie clearly offers something profound to its viewers in response. As Mashable writer Angie Han observed after the film's release, *Thor: Ragnarok* is textually about these very questions: "Specifically, it's about the bloody history of colonialism, and that history's refusal to stay buried, no matter how eager we are to whitewash our sins" (Han 2017).

Thor: Ragnarok asks us as viewers to consider our own history of violence, our propensity to cover it up rather than confront it, what we are willing to sacrifice and lose to repent from it, and what redemption we might find in the process. This process is nothing less than the formation of a postcolonial mindset. When such a process is applied to a particular history, in this case American Christian history, it yields many provocative revelations. If *Thor: Ragnarok* is about uncovering a history of sin for the purpose of moving forward, then Christians have the opportunity—perhaps even the obligation—to engage it and the ideas it elicits in a meaningful way.

COLONIAL REALITIES AND POSTCOLONIAL HOPES

Right before Thor and Loki first meet Hela, Odin describes her: "The goddess of death. . . . Her violent appetites grew beyond my control." Over the course of the film, Hela lives up to this description, ruthlessly murdering hundreds of soldiers and citizens in her quest for domination. This greed for power and resources, combined with a disregard for life, are the hallmarks of colonialism. However, before discussing colonialism and postcolonialism in *Thor: Ragnarok*, it is important to define these terms.

Postcolonialism is, as the word implies, a movement that takes place in response to, or after, colonialism. Colonialism may be identified in any number of historical periods, but is most often associated with European expansion and colonization beginning in the early sixteenth century and continuing well into the twentieth century—an undertaking which literally remapped the world. According to historian and postcolonial theorist Robert J.C. Young, "This division between the rest and the west was made fairly absolute in the 19th century by the expansion of the European empires, as a result of which nine-tenths of the entire land surface of the globe was controlled by European, or European-derived, powers" (Young 2003, 2–3).

But to truly understand colonialism, we must look beyond maps. As the world was conquered by a particular people, their ideas disseminated and became the dominant way of thinking. These ideas included a particular way of categorizing people that reinforced European dominance, leading to the dawn of global racism. Young summarizes it well in his book *Postcolonialism:*

> Colonial and imperial rule was legitimized by anthropological theories which increasingly portrayed the peoples of the colonized world as inferior, childlike, or feminine, incapable of looking after themselves (despite having done so perfectly well for millennia) and requiring the paternal rule of the west for their own best interests. The basis of such anthropological theories was the concept of race. In simple terms, the west/non-west relation was thought of in terms of

whites versus the non-white races. White culture was (and remains) the basis for ideas of legitimate government, law, economics, science, language, music, art, literature—in a word, civilization. (Young 2003, 2–3)

During this time, European colonizers' arrival to the Americas led to a triangular colonial moment that set the course for our current U.S. American reality. The indigenous populations of America were largely decimated and/or displaced and replaced with white European settlers. Simultaneously, the colonization of the African continent produced a slave trade, allowing white European settlers to develop North America using cheap, multigenerational labor. Before and after securing its independence, the United States of America colonized the new world by displacing those already living here, and using the "spoils" of a colonized Africa to build wealth and a new way of life.

The end of the period of colonization in the twentieth century did not bring about an end to its implications. Young points out that, "despite decolonization, the major world powers did not change substantially during the course of the 20th century" (Young 2003, 3). While nearly every formerly European colony achieved a measure of autonomy, a claim of "independence" may be too strong, and more adequately described as a "minor move from direct to indirect rule" or "a position not so much of independence as of being independence" (Young 2003, 3). This state of "in-dependence" remains due to the reality that power and resources continue to be controlled by colonizing governments. Colonialism is largely a movement of the past, but the ways that it reshaped the world remain intact. Similarly, in the United States, while slavery has ended, its geographic, economic, and social implications persist.

Crucial to Thor's journey in *Ragnarok* is his re-education about the history of Asgard. Similarly, postcolonialism has emerged in the twentieth and twenty-first centuries, reorienting our understanding of the world and its arrangement. Another postcolonial theorist, J. Daniel Elam, notes that "the world we inhabit is impossible to understand except in relationship to the history of imperialism and colonial rule" (Elam 2019). The world is not as it is simply by accident, nor are many of the stories that we inherit the whole truth. Angie Han again gets straight to the point regarding *Ragnarok*: "The story of Asgard has echoes all around our own world: the 'free world' built on the subjugation and slaughter of others; the sanitization of our past and current misdeeds; the younger generation raised on patriotic half-truths. Hela serves as a terrifying reminder that the past has a way of catching up to the present, no matter how desperately you'd like to erase old sins" (Han 2017).

Ragnarok reminds us repeatedly of the power of telling stories in particular ways. In an early comedic scene, Loki, disguised as Odin, reenacts his own life in a dramatic play for all of Asgard, exaggerating and fabricating his heroism. Later, on Sakaar, Thor endures a comical attempt at brainwashing when a disembodied voice tells him that Sakaar "is the collection point for all lost and unloved things, like you. But here on Sakaar, you are significant. You are valuable. Here, you are loved," all while Thor sits strapped to a chair with a device in his neck that prevents his resistance. We also learn later that the Grandmaster prefers the term "prisoners with jobs" to "slaves." The power of words, performances, and histories to shape imagination is a major theme of the film—and of postcolonialism. Such performances shape our imaginations even today, in the celebration of particular holidays that misrepresent the past, like Thanksgiving and Columbus Day, and in dramatizations that portray the founding of the United States without telling the stories of the First Nations people or the brutality of slavery. Elam recognizes the way postcolonialism's truth-telling changes everything about the way we read history: "Postcolonial theory has influenced the way we read texts, the way we understand national and transnational histories, and the way we understand the political implications of our own knowledge as scholars" (Elam 2019).

Postcolonialism encounters opposition, of course, because it challenges the established order of things and distributions of power. As Young writes, "It disturbs the order of the world. It threatens privilege and power. It refuses to acknowledge the superiority of western cultures. Its radical agenda is to demand equality and well-being for all human beings on this earth" (Young 2003, 7). Postcolonialism not only expands our imagination about the world but also threatens the advantageous position of those who have benefitted from its hierarchy.

Postcolonialism must be addressed by all those wielding power and privilege in the world. As we will come to see, Christianity in the West, and specifically in America, has been indelibly marked by colonialism in ways inconsistent with its theological roots. And so postcolonialism emerges as a necessary *theological* movement, because just as people and places have been colonized and remade through colonialism, so have theology and religious practices been scarred by a remade world. Willie James Jennings of Yale Divinity School and his work on colonialism and the Christian imagination is particularly useful in this endeavor. His thorough and provocative work, documenting the through-line of colonialism in American Church History and its implications on present theology and practice, help us to see past the false stories and structures to the truth. Additionally, his hope and anticipation of a world remade enable us to imagine and live into a world that practices a Christianity aimed toward shared life and intimacy.

Those interested in Christianity's role in shaping the world (for better or worse) can view *Thor: Ragnarok* as a meditation on Jennings' work regarding racism and American postcolonial theology. Thor's revelation that "Asgard is not a place, it's a people" allows for the survival of Asgard without the blight of Hela—but at a high cost. Thor and the Asgardians sail off into a future with no place to call home, but finally free of Hela and her seemingly indestructible power. Jennings writes, as if in response, "A Christian doctrine of creation is first a doctrine of place and people, of divine love and divine touch, of human presence and embrace and of divine and human interaction" (Jennings 2010, 248). *Thor: Ragnarok* is an invitation to explore generational sins like colonialism and racism, as well as what it will take to overcome them. It is a call to repentance that invites us to look first at our concealed history, and then to present institutions and practices that keep us in seemingly inescapable cycles of destruction. This is the hard and imperative work of postcolonial theology, explored through a comic book movie about a Norse god. Trivial as that idea may sound, as the world yearns for justice and equity, we may find these more readily in a blockbuster that successfully earned $850 million than in a philosophy lecture or a sermon.

COLONIALISM AND THE CHRISTIAN IMAGINATION

In *Ragnarok,* when Hela first enters the throne room of Asgard, she gazes in disgust upon frescos on the ceiling depicting the benevolent rule of Asgard over the nine realms. Hela quickly rips these paintings down, revealing other images beneath, which depict the truth: that Odin and Hela ruled—and dominated—through violence and war. The truth of Asgard's history is revealed to all, which is a painful but necessary step toward understanding what is at stake and what has to happen.

Willie James Jennings has written a rigorous study of the theological history of colonialism and its implications on the Christian world in his seminal work, *The Christian Imagination: Theology and the Origins of Race.* In it, he re-narrates the story of colonial expansion into the Americas through the firsthand accounts of colonizers, the colonized, and the African slave—all key players in the history of how America was formed in terms of land, but also in terms of imagination. His work lends insight into postcolonial thought from a Christian perspective and touches on many of the themes *Thor: Ragnarok* explores—how history, land, and people all might reconcile with a horrific past.

Like Young, Jennings recognizes that colonialism and the formation of race are intertwined, but goes a step further to highlight what he refers to as a "theological beginning" of race and racism (Jennings 2010, 289). Colonialism and racial formation did not happen outside the imagination of Christianity, but grew as a deformity within Christian theology. In fact, Jennings demonstrates that Christian theologies became so aligned with the colonial mindset that Christians today can hardly imagine another way.

The colonial moment, what Jennings describes as a "perfect storm" of world changes, found Christians encountering a new world that was vulnerable to them and their ambitions. Christian theology was similarly vulnerable to distortion by economic opportunity and misguided ideas of white superiority to the extent that, as the world was remade and remapped, it was often done so in the name of God. Into this encounter, Europeans brought with them the colonialist mentality described above, merged with the Christian ideals of evangelism and election. This merging into the "perfect storm" of colonialism meant that European Christians began to imagine themselves as chosen people, empowered to impose themselves (their religion, traditions, and culture) upon the new world (Jennings 2010, 60).

Technological advantages afforded these European Christians the ability to control and dominate, making the idea of election a self-fulfilling prophecy— they could dominate the people of the new world, and so they did, and therefore it must be as God intended (Jennings 2010, 254). This misuse of power is reminiscent of what differentiates Thor from Hela: Thor's journey is about relinquishing power, whereas Hela uses her power to destroy and consume. Christianity's imagination of power is often shaped more like Hela's than like Thor's.

Thus, the Christian imagination had two dangerous deformities: white supremacy and disembodied spiritualism. Put another way, American Christianity was infiltrated by the idea that its very mission and destiny were to establish its theology among all peoples and places while remaining intrinsically and racially superior to them, and thus not needing to become one with them (Jennings 2010, 166). While Christian theology spread to new areas during colonization, it was a particular Christianity that "deploys divine presence without concomitant real presence and real relationship" (Jennings 2010, 167). A Christianity without physical intimacy and togetherness is a Christianity that falls short of the story of scripture: a story in which God repeatedly joins the story and destiny of a particular people in a particular place; sharing space and touching bodies.

Because racism allowed colonizers to create a new hierarchy of humans, and those humans now occupied a shared space, Christianity became a more spiritual, less embodied religion by necessity. Far from Thor's revelation that Asgard is not a place, but a people, the Christian imagination catastrophically damaged its ability to remain centered on God's love for humankind. Jennings highlights this through the life and writings of Olaudah Equiano, a slave who managed to attain freedom, education, and even monetary success, but whose imagination and future were consistently limited by the colonial mindset. Equiano was himself a Christian, but his theology was constrained by the world in which he lived. Because of his life experiences, he had to somehow make sense of the religion that had saved his soul yet had once also enslaved his body, and all the while continued to evaluate his worth based on race. Christianity's offer of communion with God and the church could never be fully accessed by Equiano, because he "was forced to try to imagine Christian community in the face of its deepest social ruptures. This Christian faith imagined and sought belonging but was repeatedly thrown back by the dominant racial calculus to a theological isolationism in which God's providential care had to substitute for communal care. . . . In Equiano's case, visions of providential care had to be stretched to distortion, stretched to cover absurdity after absurdity" (Jennings 2010, 183). Jennings' point is simple but profound: in order to reconcile the displacement and enslavement of particular peoples, Christian theology had to move away from the physical, embodied vision of the Gospel, and replace it with a more spiritual, metaphorical reading, allowing one to be "spiritually" close to God while perpetuating absurd physical atrocities against neighbor. Both for the enslavers and the enslaved, the Christian imagination had to morph into one that could permit and even bless this disparity. This theological shift would ultimately prove to have profound implications on the intimacy and connectedness central to Christian life.

Race plays an implicit rather than explicit role in the colonial imagination of *Thor: Ragnarok*. To discuss colonial America in the past or present without acknowledging the role of race is impossible—and dangerous. After all, the film is about the danger of covering up past sins, and racism has been described by political theologian Jim Wallis as "America's Original Sin" (Wallis 2017). What the film does, however, is shift the focus more toward the roles of place and space. Colonialism is by definition about the occupation of new space and the displacement—literal and cultural—of the people who lived there previously. One of the reasons it takes Thor so long to imagine Asgard as a people rather than a place is because people and places are deeply connected—culturally, physically, and spiritually. To that point, Jennings is convinced that displacement is a theological act as well, one that led colonial Christians to abandon the importance of land to God and to theology. In fact, he argues that the emergence of racial categorization only makes sense in the loss of place. "Without place as the articulator of identity, human skin was asked to fly solo and speak for itself" (Jennings 2010, 64). As European settlers colonized the new world, displacing those who already occupied it while filling it with a subjugated people already colonized and displaced from Africa, a theology that valued land and place had to give way to something more distorted. Thus, any attempts to address race and racism that fail to address displacement and the importance of place to culture and identity will fall short.

The beginning of the end of all things for Thor is the realization of old truths—forgotten, buried, but nonetheless dangerous. Like Thor, it is easy for us to be blindsided by a history that has been overlooked and under-taught. However, armed with a deeper sense of truth and a desire to see a new future, we can engage the present with clarity and understand the moment we find ourselves in. It is impossible to reckon with our present reality and its implications if we are unable or unwilling to recognize the truth about how the world was changed—both what was at stake, and what was lost.

THE PAST IS OUR PRESENT

It is not enough for Thor and Asgard to simply learn about Hela's past. They also must figure out how to stop her, the key to which lies in understanding what gives her power and sustains her life in the present. Similarly, it is not enough to understand colonialism as a past event; we must also reckon with the ways it currently limits the Christian imagination, and what practices and institutions sustain it. In *Thor: Ragnarok,* the revelation of the past is followed closely by an exile, wherein Thor is offered the opportunity to remain hopeful while also experiencing his own displacement and enslavement.

The film doesn't necessarily spell out the source of Thor's hope; perhaps it is a naïve heroism or simply the desire for revenge. But Thor never stops believing that Asgard still has hope, as bad as things are. Similarly, Jennings has hope despite the present state of the Christian imagination. Jennings calls this current reality "the remade world," a world purposefully shaped and designed by those in power over time to benefit some at the expense of others (Jennings 2010, 287). This is a judgment, of course, but it also offers hope. If the world was made to be this way, it can perhaps be unmade. But the first step to unmaking a remade world is to recognize the ways in which that world affects our imaginations. Jennings reminds us, "Before we theologians can interpret the depths of the divine action of reconciliation we must first articulate the profound deformities of Christian intimacy and identity in modernity" (Jennings 2010, 10). We ought to be careful not to jump to cheap, superficial reconciliation, to "doing better" in a way that falls short of recognizing the deformed external and internal structures that hold this remade world together. This would be akin to what Odin does in banishing Hela; it is a temporary solution that not only delays the needed resolution but also increases the danger for those to come.

Perhaps the most glaring failure in the present is a lack of faithful awareness and teaching of the past. Like the literal coverings in the palace of Asgard that mask a shameful past, retellings of American Church history often gloss over or minimize colonialism's significance. Jennings notes that both church history and general theological education "live in conceptual worlds that have not in any substantive way reckoned with the ramifications of colonialism for Christian identity or the identity of theology" (Jennings 2010, 291). Theologian James Cone, as he often does, puts it more bluntly:

> Because white theologians live in a world that is racist, the oppression of black people does not occupy an important item on their theological agenda . . . because white theologians are well fed and speak for a people who control the means of production, the problem of hunger is not a theological issue for them. That is why they spend more time debating the relation between the Jesus of history and the Christ of faith than probing the depths of Jesus' command to feed the poor. (Cone 1997, 47–48)

But if we are willing to take this history and its ramifications seriously, Jennings beckons us to see two key areas where the Christian imagination is found wanting: intimacy and sense of place.

The planet of Sakaar illustrates the fascinating dichotomy that can occur between different peoples occupying the same spaces in terms of intimacy. Sakaar is little more than a trash dump, catching exiles and lost things, where many live in squalor and others, like the Grandmaster, live in luxury over them. The planet's social framework is maintained through a system of violence in which everyone participates, the "Contest of Champions." The Grandmaster tells a story of acceptance and love, but it is actually violence that is celebrated in the streets, even by those experiencing it. Thor's experience of this violence as a displaced and exiled individual enables him to eventually realize the source of Hela's power.

Similarly, the remaking of the world in colonialism left Christianity with a "diseased social imagination" (Jennings 2010, 9). Bad colonial theology fused with prosperity and perceived blessing made it nearly impossible for authentic intimacy between different peoples to be possible within the Christian imagination. Jennings calls it a "poverty of desire": if colonial Christians insist that particular people are intellectually inferior, and therefore in need of assimilation, how can those two peoples ever truly experience authentic belonging and relationship? "This problem has fundamentally to do with a world formed and continuing to be formed to undermine the possibilities of Christians living together, loving together, and desiring each other" (Jennings 2010, 202). As modern Christians more and more experience disconnection and isolation rather than authentic belonging with one another, it is no surprise that religious expression has become a consumer enterprise—segregated and individualized. This is the only Christian imagination that can possibly form on a national level in light of all the distortions and absurdities with which colonialism infected it. It is also a Christianity that is very easy to participate in without questioning it, like the people of Sakaar who celebrate the regime that oppresses them and kills others.

This loss of intimacy has implications beyond simply how we perceive one another. Jennings continues, "Colonialist new identity meant unrelenting assimilation and the enfolding of lives and cultural practices inside processes of commodification" (Jennings 2010, 292). In other words, the willingness to belong to one another and experience mutual submission under God lost the battle to greed. Under colonialism, the worth of different peoples became calculable in terms of how resources were plundered and redistributed to those with power. This is the most powerful of all revelations in *Thor: Ragnarok*. Whereas the previous films invite the viewer to bask in the splendor of Asgard, with all its gold and wealth and power, this film undermines that splendor with the revelation from Hela: "Odin and I drowned whole civilizations in blood and tears. Where do you think all this gold came from?" In the present, we are therefore unlikely to be willing to come together across lines of race or class with humility; not only because it is hard to imagine we are all truly equal, but also because we are afraid of what it might cost us to actually make that true. For Thor and for Asgard, it cost them all that gold and more—the very planet sustained by their prosperity.

Here the film again lacks the specificity of our current condition, in which space is shared by both the colonizers and the colonized. But in addition to helping us understand the significance of place to identity and wealth, it can offer us a jumping-off point into a conversation about place and race in America today. A cruel irony of literal and cultural displacement is that when colonized peoples are stripped of their spaces and the identities built on them, they are often re-placed into spaces that are then racialized. In the same way colonialism "re-mapped" the world and left it that way in perpetuity, cities and neighborhoods in America were mapped for racist purposes, and they largely remain segregated today. As Richard Rothstein argues in *The Color of Law,* this intentional segregation has happened throughout American history, but was particularly precise and consequential in the early twentieth century, when private prejudice was supported by thinly veiled public policy (Rothstein 2017, xii).

As a result, the disparities created by racial remapping in wealth, education, investment, and other resources leave many of those maps looking the same today as when they were made that way on purpose nearly a hundred years ago. These disparities reinforce and perpetuate on a generational scale the wealth and education gap between people of color and whites, and the hierarchies that these realities create. While the Fair Housing Act was passed in 1968, it has done little to undo the damage done prior to its passing. A recent study by the Institute for Policy Studies shows that "over the past 30 years the average wealth of white families has grown by 84%—1.2 times the rate of growth for the Latino population and three times the rate of growth for the black population. If that continues, the next three decades would see the average wealth of white households increase by over $18,000 per year, while Latino and Black households would see their respective wealth increase by only $2,250 and $750 per year" (Holland 2016). Because place and land are rendered as property which increases in value and is passed down through generations, there remains a direct link from colonialism's seizure of land, twentieth-century segregation of that land, and the racial wealth disparities of today.

Painting an honest, if dispiriting, picture of the modern imagination and its practice is a necessary step in the journey of postcolonial Christian work. It is no small decision for Thor, Valkyrie, and Loki to return to Asgard and face Hela, knowing the extent of her power but not yet knowing what it might take to defeat her. Thor knows that "The longer Hela's on Asgard the more powerful she grows." In the same way, the longer we leave alone the legacy of colonialism and intergenerational wealth disparities, the more powerful and insurmountable they seem. But the courage to fight back comes from a place of hope and responsibility. Particularly, Thor understands that his responsibility is to the people of Asgard. "This isn't about the crown," Thor says firmly, "This is about the people." Thor learns, as we may hope to, that intimacy with people, more than systems and traditions, is what beckons us forward.

RECLAIMED IMAGINATION

To defeat Hela, Thor must complete the lesson he has gradually been learning throughout his film appearances: that leadership, in his case kingship, is about valuing the people who make up a community more than the inherited institutions and traditions that the people inhabit. For Thor, this is encompassed in the realization that "Asgard isn't a place, it's a people." This revelation comes at a cost, however. Thor must be willing to destroy the planet and all of its riches, institutions, and meaning, from which Hela draws her power. "*Ragnarök,*" the end of all things, is in actuality only the end of *old* ways and *old* things. Despite an immense loss, it opens up a new future without Hela and Asgard's destructive ties to the past.

But to get to this point of decision, Thor and his allies have to fight. Because *Thor: Ragnarok* is a superhero action movie, even though the stakes are philosophical, their struggle is represented in a literal fight, full of CGI spectacle and memorable moments. There is for us, though, no rainbow bridge on which we can wage a battle for the soul of the Christian imagination. Instead, this "battle" must be waged on multiple fronts upon which the Christian imagination can be confronted and reclaimed, many of them theological but with practical implications. Additionally, the sacrifice that Thor makes to destroy Asgard can be emulated in many ways that demonstrate the need for sacrifice and loss to accompany redemption.

One site of Christian struggle is in the use of scripture. To imagine the future of the Christian imagination beyond colonialism necessitates a fresh look at the Bible, which offers a richer story than dominance and displacement. The collective Christian imagination has the ability—indeed, the duty—to understand itself beyond the colonial moment following the destruction of the institutions and practices of colonialism. Some may be tempted to think that to destroy colonial Christianity means that no Christianity will be left. Like Valkyrie, the exiled warrior who knows the truth but cannot bear it, it is tempting to abandon lost institutions altogether—including the people entangled in them. However, Jennings suggests with hope that "Christian life is indeed a way forward for the world" and that the Gospel itself contains the very way out of the colonial deformities of imagination (Jennings 2010, 294).

If we refuse the colonial lie that people and places are not connected, then what is true about people and place from a Christian perspective? A responsible biblical theology of land suggests that people and land are indeed connected, but only through God. In the Old Testament, whether in Abraham's search for a home, the Exodus journey to the promised land, or the exile to Babylon, "God stood always 'in the way' as it were, between Israel and the desire for land, reordering its identity first in relation to the divine word and then to the land" (Jennings 2010, 212). Additionally, in the New Testament, Jesus disappoints expectations that he will reclaim the land from Roman rule, and instead understands Israel's salvation differently. This is disorienting to an American (and Christian!) sense of ownership of land and property, which stems from colonialism. Instead, a robust Christian theology always understands "the God of Israel as the creator who 'owns' all land and therefore claimed all peoples" (Jennings 2010, 213). In practice, this means that Christians act in different ways regarding land and space. Jennings considers this "a crucial point of discipleship. Where we live determines in great measure how we live" (Jennings 2010, 287). Where Christians live, and how they live there, ought to be as much a Christian consideration in a postcolonial imagination as how one prays.

Christians ought to enter and live in new spaces with intimacy and humility, two other great theological losses of colonialism. The Christian posture in this way is perhaps best characterized by a God who washes the dirty feet of the disciples. This is a physical act, the job of a lowly servant, to touch and be touched by calloused, dirt-stained feet—all performed by the Son of God. Throughout his ministry, Jesus made a habit of touching and being touched by people in encounters that were always transformative. There are a few stories in which Jesus heals without touch, which suggests that perhaps while it was within his ability, it was not his preferred method of transformation. Jesus tells his disciples to go and do likewise, a command that, like many texts that involve intimacy and physicality, has been rendered inert by colonialism's propensity toward isolation and disembodiment.

Intimacy and community are thus strategies valued within a postcolonial imagination. These concerns, for Jennings, are "the desired telos of the Christian gospel" (Jennings 2010, 214). Additionally, Jennings has written an excellent commentary on Acts that is especially attuned to postcolonial concerns. For Jennings, beginning with the Pentecost event in Acts 2, this early story of Christianity spreading without dominating is instructive for how the Church should understand its role among peoples—he calls it "the epicenter of revolution," a specific "revolution of the intimate" (Jennings 2017, 27). These stories can serve as archetypes for Christians interacting in the world—not dominating or condescending, but being humbled as "a community broken open by the sheer act of God" (Jennings 2017, 27). The Gospel demands that Christians be willing to move, change, and adapt for the sake of joining—the opposite of colonialism.

If the Christian imagination enters new spaces to interact humbly with new peoples, theology and church history will necessarily be shaped and changed by new voices that were historically ignored or relegated to smaller, separate areas of study. In this way, the Christian imagination widens to see more of a universal vision, to see more of God. Cone writes, "The only way people can enhance their vision of the universal is to break out of their cultural and political boxes and encounter another reality" (Cone 1997, 49). Theology, wherever it is practiced, must be broken open to the diverse expressions of faith and practice in God's vast world. This is exemplified in the trajectory the Book of Acts takes, toward the baptism of an Ethiopian eunuch, to the inclusion of Gentiles in the church. In *Ragnarok,* when Thor forms "The Revengers" to escape from Sakaar and return to Asgard to fight Hela, a similar inclusiveness among surprising peoples takes place. The team is composed of a disgraced Asgardian (Loki), an exiled one (Valkyrie), but also characters like Hulk, Korg, and Miek who have no real tie to Asgard, but who understand themselves nonetheless joined together in the larger story of freedom and redemption.

In the remade world, there are many obstacles to what God in scripture imagines as intimate life together, including separation, inequity, and fear. As Jennings says, "We are in need of a vision of the journey of faith imagined as the joining of peoples now separated by violence, poverty, or race" (Jennings 2010, 286). The word "joining" is crucial, because it implies a necessary act or series of acts, rather than a mere posture or change in thought. In fact, Jennings continues, "This joining also involves entering into the lives of peoples to build actual life together, lives enfolded and kinship networks established through the worship of and service to the God of Israel in Jesus Christ" (Jennings 2010, 287). Just as the formation of "The Revengers" includes different creatures with diverse histories and trajectories, so a new Christian imagination sees all people as members of a divine community, to shape and be shaped by one another in relationships exemplifying sacrifice and vulnerability.

The "way forward for the world" that Jennings believes Christianity offers is most distinctly characterized as "a compelling invitation to life together" (Jennings 2010, 294). However, it also entails sacrifice. As Young notes that postcolonialism "threatens privilege and power," so Thor learns that it involves losing and destroying "all this gold." Is the Christian response, then, to destroy property and wealth in a destructive act of response? *Thor: Ragnarok* falls short of demonstrating how Asgard might reconcile itself to the universal implications of its imperial rule. Postcolonial Christians, however, share space with the victims of colonialism, and perhaps have an opportunity to build rather than destroy.

As the Christian imagination endeavors to respond to the legacy of colonialism, it may find itself drawn to biblical concepts like Jubilee, wherein every fifty years debts were forgiven, resources redistributed, and people released from bondage. In "The Biblical Case for Black Reparations," Ulysses Burley III and Nathan Robinson connect the concept of Jubilee to the modern one of black reparations—the idea that actual money might be redistributed to black communities and black people to repair and reverse generational inequity and close the racial wealth gap outlined above (Burley III and Roberts 2016). Whatever the details of the strategy, it is clear that a Christian imagination that has severed its ties to the colonial inheritance would emulate the self-giving sacrifice of Christ. James Cone beautifully describes Jesus as "the Liberator of the oppressed from social oppression and to political struggle, wherein the poor recognize that their fight against poverty and injustice is not only consistent with the gospel but is the gospel of Jesus Christ" (Cone 1997, 74–75). Reparations are one potential way that white Christians might consider sacrificing their colonial inheritance in order to remake the world, given that it was made to intentionally limit the access to and accumulation of wealth for black Americans.

In the same way that Thor and Asgard have to relinquish their understanding of Asgard as a place, so Christians must relinquish the colonial mindset regarding space and place. Only then can Christians develop new social, racial, and economic views, looking toward a Christian imagination freed from colonialism. More than that, Christians must understand that the Gospel beckons its followers toward intimacy and joining in all spaces. Thor and the Asgardians learn that such a revelation comes at a high cost, but the reward is a future with hope. In chapter 29 of the Book of Jeremiah, God calls the exiled people to "seek the welfare of the city . . . for in its welfare you will find your welfare" before famously assuring them, "For surely I know the plans I have for you, says the Lord, plans for your welfare and not for harm, to give you a future with hope" (Jeremiah 29:7, 11, *NRSV*).

CONCLUSION

The complexities of race, place, and intimacy should not be understated. No one work of theology, nor one theologian, nor film or filmmaker can capture or reconcile thousands of years of collective history. But there are recognizable differences between the way things are and the way we imagine they could or should be. As a pastor of mine once said, the greatest Christian task is to look at ourselves and our world, then look to Christ, and confess the difference. That confession, though, is not a disembodied hope, nor a passive shrug regarding how those differences came about, or what it might cost to rectify them.

Christian hope and postcolonialism both consider seriously the state of the world and how it came to be, but also believe that it does not have to remain this way. As Young describes the work of postcolonialism as "turning the world upside-down," a renowned Christian text by Richard Kraybill in 1978 also describes the Kingdom of God as "The Upside-Down Kingdom." James Cone, too, reminds us that the work of turning the world upside-down on behalf of the oppressed is a deeply biblical and Gospel-driven work:

> The God of Abraham, Isaac, and Jacob and of Peter, James, and John is not an eternal idea, and neither is the divine an absolute ethical principle to whom people ought to appeal for knowledge of the Good. Rather, Yahweh is known and worshiped as the One who brought Israel out of Egypt, and who raised Jesus from the dead. God is the political God, the Protector of the poor and the Establisher of the right for those who are oppressed. To know God is to experience the acts of God in the concrete affairs and relationships of people, liberating the weak and the helpless from pain and humiliation. For theologians to speak of this God, they too must become interested in politics and economics, recognizing that there is no truth about Yahweh unless it is the truth of freedom as that

event is revealed in the oppressed people's struggle for justice in this world. (Cone 1997, 57)

A movie like *Thor: Ragnarok* compels us to be caught up in its story, offering a deep reflection on humanity. We are invited along as it grapples with notions of our shared life in the real world, and it offers perspective on a way forward. Perhaps unintentionally, it also welcomes reflection by Christians who find themselves called by God to deeply love and participate in the redeeming of the world, despite feeling powerless in the face of inequity and injustice. Like Thor and "The Revengers," we may find ourselves compelled to reckon with the sins of the past and the ways we, knowingly and unknowingly, sustain them, ignore them, or draw power from them to hurt others.

As *Ragnarok* draws to a close, with Hela defeated, the people of Asgard look to Thor and ask an anxious but hopeful question: "Where to?" I believe, like Jennings, that Christianity can not only be distinguished from and reconciled with our history of colonialism, but that Christ's actions and teachings offer a roadmap out of that past and toward the ultimate answer to the existential question, "Where to?" A liberated Christian imagination offers an invitation to a truly remade world: the Kingdom of God, a new kingdom of peoples captivated by Christ's teachings, practicing humble intimacy with all peoples in all places, under the unifying rule of the God of the Oppressed. It is this Christian hope that compels us to intimate life together, characterized by radical sacrifice and immense joy.

Chapter Thirteen

Savage Monster or Grieving Mother? Sabra and Marvel's Political Theology of Reconciliation in Israel-Palestine

Amanda Furiasse

The Marvel superhero Sabra, also known as Ruth Bat-Seraph, remains among Marvel's most divisive yet little-known comic book characters. Although Sabra is no longer a mainstay in Marvel comics, she was once one of Marvel's most popular comic book characters. Created in the aftermath of the 1967 Arab-Israeli War, Sabra first appeared in the *X-Men II* and *Incredible Hulk II* series where she was introduced to readers as an Israeli citizen living with mutant powers, including the ability to fly at jet speed, super-human physical strength, and fluency in more than four languages. After her initial appearance on the comic book pages as a minor character in the *Incredible Hulk II* series, the character soon evolved into a major character in the *X-Men II* series where she appeared as a supporter of the mutant cause. Professor Xavier invited her to join his elite team of mutants, though she never took them up on the offer. Decades later, she remained a popular mutant character well into the 90s and early 2000s where she appeared in some of Marvel's most popular comics, including *Civil War* and *Secret Invasion*.

To date, little has been written about Sabra and her crucial role in the Marvel Universe. This is largely the result of her character's divisive and controversial legacy. However, during the late seventies and early eighties, Sabra was expected to allay enmity between Israelis and Palestinians with the former taking responsibility for arousing violence as opposed to merely being subjugated to it. One of the most formative moments of her life was grieving the loss of her son to a terror bombing. Sabra sought to avenge his death by marshalling her super powers. The past however complicated her pursuit for justice, reminding her that the violence she wanted to overcome was inflicted by her as well. To redress the pain caused by her son's tragic death, Sabra prioritized diplomacy over revenge. I draw on Sabra's liminality as a grieving mother as well as a savage monster to highlight limits to the theology of reconciliation that gained impetus after the Camp David Accords in 1978 and started to wither away after the Oslo Accords in 1993. The assumption that peace would ensue once Israelis reconcile with their worrisome past advances representations of Arab communities as defenseless victims in need of Israel's motherly protection and diplomatic genius. Sabra's American authors ultimately forefront a complex and contradictory portrait of the Israeli state's role in the Israeli-Palestinian conflict with the Israeli state simultaneously represented as a savage monster who incites anarchy and a grieving mother who fulfills our messianic expectations for a just and lasting peace in the Middle East. Her story forefronts a distinctive liberalism that informed how Americans during the late seventies and early eighties understood the Israeli-Palestinian conflict, with diplomacy as a panacea to such regional conflicts its defining marker.

Ruth Bat-Seraph's story follows common American stereotypes about young Israeli Jews. She is born near Jerusalem to an Israeli war hero who raises her on a special government-run kibbutz. Her mutant powers first manifest themselves in her youth, and they include enhanced physical strength, agility, stamina, reflexes, and the ability to fly. Her body can also withstand impacts of high-caliber rifle fire.

The Israeli government exploits Sabra to bolster Mossad, the Israeli Intelligence Agency. She spends most of her youth away from her family, training with Mossad to become a weapon in their war against local terrorist groups. Her special abilities should have enabled her to withstand Mossad, but instead they became the reason why Mossad manipulated her to serve its interests. Periodically, the contradiction of being powerless amid having super abilities overwhelms Sabra. She fails to consolidate the ideal mutant as imagined by the Israeli government, fluctuating instead between naïve trust and skepticism of governmental institutions.

The government weaponized her mutant abilities, representing some obvious similarities to the stories of other mutants, including both Magneto and Wolverine, who like Sabra were routinely subjected to government manipulation and surveillance. As in the case of other X-Men stories, the government intervenes and subjects her to persistent testing and manipulation. Rather than enjoy a relatively peaceful and normal childhood, Sabra instead undergoes intense military training to become a highly skilled Mossad operative. The presence of government surveillance and manipulation remains an early and recurring source of Sabra's anger. Her frustration and rage over her manipulation at the hands of government officials in turn moves Sabra to fluctuate between naïve trust and critical skepticism of government institutions.

For instance, in *X-Men II* #67, Sabra is manipulated into supporting Operation Zero Tolerance, a global anti-mutant campaign committed to completely eradicating mutants. Her participation in Operation Zero Tolerance's persecution and even genocide of other mutants eventually leads her to confront her deeply held assumptions about herself and her relationship to her government. She eventually betrays Mossad and provides classified information to Professor Xavier's students that ultimately helps them escape government surveillance. While the government effectively transforms her into an instrument of violence that they can use against individuals and organizations deemed to be a threat to Israel's national interests, Sabra, however, routinely draws on her superpowers to defy the government as well.

Her relationship to Windstorm further represents the fragile boundary between embodying state surveillance and anarchy. In *Marvel Super-Heroes* #6, Sabra saves Windstorm from dying of a drug overdose on the streets of Tel Aviv. Like Sabra, Windstorm remains haunted by traumatic experiences in her past, using drugs as a mechanism to drown her sorrow and even attempts to kill herself. Sabra refuses to allow Windstorm to die and uses her regenerative powers to restore her back to life. While her regenerative powers are a crucial component of her mutant powers, this marks the first time in the comics that Sabra uses them to save someone. In the process, Windstorm is bestowed with mutant powers, including the superhuman ability to control the winds. Upon being restored to life, Windstorm decides to join the Israeli military where she is trained to become a soldier. However, in the process of training to become a soldier, Windstorm transforms. She rejects her savior and establishes a terrorist group called Israelis for Anarchy to threaten Israeli leaders and international politicians working for peace and reconciliation in the region. For instance, the organization targets Israel's most sacred and historic institutions, including a kibbutz, where Windstorm holds the U.S. ambassador's son hostage (*Marvel Super-Heroes* #6). Comic book authors make clear that Windstorm's hatred for Israel and disdain for the entire international peace process builds on Sabra's own recurring struggle to trust and support international institutions. Amid Windstorm terrorizing the international peace process, Sabra neither kills nor strips her of her superpowers (*Marvel Super-Heroes* #6). Sabra after all distrusts the peace process as well.

A watershed moment transpires in Sabra's Israeli identity and commitment to the state when she encounters the Hulk. In *Incredible Hulk II* #256, Sabra mistakenly assumes that the Hulk is working with Arab terrorists. After his plane crashes near the city of Tel Aviv, Sabra confronts the Hulk and assumes that he was responsible for a recent terrorist attack against local communities. However, as Sabra begins to drain the Hulk of his power, she discovers that the Hulk had in fact been trying to protect a young Arab boy, named Sahad, from her violent wrath. The young Arab boy reminds her of her own son who died in a tragic terrorist attack. In *X Men II* #67, a group of Palestinian terrorists ambushed her son Jacob along with several other Israeli school children on their school bus. She avenged her son's death by arresting the accused terrorists in Palestinian territory, without waiting to receive government clearance. She made no secret of her son's emotional impact on her, describing her life as entirely "empty" and "devoid of hopes and dreams" (*X-Men II* #67). Witnessing the Hulk's grief over the young Arab boy's tragic death, Sabra suddenly realizes that while she had assumed that she was a savior, she was in fact the true villain all along.

The author Bill Mantlo makes clear to the reader that grief over the tragic loss of her son has turned her into the very thing that she seeks to fight and destroy. Now upon witnessing the Hulk's sorrow and grief over Sahad's tragic death, Sabra questions who was the true monster all along. She falls on her knees in disgust of herself and struggles to find any words to describe her grief. Mantlo describes the scene in the following way: "It has taken a monster to awaken her own sense of humanity" (*Incredible Hulk II* #256). Rage binds Sabra to a contradictory character who both grieves the loss of human life and causes similar grief for others, an Israeli mother seeking to kill the monster who is no one else but Sabra herself.

This is not the only instance where Sabra routinely straddles the line between savior and villain in the comics. In addition to her confrontation with the Hulk, her encounter with the Syrian national hero Batal also subverts the reader's assumption that Sabra is in fact the clear hero of the story. In *New Warriors* #58, Sabra first encounters Batal when she is assigned to protect the Israeli prime minister Yitzhak Rabin at the United Nations to ensure Rabin brokers a successful peace deal between Israel and Syria. However, an unknown force takes over her mind and turns her against international peace-keepers and Batal. Sabra's mind control is only broken when she hears someone reciting the traditional Jewish prayer of the dead, the Mourner's Kaddish. Through recitation of Jewish prayer, Sabra regains her ability to think clearly and realizes that she had become a monster and nearly destroyed the entire peace process between Israel and Syria.

This inversion of the common superhero trope of a clear good hero and evil villain makes Sabra unique in that her story does not follow a traditional superhero arc. It is perhaps possible that this inversion of a very common superhero trope represents an attempt on the part of her authors to both innovate the superhero genre and deliver a poignant political critique of the Israeli-Palestinian conflict. As her initial creator, Bill Mantlo was well known for his creative ability to innovate the superhero genre and deliver complex social critiques of American politics and ethics.

At Marvel Comics, Mantlo forged a reputation for his very public commitment to social justice and even earned his law degree from the Brooklyn

Law School (Staley 2017). However, he often found himself at odds with the executive staff at Marvel Comics. By the 1970s, Marvel Comics was increasingly moving toward a corporate-minded, profitability model. This shift caused a mass exodus of creative talent as writers increasingly left and tried to start their own independent comics. Mantlo was among the few talented writers who remained loyal and committed to the company. This was despite the fact that Marvel executives only offered him a freelance contract with few benefits (Staley 2017).

He also remained committed to writing comic book characters that exemplified the core struggles of America's underclass. For example, Cloak and Dagger, which Mantlo created around the same time as Sabra, featured a black and white teenage superhero duo who battled drug dealers and traffickers to redress complex social issues plaguing New York City streets. Social institutions, specifically the police and law enforcement agencies, are subject to constant criticism as Mantlo routinely assesses the law's failure to protect the most vulnerable members of society. Mantlo thus inverts the reader's ethical expectations and represents society's most trusted institutions as in fact completely inept and unable to serve and protect the most vulnerable members of society.

Mantlo explained that his characters' moral complexity represented an attempt to redress the suffering and experiences of immigrants in America (Shayer 2010). With political and social institutions commonly vilifying immigrants, he wanted to offer a nuanced and complex portrait of daily life for immigrants as they struggled to survive and prosper in a society where the law failed to protect them. His characters are thus forced to openly defy the law and operate in morally complex worlds where the apparent line between good and evil is not always clear.

This perspective on American institution also seems to shape Mantlo's understanding of Sabra's inner struggle to trust government institutions. For example, Sabra defies her orders from Mossad when she discovers that they are working in concert with other governments to murder every living mutant (*X-Men II* #67). She offers important intelligence to Professor Xavier and his X-Men team that ultimately helps them escape capture. Sabra then is not the only morally ambiguous character, but government institutions are as morally ambiguous as Mantlo's characters with institutions commonly unable and unwilling to protect society's most vulnerable members. Rather than depict the villain as an outside or completely evil character or institution, the comics instead represent Sabra and the institutions that she works for as the chief villain.

In addition to reflecting Mantlo's own complex understanding of American society, this poignant inversion of the common superhero trope of a clear moral line between good and evil might also represent an attempt on the part of Sabra's authors to deliver a political critique of the U.S. government's inability to effectively work with Israel and redress the ongoing Israeli-Palestinian conflict. The comics make this point explicitly clear with both the recurrent use of political symbols and Sabra's relationships to American and international governing bodies.

In the case of political symbols, Sabra literally wears the star of David, the Israeli state's central political emblem, across her chest and flies over the skies of Israel alongside Israeli fighter jets as local Israelis herald her as "The Super Heroine of the State of Israel." In *Contest of Champions* #2, Sabra also explains that she derives her superhero alter-ego name, "Sabra," from the people of Israel. As she explains to Iron Man, "Like the spiny pear that is the symbol of the Israeli people from which I derive my name" (*Contest of Champions* #2).

Serving as a literary representation of the Israeli state, her relationships to other characters and actions typifies Israel's complex and often contradictory relationship to American institutions. For example, Sabra never completely accepts Professor Xavier's invitation to join the X-Men but also never entirely rejects the invitation and agrees to aid the X-Men at various points in the comics. In addition to providing crucial intelligence to the X-Men, she also provides protection to Storm and other X-Men when she discovers them in dire need of help after fighting off an attack in the North Sea (*X-Men III* #31). However, she also remains an outsider to the X-Men and even maintains a divisive relationship with other members. In one instance, she purposely aggravates members and expresses a continual interest in exposing their greatest personal flaws and weaknesses (*Excalibur I* #121).

When she does agree to fight alongside American mutants and superheroes, she often ends up causing more damage with her vulnerability to mind manipulation continually threatening her commitment to international peace. For example, when she is assigned to protect the Israeli prime minister Yitzhak Rabin while he is in New York trying to broker peace talks with Israel's Middle East neighbors, an unknown force takes a hold of her mind and turns her against international peace keepers (*New Warriors* #58). In the end, the peace talks are an abysmal failure with Sabra the primary one responsible for their failure. While she might be an ally to American mutants and superheroes as they work collaboratively to redress international conflicts, she remains a completely unreliable ally who jeopardizes the entire peace process.

Her relationship to other Arab characters in the comics is even more divisive and complicated. Although Marvel Comics in the early 1980s created only a few central Arab characters, the Arabian Knight remained among the few examples of a strong and independent Arab superhero. Created by Bill

Mantlo at the same that he created Sabra, the Arabian Knight first surfaces as Sabra's counterpoint in Saudi Arabia. Like Sabra, the Arabian Knight is one of Saudi Arabia's greatest and most beloved national heroes who works on behalf of the Saudi Arabian government to redress conflicts in the region. He derives his power from three magical weapons which he discovers once belonged to his ancestors (*Incredible Hulk* #257). In *Contest of Champions* #2, the Arabian Knight partners up with Sabra and Iron Man but initially resists working with her, citing her Jewish background as problematic to him. In later comics, their divisive relationship is peppered with even more harmful stereotypes about Arab communities. In *Union Jack* #1, the Arabian Knight rejects the idea of working with Sabra, arguing that her true social role is that of wife and mother.

Sabra's relationship to other American and Arab characters seems to mirror Israel's complex and evolving role in international politics. In the decades leading up to Sabra's first appearance in the comics, Israel was continuing to grapple with the lasting effects of the 1967 Arab-Israeli Yom Kippur War. This war was historically unprecedented in that Saudi Arabia played a crucial and important role in contributing key military equipment, including helicopters, armored cars, artillery batteries, and guns, as well as highly trained troops to the region (Sela 2000, 37). While the Israeli military might have halted the Egyptian military's offensive after they crossed the Sinai Peninsula, the war highlighted the emergence of Saudi Arabia as a competitor to Israel in shaping the future of the Middle East.

This vulnerability was further exacerbated with the United Nations' historic 1975 declaration. A few years after the Yom Kippur War, the United Nations General Assembly issued Resolution 3379, declaring Zionism to be "a form of racism and racial discrimination." For Israel, the declaration served as irrefutable evidence of Saudi Arabia's growing influence in shaping international governance with officials blaming the UN's decision on pressure from Saudi officials (Bennis 1997, 49). The UN's decision delivered a particularly significant blow to Israeli confidence with the international declaration attacking the state's historic and formative ideological pillars.

In the aftermath of these political humiliations, Israeli officials increasingly agreed to negotiate with their neighboring Arab states with the U.S. government playing a crucial role in brokering these early agreements. In 1978, the first of these negotiations ushered in the Camp David Accords which were signed by the Egyptian president Anwar Sadat and Israeli prime minister Menachem Begin (Quandt 1986, 357). A year later, Egypt and Israel signed the Egypt-Israel Peace Treaty which included not only a cessation of war, but a promise from Israel to completely withdraw its forces from the Sinai Peninsula (Quandt 1986, 357). The peace talks were internationally heralded as the beginning of a new era for Arab-Israeli relations, and Sadat and Begin even received the 1978 Nobel Peace Prize in what appeared to be a sign of things to come.

However, in the 1980s these peace agreements were persistently breached and in some cases even completely broken. By 1982, the Israeli military launched a strategic military operation in Southern Lebanon to attack and remove PLO forces encamped in the region. The operation defied international peace treaties with the UN general assembly years earlier recognizing the PLO as a representative organization for the Palestinian people and even granted the PLO the right to participate in deliberations on Palestine (James 1983, 613). The conflict in Southern Lebanon continued to escalate and in September of 1982 Lebanese soldiers massacred Palestinian and Lebanese Shiite civilians living in the Sabra and Shatila refugee camps (al-Hout 2004, 272).

Although just a few years earlier international officials celebrated and awarded Israeli officials with the Nobel Peace Prize, by the 1980s UN officials were investigating Israeli officials for their role in the genocide of Palestinian and Lebanese civilians. The UN general assembly castigated Israel for their negligence and breach in their international peace negotiations. Israel increasingly proved to be an unreliable ally in the region who pioneered international peace treaties while simultaneously and contradictorily jeopardizing the entire peace process.

Sabra embodies this complicated understanding of Israel's role in international politics. Like the modern Israeli state, Sabra sometimes puts aside her differences and works collaboratively together with American and Arab peace keepers to fight global injustice. In *Contest of Champions* #2, the Arabian Knight recognizes Sabra's importance as the two slowly grow to respect each other. Sabra also plays an important role in the formation and maintenance of international peace-keeping agency devoted to bringing together superheroes and mutants to redress international conflicts, such as the X-Men and SHIELD. In the case of Operation Zero Tolerance, Sabra enables SHIELD and the X-Men to stop the army of Prime Sentinels hunting mutants around the globe (*X-Men II* #69). Sabra's commitment to international peace-keeping even forces her to break her commitment to Mossad as she decides to hand over secret intelligence that Mossad has gathered about the X-Men to Professor Xavier (*X Men II* #67).

However, her cooperation with international peace keepers and organizations such as SHIELD and the X-Men remains limited with her vulnerability to mind manipulation and commitment to Mossad impeding her capability to fully commit herself to international reconciliation. Since she declines membership into both the X-Men and SHIELD, Sabra sporadically surfaces in varying stories. When she does appear, it is typically to gather intelligence on other mutants and superheroes who often express a disinterest and even distrust in her perceived motives.

Despite Sabra's inability to fully commit herself to international peace, she continues to manifest an explicit hope for future reconciliation and peace in the Middle East. She always defers to the counsel of international governing bodies when faced with the threat of regional and international conflicts. In stark contrast to Sabra, Windstorm expresses a very clear pessimism and distrust for the international system. For example, in *Marvel Super-Heroes* #6, Windstorm stages a coup against the Israeli government as they attempt to negotiate with international peace keepers. When she kidnaps the U.S. ambassador's son who has disabilities, Sabra is finally forced to end her creation and strips Windstorm of her powers. In the end, Sabra's commitment to international governance takes precedence over her personal relationships and commitments.

This naïve optimism and belief in international governance's capability to overcome personal evils and national conflicts reflect her American authors' belief in the stability of the international system. In the aftermath of the U.S. military's humiliating defeat in Vietnam, President Carter devoted his presidency to normalizing relations between Communist governments and governments seemingly at odds with U.S. foreign policy (Hargrove 1999, 153). President Carter's faith in the peace process was thus predicated on a certain optimism about the undaunted stability of the international system. In the case of the Israeli-Palestinian conflict, the Carter administration viewed the conflict as a crucial witness test to his foreign policy's efficacy in the Middle East (Terry 1990, 153–55). For the Carter administration, the Camp David Accords ultimately proved that his policy of normalization and calculated strategy of deferring to international governing bodies was effective for protecting human rights and facilitating the peace process in the Middle East (Alam 1992, 76). The Reagan administration did not necessarily defer from this strategy and continued to forge international treaties with states once deemed to be irreconcilable enemies. In the case of the Israeli-Palestinian conflict, President Reagan issued an international peace plan that demanded self-government for Palestinian communities and a cessation of Israeli settlements in Palestinian neighborhoods. In the end, Reagan's treaty prohibited Israel from exercising permanent sovereignty over Gaza and the West Bank and deferred to the peace plan put forth in the UN Security Council Resolution 242.

This optimistic hope in the possibility and even inevitability of reconciliation is also predicated on a liberal American Christian belief in Jewish suffering's redemptive potential. In her first appearance in the comics, Mantlo describes Sabra as enduring a tragic and horrifying loss, the murder of her young son, Jacob. Although Sabra is immensely powerful and can even save those near death, she cannot save her son. Moments after she witnesses her son get on a bus for school, a Palestinian terrorist group randomly selects that bus as their next target. Sabra finds herself completely powerless to stop the attack or save her son and other schoolchildren on the bus. The grief and suffering endured from her son's death drives Sabra's commitment to protecting and facilitating the international peace process.

However, her suffering also simultaneously jeopardizes and threatens her commitment to the peace process. In the *Incredible Hulk II* #256, Sabra's transformative confrontation with the Hulk forces her to reassess how her grief and suffering has transformed her into the very thing she sought to fight and defeat. While she initially jumps to the conclusion that the Hulk is a mindless monster like Goliath and threatening innocent civilians, her initial assumption is flipped on its head when Sabra witnesses the Hulk grieving over the tragic death of the young Palestinian boy, Sahad. Like Sabra's own son, Sahad died in a seemingly senseless and random terrorist attack. As the Hulk weeps over the tragic and senseless loss of Sahad, the Hulk voices aloud to the reader that the young Arab boy died "because of what some holy books had to say." In response to the Hulk's conclusion, Sabra confirms to the reader that the young Palestinian boy's senseless murder reminds her of her son Jacob's tragic death and acknowledges that she is not only culpable in his death but that she has become a monster.

This transformative confrontation between the Hulk and Sabra might blame the Israeli-Palestinian conflict on senseless religious squabbles, but it also implicates Israeli Jews in the ongoing conflict and death of innocent Palestinian civilians. For Mantlo, Israeli Jews' grief and suffering has not transformed them into heroes but has instead turned them into the very monsters that they once sought to eradicate from the world. This representation of the conflict might initially invert the reader's expectations and critique suffering's redemptive potential, but the confrontation ultimately ends with Sabra recognizing her culpability and role in Palestinian suffering. Sabra's suffering thus ultimately enables her to recognize that she is as culpable for the ongoing violence and fulfills a redemptive character arc.

Unlike Sabra, Windstorm is unwilling to allow her suffering to transform her into a better person. She instead prefers to exist as a monster who is unwilling to evaluate how she has become the cause of others' suffering and grief. While the reader might expect Windstorm to express gratitude for Sabra's life-saving efforts, Windstorm instead rejects her savior and goes on to start a terrorist organization committed to destroying the entire Israeli-Palestinian peace process (*Marvel Super-Heroes* II #6/4). In the end, Sabra's commitment to saving a suffering drug addict ultimately leads to the creation of a super-villain. The reader is never told why Windstorm turned to drugs and found herself dying on the streets of Tel Aviv. However, it can be inferred that Windstorm endured some sort of trauma in her past. As Sabra's creation, Windstorm perhaps represents what Sabra could become if she refuses to reconcile with her past and evaluate her culpability in Palestinian suffering.

This emphasis on suffering's potential to transform Sabra is again heightened with comic book authors' use of the Mourner's Kaddish. The Mourner's Kaddish is a traditional Jewish prayer used in burial rituals. The Book of Job serves as the prayer's central inspiration with the prayer's final quotation, "May the One who creates harmony on high, bring peace to us and to all Israel," lifted directly from Job 25:2 (Diamant 2007, 20). In the Book of Job, this final quotation refers to the possibility that Job's tragedy can ultimately be "transformed into a hard-won blessing" (Diamant 2007, 20). The prayer thus emphasizes the transformative potential of suffering, promising mourners that their grief over the loss of a loved will one day become a blessing. Moreover, the Mourner's Kaddish also calls upon those who mourn to forgive themselves and the dead with the demand to forgive a central aspect of the prayer's emphasis on suffering's redemptive potential (McLoughlin 2006, 4).

This emphasis on suffering's redemptive potential ultimately provides an important window into the processes by which Sabra's American authors were trying to make sense of Jewish suffering. In the aftermath of the Holocaust, American Christian theologians increasingly tried to make sense of Christendom's historical failure to protect Jewish communities and even contribute to Jewish suffering. Some Christian theologians chose to apply a Christian framework on the Holocaust and interpret the suffering of Jews during the Holocaust as redemptive (Buhring 2008, 101). If the suffering of Jews during the Holocaust was not in fact redemptive, then what purpose could it possibly serve? Some Christian theologians argued further that the suffering Jews endured during the Holocaust enabled Jewish communities to become like early Christian martyrs and cultivate the "divine quality of self-giving love" (Raphael 2003, 12). For American Christian theologians, the application of a redemptive framework to the Holocaust ultimately redressed the problem of Jewish suffering in Christian theology (Haynes 1994).

Sabra's American authors apply a similar theological framework to Sabra's tragic past. Typifying the suffering of Jewish communities in the aftermath of the Holocaust, the horrific murder of Sabra's son ultimately fosters her commitment to protect and defend the Israeli state. However, Mantlo also subtly critiques this framework and represents her suffering as obscuring her ability to fully recognize Palestinian suffering. Mantlo's critique demonstrates how liberal Americans in the 1980s were beginning to critically assess Israeli

Jews' role in the Israeli-Palestinian conflict and trying to imagine a framework of peace that assigned culpability to the Israeli state.

Although Mantlo critiques a simplistic framework for redemption, Sabra nevertheless reconciles with her past and ends up reinforcing the assumption that Jewish suffering is inherently redemptive. This belief in redemption ultimately ushers in a theology of peace that promotes the assumption that reconciliation between Israeli Jews and Palestinians requires a process of forgiveness, repentance, and justice. This theology of peace is deeply reminiscent of global political theologies of reconciliation.

By the late 1970s and early 1980s, Christian theologians were increasingly reinterpreting the theological concept of reconciliation and applying it to global political conflict zones, including Vietnam, Northern Ireland, Korea, Palestine, and South Africa. Reconciliation theology was unique in that it reassessed theology's political significance and the processes by which certain theological concepts could influence historical and political conditions on the ground in conflict zones. This emphasis on the historical and political in turn reassessed the conditions and experiences of the oppressed and how the oppressed and oppressor could ultimately achieve some form of reconciliation.

In the case of South Africa, Desmond Tutu and Nelson Mandela were pioneering new strategies to facilitate truth and reconciliation between black and white South Africans. By the early 1980s, global news coverage of the struggle over apartheid in South Africa rapidly transformed Desmond Tutu into a global icon and household name with Tutu awarded the Nobel Peace Prize in 1984. Tutu's reconciliation theology remained grounded in the African theological concept of Ubuntu. Popularizing this local African tradition to Western audiences, Tutu described Ubuntu as the process whereby oppressor and oppressed can facilitate interracial reconciliation in South African society (Tutu 1999, 162). However, reconciliation is not merely about the oppressed forgiving their oppressor or the oppressor trying to spin what Tutu calls an "exculpatory self-justifying tale" (Tutu 1999, 163). Rather, reconciliation requires that the oppressor recognize the hurt and pain that they have caused to others and repent for that injustice. According to Tutu, Ubuntu is the central core of being human, because it allows human beings to "belong to a community and achieve a social harmony which is the essence of community" (Waldmeir 1998, 254). Without forgiveness, the desire for revenge threatens to undermine a community's harmony and thus harms both the oppressed and oppressor.

This concept has in turn been applied to varying conflict zones, including Israel-Palestine. For example, Donald Shriver in the late 1970s was trying to facilitate a theology of reconciliation that could reconcile Israelis and Palestinians. For Shriver, reconciliation required that Israelis confront the collective shame of their nation's true history. Shriver uses the example of an Israeli woman that fled rising anti-Semitism in Eastern Europe along with her family to seek refuge in Israel. Although she had always believed that her home in Israel was voluntarily abandoned by Palestinian families in the aftermath of 1948, decades later, when the Palestinian family that once owned the home revealed that Israeli soldiers forcibly removed them from the home, she felt shame and disgust over her nation's true history (Shriver 2008, 164–65). In the woman's own words, "I didn't stop loving my country, because of that, but my love lost its innocence" (Shriver 2008, 166). According to Shriver, this capacity to recognize one's true national history and repent for this shameful past was the key to facilitating an authentic process of reconciliation between Israelis and Palestinians.

Sabra's transformative encounter with the Hulk seems to typify this process of reconciliation. Like Israeli Jews or white South Africans facing their nation's shameful history, Sabra realizes that she is a monster who is responsible for the death and suffering of young Palestinian children, such as Sahad. The image of the young dead Palestinian boy in turn reminds Sabra of her own son as she realizes that her desire for revenge and anger over her tragedy has caused her to facilitate even more violence and tragedy. Representative of Jewish suffering in the aftermath of the Holocaust, Sabra's process of reconciliation suggests that Israeli Jews cannot allow their tragic past and suffering to transform them into monsters who are incapable of understanding the experiences of Palestinian communities. Reconciliation between Arabs and Israeli Jews is thus represented as a process whereby Israeli Jews unmask their pride and shame.

Sabra's process of reconciliation is also imbued with messianic imagery and tropes as her American authors apply clear parallels between her struggle and that of other messianic characters in Jewish and Christian theology, including both King David and Christ. Wearing the messianic star of David across her chest, Sabra facilitates truth and reconciliation not necessarily through her physical strength but instead successfully facilitates truth by acknowledging her own weaknesses and personal failings. Rather than represent her physical strength as her greatest asset, her authors instead invert the reader's expectations and represent her physical strength as in fact her greatest weakness. Sabra's capacity to recognize her weakness and repent for her past crimes while also forgiving Arab communities for the murder of her son ultimately allows her to resolve conflicts and facilitate peace.

Sabra's character draws the reader to an alternative eschatology to the one espoused by white evangelical Christians such as Hal Lindsey in his wildly popular novel *Late Great Planet Earth*. Published in 1970, the *Late Great Planet Earth* also paints a world where Jewish suffering allows for the possibility of redemption. But this world is imagined as one prepared for Christ's return. While Jews will have regained the opportunity to repent for their sins to Christ, others, including Muslims, are painted as eternally damned. The novel mentions Islam only once in response to Egypt's Nasser proclaiming "Our Basic Aim will be to Destroy Israel" (Lindsey 1970, 72), and explicitly ignores Palestinians and other Arabs all together. Sabra's American authors differ sharply from Christian millenarian novelists such as Lindsey in imagining a redemptive future that includes Palestinians and other Arab communities. While they mention Palestinians and Arabs, however, they fail to offer them a voice. For example, the young Arab boy Sahad does not even speak to Sabra and remains mute as Sabra confronts her culpability in his death. When Arab characters are finally given opportunities to speak and engage with Sabra, they usually reject any opportunity for real engagement with the Israeli Jewish superhero. The relationship between Sabra and the Arabian Knight remains superficial at best as the two resort to bickering and the Arabian Knight argues that Sabra belongs in the home where she can fulfill her prescribed social roles as wife and mother (*Contest of Champions* #2).

Palestinian leaders are also completely absent from Sabra's story. This complete dearth of Palestinian leaders from her story renders few if any roles for Palestinians. The only roles typically allotted to Palestinians involve being either a defenseless child or evil terrorist killing innocent children. Palestinian characters are consequently not imbued with any agency in Sabra's story. The absence of Palestinian voices renders this political theology of reconciliation devoid of an authentic Palestinian perspective. Her American authors consequently create their reconciliation theology from their own limited racial, national, and religious perspective. Furthermore, Mantlo's critical assessment of Israel's contribution to the Israeli-Palestinian conflict is devoid of any Palestinian voices or any Arab perspective on the conflict.

Although Sabra's story was replete with many flaws, including the use of racist stereotypes about Arab communities, her authors tried to imagine that peace was in fact possible for Israelis and Palestinians. Living in the aftermath of the Camp David Accords, Mantlo created the character of Sabra in a historical era in which the United Nations and international law agencies seemed to be ushering in a new era of peace and reconciliation between Israelis and Palestinians. The work of political activists and theologians in South Africa and Northern Ireland further proved that reconciliation was possible if only leaders facilitated a process of forgiveness and repentance between oppressors and oppressed. Sabra's story thus serves as a testament to Americans' faith in the international system's capability to advance global peace.

However, decades after Sabra first appeared in the *Incredible Hulk II* series, she suddenly disappeared as a prominent character in the Marvel Universe. Although Marvel authors attempted to reimagine the character in *Astonishing Tales II* #6 which was released in 2009, this reimagining of the character politically sanitized her story. The tragic death of her son Jacob in a terrorist attack was removed from her story and replaced with a story about her father's sacrificial death in a Hydra-directed plot to kidnap her. This reimagining of the character contains absolutely no reference to Sabra's ongoing struggle to forgive and reconcile with her Arab neighbors nor to her internal struggle to redress her monstrous impulses. Rather than focus on Sabra's relationships to Arab communities and other Arab characters, her authors are more concerned with her relationship to the fictional global terrorist organization Hydra.

More than a decade has passed since this final appearance of the character in 2009. If her continued absence from the Marvel Universe is any indication of Americans' attitudes about the Israeli-Palestinian conflict, American authors cannot even imagine that peace is still possible between Israelis and Palestinians today. As Sabra's memory and legacy continues to dissipate, any hope of a peaceful and just resolution to the Israeli-Palestinian conflict also continues to fade with it. Can Marvel authors reimagine the character to redress the Israeli-Palestinian conflict's current political circumstances? Could this reimagining of the character incorporate the diverse experiences and perspectives of Palestinian communities? Only the future will tell if Marvel authors will one day reimagine how the dynamic and multifaceted character of Sabra could once again serve as a poignant reminder to Marvel's growing global audience that reconciliation is always possible.

Chapter Fourteen

Modern Re-Enchantment and *Dr. Strange*

Pentecostal Analogies, the Spirit of the Multiverse, and the Play on Time and Eternity

Andrew D. Thrasher

Can science answer all the questions of the cosmos? Many may assume, whether explicitly or implicitly, that science can and will reveal all truth. By its location within the historical paradigms of the modern scientific disenchantment from a pre-modern enchanted worldview, *Dr. Strange* presents to us the limits of science and a cultural reflection of modern re-enchantment.[1] The character of Dr. Strange reflects a playful and imaginative process of combining both the modern disenchantment from religion and the progress of science with the late-modern process of re-enchantment. *Dr. Strange* develops an imaginative portrayal of late-modern spirituality that re-enchants modernity by playing with notions of time, eternity, science, and nihilism. *Dr. Strange* "plays" with late-modern conceptions of spirituality by creating new imaginative forms of conceiving and imagining reality. This chapter argues that the play of modern re-enchantment in *Dr. Strange* also highlights theological analogies by leaning on the thought of Augustine and the work of Pentecostal scholars James K. A. Smith and Wolfgang Vondey.

Analyzing the mystical and spiritual nature of the multiverse in *Dr. Strange* develops a late-modern spirituality open to the experience of transcendence as an imaginative portrayal of theological re-enchantment. When viewed in light of Tone Svetelj's synopsis of Charles Taylor's analysis and diagnosis of modernity, *Dr. Strange* embodies not a naive belief in transcendence characteristic of pre-modern religiosity but rather a re-enchantment of modern sensibilities (Svetelj 2012, 394–424). In turn *Dr. Strange* represents residual effects of the modern ideal of progress in medicine and reason that re-enchants the modern via the mystical arts. By creating a Pentecostal analogy on the notion of "spirit" and "play" in the mystic arts, and a modern mechanistic view of science and instrumental reason that progresses via the supernatural as an example of modern re-enchantment, I will argue that *Dr. Strange* embodies the cultural reflection of the resurgence of spirituality that leaps beyond the modern bounds of science and reason to reflect a late-modern spirituality that yet remains paradoxically modern.

The final section of this chapter addresses the relationship between time and eternity and compares and contrasts Kaecilius' nihilistic understanding of Dormammu and the Dark Dimension with Augustine's notion of time as participating in the fullness of eternity. If *Dr. Strange* offers an example of our late-modern imaginary—how we conceive, perceive, and imagine ourselves, society, and culture through the various stories and myths that shape who we are and what we believe about ourselves—it demonstrates through Kaecilius a nihilistic embrace of eternal nothingness beyond time as a source of liberation from time. But underlying it is a logic of nihilism reflected in late-modern culture that realizes that as we embrace a nothingness beyond time, we are embracing our own negation. The embrace of eternal nothingness implies the negation of time and meaning as it is consumed by Dormammu and the Dark Dimension. Contra Kaecilius, an Augustinian perspective on time and eternity shows how time participates in eternity in such a way that affirms time's meaning and significance because it participates in God.

DR. STRANGE AS SECULAR HUMANIST

At the heart of modernity is the efficient role of instrumental reason guided by a mechanistic conception of the cosmos and governed by the scientific method in uncovering, re-ordering, and controlling the natural world. Modernity is marked by a certain naturalism, a certain understanding of the role of reason, and a certain methodology that uncovers the laws of the natural world in a way that progressively improves human life, society, and culture. If what marks modernity is the instrumental role of scientific reason, it is undergirded by a progressive view of nature and a positive view of human dignity. The modern progressive view of nature sees the world as ordered by natural mechanistic laws that are teleologically ordered to a certain end. This end goal (*telos*) is achieved by the use of instrumental reason in producing the means to the desired ends. Tied to the natural world, humans must act according to the use of instrumental reason in such a way that protects and respects human dignity as inherently ordered to human flourishing. Between a progressive view of the natural world and a positive appraisal of human dignity is the goal for bettering the conditions for human life.

This describes what Charles Taylor calls the "secular/exclusive humanist," one of the four options in which moderns may find themselves (Taylor 2007, 636–37).[2] The mark of the secular humanist is someone who is autonomous and buffered against the supernatural, creating a buffer between him/herself and the supernatural in such a way that a boundary is established and ruled by natural laws and the efficiency of scientific instrumental reason. Thus, Charles Taylor's buffered self of the secular humanist not only sees himself as invulnerable from the supernatural world's ability to affect him, becoming the master of himself, but the buffered invulnerable self is also buffered to the natural world as an autonomous agent concerned with human flourishing (Taylor 1989, 143–76; Taylor 2007, 159–211, 303–9; Taylor 2011, 220; Smith 2014, 64). Thus modernity understands itself as fundamentally natural, and creates an unbridgeable dualism between the natural and the supernatural. This naturalism, devoid of its relation or interaction with the supernatural, reduces its self-understanding to the realm of the natural world, governed by scientific rationality and instrumental reason in efficiently uncovering the laws of the natural world for the betterment of humanity.

Dr. Strange personifies this modern sensibility of the secular humanist, who buffers himself from the effects of the supernatural and reduces his conception of the world and its possibilities to pure naturalism. Dr. Strange's naturalism is one that not only discounts the supernatural, but reduces the natural to the physical functions of the mind and body. For Dr. Strange, the Hippocratic Oath represents his naturalism: to save human life with the help of medicine, science, and reason.

But while the medical knowledge and skill of Dr. Stephen Strange symbolizes the heights of secular humanism, his ego and pride reflects the lowest of secular humanism. Dr. Strange's ego and showy pride not only lead to his downfall through a tragic accident where he loses the use of his hands through severe nerve damage, but ultimately also to his redemption. At the limits of medicine and science, Dr. Strange comes to the brink of despair, cynicism, and lost hope. But when Dr. Strange is exposed to the mystic arts, the strangeness of manipulating time, space, mind, and reality, a gap is filled, and he must re-orient his understanding of reality. No longer is reality reduced to the physical and natural, but Dr. Strange begins the strange and fascinating exploration into the supernatural nature of the multiverse. Underlying this multiverse is an enchanted naturalism that represents theological analogies with Pentecostalism.

PENTECOSTAL ANALOGIES

Pentecostalism offers a helpful analogy for understanding *Dr. Strange* and the idea of modern re-enchantment. *Dr. Strange* offers an imaginative portrayal of Pentecostalism's notion of an enchanted naturalism as developed by James K. A. Smith, while also developing a Pentecostal/scientific concept of "spirit" developed by Wolfgang Vondey. Thus the mark of modern re-enchantment in *Dr. Strange* is characterized by two forms of Pentecostalism where the natural world is seen as inherently enchanted by the supernatural and where there is a certain scientific spirit to the cosmos that orders the natural world to its completion in the supernatural. The following unpacks the *telos* (end goal) of nature, James K. A. Smith's understanding of an enchanted naturalism, and Wolfgang Vondey's analysis of the "spirit" in Isaac Newton and Albert Einstein. After these analyses, the "spirit" of the multiverse is examined as an understanding of the supernatural in *Dr. Strange*.

Enchanted Naturalism: Pentecostal Analogy #1

The modern conception of nature is one that eschews the possibility of the supernatural's interaction and intervention with the natural world. In the science vs. theology debate, James K. A. Smith offers a distinctive Pentecostal ontological vision which sees science and theology as not only compatible, but one in which the supernatural constantly charges the natural world in what he calls an enchanted naturalism. Smith highlights that for most moderns the notion of the supernatural intervening into the natural word is impossible insofar as it defies the laws of nature (Smith 2010, 89–99). Within this mechanistic view of the universe a deistic divine clockmaker establishes ordered natural laws that govern the natural order of the cosmos.

Within the modern deistic view of the universe, the natural world has inherent and intrinsic laws that govern the possibilities within the natural world, and anything that defies or suspends them is, quite bluntly, *not possible*. In this sense, the modern conception of nature not only disdains the possibility of the supernatural interacting in the natural world, but views the supernatural as irrelevant to the natural world and unreachable. But, as Smith argues, if the natural world is always already enchanted, participating in the supernatural because the supernatural is implicit within nature, then the interface between the natural and the supernatural is not at odds. Rather the natural world is constantly marked by the presence of the spirit of the supernatural. By denying the autonomy of nature and seeing it as participating in the supernatural, Smith argues that a Pentecostal enchanted naturalism views nature as "primed" for the spirit of the supernatural (Smith 2010, 99–103).

Dr. Strange holds similar views of nature. Dr. Strange originally saw nature as autonomous and governed by science and reason. However, after his exposure to the mystic arts, he adopted a view of nature as being shaped and charged by the spirit of the multiverse. There is also the sense that the natural world finds its progressive completion in the supernatural. There is a paradox in *Dr. Strange*: the modern progressive view of nature as governed by mechanistic natural laws is combined with an enchanted naturalism where nature is infused with the spirit of the multiverse. An enchanted naturalism implies that the natural world is not all there is. Rather the natural world is already charged by the supernatural in such a way that the natural world is deepened by the supernatural where the "mind expands, the spirit elevates, and the body heals" through its participation in the spirit of the multiverse through the mystic arts.

The Spirit of Science: Pentecostal Analogy #2

A second Pentecostal analogy builds on the work of Wolfgang Vondey and connects the intersection between enchanted naturalism and a spirit of nature. Vondey's work on understanding the potential intersection of modern physics and Pentecostal practice leads him to engagement with Newton and Einstein where he unpacks their modern notions of "spirit"—Einstein's and Newton's understanding of "spirit" highlights panentheistic views of a rational spirit or principle ordering the cosmos. For Newton, this "spirit" is distinctively mechanistic and a universal principle and cohesive force that serves a mediatorial role between time and space, ordering it as an intermediate agent in ordering creation to God (Vondey 2010b, 82). For Einstein, the role of the spirit adapts to twentieth-century scientific knowledge, where this spirit is the universal principle rationally ordering the universe, ordering the symmetry of the space-time continuum (Vondey 2010b, 83). According to Vondey, for these two physicists, the concept of spirit offers implications for understanding the physical universe (Vondey 2010b, 84). In this sense, the modern development of physics in Newton and Einstein provides tangible implications in which the natural world is ordered by spirit in a way that is understandable and linked to the supernatural.

The notion of the spirit translates into *Dr. Strange* in such a way that not only is the natural world enchanted or "en-spirited" but that there is a rational principle ordering it to its completion in the spiritual dimensions of the multiverse. In *Dr. Strange* not only do the mystic arts allow one to manipulate the natural world, but they do so in a way that allows one to reshape the natural world through tapping into the spirit of the multiverse. By both understanding the spirit of the multiverse and tapping into its power, *Dr. Strange* re-enchants the natural world supernaturally, shaping it toward its progressive completion.

Modern Re-Enchantment: Mystic Arts and the *Telos* of Nature

In *Dr. Strange*, the sense of modernity is one bound by progressive scientific and medicinal advancement through the use of instrumental efficient reason and scientific rationality. Surprisingly, Dr. Strange, even when he is confronted with the supernatural, remains quite modern in his understanding of the natural world as mechanistically ordered. Between the pre-modern teleological understanding of the cosmos as finding its completion in Christ and the modern mechanistic conception of the cosmos as no longer bound to a cosmic teleology that finds its completion in the supernatural, we find Dr. Strange somewhere between the two in the conception of medicine as potentially finding its actual *telos* through the supernatural. Within the comics, Dr. Strange sees the natural world and especially medicine as progressive. Dr. Strange sees the supernatural as the progressive end of medicine and science where they will eventually find their completion and actualization in a universal cure (Vaughan 2007).

In *Dr. Strange*, the natural world finds its completion via the supernatural in the spirit of the multiverse and the mystic arts. In *Dr. Strange*, the potential of medicine, science, and reason may be actualized via the supernatural. In the comic *Dr. Strange: The Oath*, Wong is diagnosed with terminal cancer and Dr. Strange seeks to find a universal cure in the multiverse. The comic describes the universal cure progressively in such a way to state that medicine, even without the supernatural, will find a universal cure through scientific and medicinal research (Vaughan 2007). But while the supernatural charges the natural world, it also actualizes the natural world's potential in progressively completing it. The modern progressive view of nature in *Dr. Strange* implies that though nature is enchanted, the *telos* of nature will be naturally completed in its own time through scientific development: the universal cure Dr. Strange finds in the multiverse implies that the *telos* of medicine will come about naturally through the progressive development of scientific and medicinal research. While the supernatural seems unnecessary or irrelevant in this context, for Dr. Strange medicine has a progressive *telos* it will naturally achieve. But the reality of finding a universal cure in the multiverse implies that the supernatural has already actualized the natural ends of medicine. The supernatural and mystic arts are a way of actualizing the natural world's progressive potential.

DR. STRANGE AND THE SPIRIT OF THE MULTIVERSE

The following describes a "theology of the multiverse" by articulating four central theological or spiritual themes that mark the conception of the cosmos in *Dr. Strange*. These four themes are: a) the spirit of the multiverse; b) the mirror dimension; c) the natural law or space-time continuum; and d) Dormammu and the Dark Dimension. Undergirding these four themes is the preceding analysis of modern re-enchantment and Pentecostal analogies. As such, an enchanted naturalism and the *telos* and spirit of nature is assumed and further developed below in the context of *Dr. Strange.*

The Spirit of the Multiverse

Contra our understanding of reality, the Marvel Universe depicts the cosmos not as a *uni*verse, but rather as a *multi*verse. Within this conception of the cosmos not only are there multiple dimensions *to* reality, implying layers to understanding the complexity of reality, but also multiple dimensions *of* reality. An enchanted naturalism thus becomes more complex in the schema of a multiverse. That is, not only is the natural world en-spirited by a supernatural dimension, but there are multiple supernatural dimensions and layers to our understanding of the spirit of the multiverse.

The spirit of the multiverse, then, is not only multiple in its possibilities of ordering the natural world, but the spiritual dimensions in and to this multiverse can affect the natural world in ways that bend and re-shape time, space, and reality. Within this framework the mystic arts tap into the spiritual dimensions of the multiverse to bend time or space, allowing, for instance, the sorcerers with their sling-rings to move across vast reaches of space. These sorcerers are also tasked to guard and protect the space-time continuum from the darker forces within the multiverse. This is where the mirror dimension comes in, a dimension that reflects the natural world without distorting it.

The Mirror Dimension

Described above, the multiverse implies the multiple dimensions of the cosmos, and how these multiple dimensions may be manipulated and tapped into. The mystic arts provide not only the training in how to manipulate the spirit of the multiverse but provide pathways in which one is able to alter the natural world. Within the Marvel Universe one gets the sense that the multiverse is inhabited by spiritual realities that are far greater and more powerful than one can imagine, but there is also the sense in which the multiverse is something that reflects or mirrors the natural world as we conceive it. It is within this mirror dimension that one is able to manipulate space, time, shape, and form in such a way that one can create an alternate reality that mirrors the physical world of our own universe, while also allowing that world to bend without distorting the natural law of the space-time continuum.

But the mirror dimension is also a space where one can tap more strongly into the powers and spirits of the multiverse. When Dr. Strange and Mordo enter into the mirror dimension and are pursued by Kaecilius and his followers,

Mordo comments that they are stronger there, being able to tap into the powers of the Dark Dimension. Thus, the mirror dimension is a place where the strength of the spirit of the multiverse allows one the ability to alter time, space, form, shape, and reality. In a sense, while the mirror dimension is without the natural world, it mirrors it in such a way that the natural world is reflected in and can be manipulated by tapping into the mystic arts and the spiritual dimensions of the multiverse.

"Playing" with Natural Law

In *Dr. Strange*, the sorcerers are called the guardians of the natural law. When Dr. Strange first uses the Eye of Agamoto to restore the ripped pages that tell how to connect with Dormammu, and he begins to conduct the spell, Wong and others come in and stop him from fulfilling the ritual, commenting that he was breaking the natural law of the space-time continuum. When he becomes the sorcerer supreme, Dr. Strange is called to guard the natural world from the evil powers of the multiverse that seek to destroy the natural world. In "playing" with the natural law by using the Eye of Agamoto, Dr. Strange not only has the ability to distort or alter reality, but he also has the power to save the world from Dormammu by binding him to time.

The space-time continuum or the natural law, as I understand it, is linear and ordered by the laws of the cosmos in such a way that there is a sort of naturalness to time and space that should not be distorted. Through their ability to conduct the mystic arts, however, the sorcerers are able to bend and distort time and space and the mirror dimension is the proper place in which this is allowed to be done. The Eye of Agamoto provides a proper means of bending natural law. While the Infinity Stones embody the elemental laws of the cosmos, they also empower the wielder to alter the element those stones embody. As the Eye of Agamoto holds the time stone, Dr. Strange has the ability to alter or "play" with time, to bind eternal timelessness to time in such a way that the "play" of time allows Dr. Strange to save the natural world from its subversion into the timeless death and decay of the Dark Dimension.

Dormammu and the Dark Dimension

Governing the Dark Dimension of void and timelessness is the world destroyer Dormammu. Dormammu is a being of infinite power and craves the destruction of all worlds—earth most of all. Guarding earth from its destruction by Dormammu are the sorcerers of the mystic arts who guard the sanctums in Hong Kong, London, and New York from destruction. If these sanctums are destroyed, Dormammu will be able to consume this world into the destruction, death, and decay of the Dark Dimension. The Dark Dimension is a void beyond time where death and decay mark all that dwells within it. Kaecilius sees this Dark Dimension as the ultimate end of the natural world, in that time kills everything, and he argues that one must embrace the inevitable void of time. Dr. Strange and the Ancient One, however, see that this embrace of "eternal life is not paradise but torment." For Kaecilius the Dark Dimension implies the return of the many into the one beyond time, the consumption of the natural world by an eternity of death and decay, an embrace of the void beyond time as life everlasting in the void of destruction and timelessness.

DORMAMMU AND AUGUSTINE: PERSPECTIVES ON TIME AND ETERNITY

This final section compares and contrasts two notions of time and eternity in *Dr. Strange* and Augustine. The following contrasts the notion of eternity as void vs. fullness, and the embrace of nihilism vs. participation. It does so by challenging the seemingly late-modern nihilism of Kaecilius' understanding of eternity as the void of time with an Augustinian perspective that sees time as participating in the timefulness of eternity. In a sense, is time voided into the nothingness of the Dark Dimension or is time affirmed to dwell and participate in the eternity of God? Thus below I discuss time and eternity as void vs. fullness to argue against the nihilism of Kaecilius and for an Augustinian perspective on participating in the timefulness of God's eternity.

The Eternal as Void

Kaecilius' embrace of the Dark Dimension reflects what could be called the dark reflection of the logic of nihilism. Conor Cunningham's analysis of the logic of nihilism ties it to the emphasis on non-being in such a way that nothing is affirmed as something because nothing always is, and so late-modern nihilism is merely the realization of creation as nothing. The logic of nihilism entails the voiding of something as nothing, and in the search of affirming nothing as something, we realize that nothing is still nothing and we end in the logical embrace of this nothingness (Cunningham 2002). Kaecilius' embrace of the Dark Dimension is grounded in his nihilistic understanding that time kills everything, and in a sense he is entirely correct. Death is inevitable and time is the law that leads to death. To embrace death is to embrace the nothingness and void of our existence regardless of the life that we live.

In understanding Kaecilius' nihilism we must understand that he conceives of the Dark Dimension not as a place of void to which the dead go but rather as a place of eternal life beyond time. However, the Dark Dimension is not a place of eternal life, but rather a place of eternal death and torment under the rule of Dormammu. If time and death are the enemy, however, according to Kaecilius one must embrace them for there is a sense of liberation in accepting the truth that nothingness is the true character of the natural world. On the opposite end of the spectrum lies an Augustinian perspective on eternity and timefulness that revalues life and the natural world.

Augustine on Time and Eternity

Contrary to Kaecilius, Augustine offers an affirmation of time in its participation in the timefulness of eternity. Augustine's notion of God involves an ontological distinction between God and creation in which God eternally exists prior to creation and time (Augustine 1991, 281). For Augustine, to be created means to be marked by time, in contrast to God who, being uncreated, is not bound by time. The doctrine of God's simplicity or aseity is helpful in understanding how the uncreated creator both affirms time eternally and exists timelessly in eternity while also allowing time its own fullness in its participation in eternity. At the heart of the Christian notion of time and creation is the sense that at all moments of time, God is present. In the Augustinian perspective time participates in God's timelessness insofar as every moment of time is encompassed by the presence of God's eternity. Augustine asks of God's eternity: "that in the Eternal nothing passeth, but the whole is present; whereas no time is all at once present: and that all time past, is driven on by time to come, and all to come followeth upon the past; and all past and to come, is created, and flows out of that which is ever present?" (Augustine 1991, 285).

By understanding time in terms of past, present, and future, Augustine's refining of the concept of time is one wherein the past always leads into the present moment, and the future is anticipated in the present moment in such a way that time is always distended into the present. The past is remembered in the present and the future is anticipated by the present. According to Neville the notion of time's flow "is the actualizing of possibilities and the putting into the past of that actuality" (Neville 1993, 103). In turn, Neville discusses the link between eternal togetherness and temporal togetherness. Temporal togetherness describes the connection between the present moment passing into the past and anticipating the future. Temporal togetherness finds in the present moment a movement forward and backward. The present moves backward into the past, while the forward movement of time anticipates the future. Eternal togetherness implies the infinite possibilities of a future based on present moments and past conditions. Eternal togetherness implies the movement of the past through present into the future, just as future possibilities are based on present and past conditions. For Neville, temporal togetherness participates in eternal togetherness because the present moment anticipates the possibility of the future's actuality. In this sense, eternal togetherness is "the condition for and inclusive of all changes involved in temporal togetherness. Eternity is the condition for and inclusive of time's flow" (Neville 1993, 112). Hence, Neville states:

> Time's flow requires actualizing something that is thus transformed from future possibility to past actuality. Time's flow changes the structure of the future and the content of the past. Time does not flow at a time but through time, through dates that successively are future, present, and past. Time's flow requires the death of the now and the birth of new possibilities. Time does not flow within time but within eternity. (Neville 1993, 119)

From time's participation in the eternal, all that is within time is present to and in eternity. In this notion of eternity, God is present to all time, implying that in his aseity (simplicity) God experiences eternally all moments of time in such a way that time is given life in and through its participation in eternity.

Dr. Strange and the Play on Time and Eternity

Augustine's account of time and eternity provides an analogy to Dormammu and the Dark Dimension. Both Dormammu and Augustine's God are beyond time. But Augustine's God and Dormammu differ in their affirmation or negation of time. Whereas for Augustine, God's eternity encompasses time in the sense that God's eternity is always present, Dormammu's eternity denies time in the sense that a timeless eternity encompasses the negation or voiding of time.

At the end of the film, Dr. Strange has quite a strange idea. If Dormammu is beyond time, what would happen *if he was bound to time*? Dr. Strange enters the Dark Dimension and confronts Dormammu, binding Dormammu to an infinite loop of time until he concedes. Since Dormammu kills Dr. Strange every time he appears in this loop, Dr. Strange embraces the possibility of an eternity of repeatedly dying. Dormammu's frustration is apparent in the film. Never has he experienced time before, and now he is bound in an infinite loop to the same experience eternally until he concedes to Dr. Strange's bargain to save the earth from its consumption into the Dark Dimension. By bending the natural law and "playing" with time, Dr. Strange not only saves the world from its consumption by Dormammu into the Dark Dimension, but he also experiences the possibility of an eternity of dying. What heroism and sacrifice.

Through this action, Dr. Strange binds Dormammu to the experience of time. Dormammu despairs as he realizes his eternity is now bound in time. The theological notion of play is linked in *Dr. Strange* to the quest for actualizing the potential of time in its binding nature to Dormammu and the Dark Dimension. Dormammu, whose intention is to consume all worlds into his timeless and eternal void, must then bargain with Dr. Strange for the salvation of the earth because he could not escape time until he was unbound.

The openness of the multiverse implies the playful interface of time and eternity in such a way that articulates the notion of "play as the connectivity of order, dynamics and indeterminacy, represents the capacity for something new, the creative possibilities of new beginnings, and surprising shifts to different levels of flourishing" (Wariboko 2012, 164). This notion of play implies that in a multiverse, there are multiple possibilities and spiritual dimensions where the natural world is not all there is. Rather the natural world is one reality within the multiverse and an enchanted naturalism implicates the openness of the natural world to the multiverse. The possibility of dynamic interplays and interpenetrations in the multiverse implies an infinity of potential possibilities and multiple supernatural dimensions that may transform the natural world and the space-time continuum. These potentials are thus actualized by the spiritual dimensions of the multiverse in such a way that Dr. Strange's play on time not only altered the natural law and space-time continuum but saved humanity from being consumed by the Dark Dimension.

CONCLUSION

Dr. Strange reflects an interesting play on both the notions of time and eternity, and an enchanted naturalism marked by the spirit of the multiverse. If the natural world is charged with the spirit of the multiverse, not only do we get echoes of Pentecostal analogies that reflect the en-spirited nature of the multiverse, but in the context of time, we also receive an Augustinian analogy that affirms time in the experience of eternity contrasted with Dormammu and the Dark Dimension. At the heart of *Dr. Strange* is a modern re-enchantment that reflects analogously the limits and *telos* of modern science, and yet reflects the heart of late modern nihilism in its embrace of the possibility of eternal nothingness. In this way, Christian theology not only analogously plays with the theology of *Dr. Strange*, but it offers answers that counter the theology of *Dr. Strange*.

Characteristic of fantasy, *Dr. Strange* is a reflection of our cultural imaginary—the cultural narratives and imagined ways of understanding ourselves and existing within our world—and it also "plays" with the spirit of our world, reshaping how we imagine our world in ways that create new imaginative possibilities for our world. It is in the context of "play" that *Dr. Strange* "takes on a central position" of "creative spontaneity and randomness that make possible novelty and surprise. Here, theology is not the dramatic performance of a script in which we find ourselves inevitably involved but a voluntary, and not always determinative, activity that is meaningful within its own imaginative freedom" (Suurmond 1992, 249–50).

Within this context, the power of the imagination in *Dr. Strange* to alter our theological and cultural imaginaries represents a new way of stretching how we conceive of the natural world, time, and eternity in a way that re-enchants the modern conceptions of nature and the supernatural. The imagined world of *Dr. Strange* has the ability to alter and transform our reality by challenging traditional and scientific notions and thereby open us to new ways of imagining our world. Thus the notion of play and the imagination in *Dr. Strange* implies a theological re-scription of our cultural imaginary in ways that re-enchant our late modern scientific sensibilities with an alternate imaginary—that of our cultural fantastic/virtual imagination—in ways that not only ground our imaginaries theologically, but also re-enchants theologically the imagination found within *Dr. Strange* (Vondey 2010a, 46; Vondey 2018).

NOTES

1. For citing the film throughout the chapter, cf Scott Derrickson, *Dr. Strange*. DVD. Directed by Scott Derrickson (Burbank, CA: Walt Disney Studies Motion Pictures, 2016).

2. The other three options according to Taylor are: a) the Neo-nietzschean; b) the expressive individualists; and c) the theistic believer.

Bibliography

COMICS, FILM, AND TELEVISION

Amazing Fantasy #15. 1962. Written by Stan Lee. Illustrated by Steve Ditko. New York: Marvel Comics.

The Amazing Spider-Man #3. 1963. Written by Stan Lee. Illustrated by Steve Ditko. New York: Marvel Comics.

———. #252. 1984. Written by Tom Defalco and Roger Stern. Illustrated by Ron Frenz. New York: Marvel Comics.

———. #253–54. 1984. Written by Tom Defalco. Illustrated by Rick Leonardi. New York: Marvel Comics.

———. #255–59. 1984. Written by Tom Defalco. Illustrated by Ron Frenz. New York: Marvel Comics.

———. #298–300, 315–17. 1988–1989. Written by David Michelinie. Illustrated by Todd McFarlane. New York: Marvel Comics.

———. #330–33, 344, 346–47. 1990–1991. Written by David Michelinie. Illustrated by Erik Larsen. New York: Marvel Comics.

———. #345, 375. 1991, 1993. Written by David Michelinie. Illustrated by Mark Bagley. New York: Marvel Comics.

———. #569. 2008. Written by Dan Slott. Illustrated by John Romita. New York: Marvel Comics.

———. #645. 2010. Written by Mark Waid. Illustrated by Paul Azaceta. New York: Marvel Comics.

———. #648, 671, 700. 2010–2012. Written by Dan Slott. Illustrated by Humberto Ramos. New York: Marvel Comics.

———. #789. 2017. Written by Dan Slott. Illustrated by Stuart Immonen. New York: Marvel Comics.

———. #790. 2017. Written by Dan Slott and Christos Gage. Illustrated by Stuart Immonen. New York: Marvel Comics.

——. #795. 2018. Written by Dan Slott and Christos Gage. Illustrated by Mike Hawthorne. New York: Marvel Comics.

——. #798–800. 2018. Written by Dan Slott. Illustrated by Stuart Immonen. New York: Marvel Comics.

——. #801. 2018. Written by Dan Slott. Illustrated by Marcos Martin. New York: Marvel Comics.

The Amazing Spider-Man (2014) #15. 2015. Written by Dan Slott. Illustrated by Guiseppe Camuncoli. New York: Marvel Comics.

——. #18. 2015. Written by Dan Slott. Illustrated by Humberto Ramos. New York: Marvel Comics.

The Amazing Spider-Man (2015) #1, 4, 12–16, 22. 2015–2016. Written by Dan Slott. Illustrated by Guiseppe Camuncoli. New York: Marvel Comics.

——. #17. 2016. Written by Dan Slott. Illustrated by R. B. Silva. New York: Marvel Comics.

——. #26, 29, 31. 2017. Written by Dan Slott. Illustrated by Stuart Immonen. New York: Marvel Comics.

The Amazing Spider-Man Annual #25. 1991. Written by David Michelinie. Illustrated by Guang Yap et al. New York: Marvel Comics.

The Amazing Spider-Man (2018) Annual #1. 2018. Written by Saladin Ahmed. Illustrated by Garry Brown. New York: Marvel Comics.

The Amazing Spider-Man Presents: Anti-Venom: New Ways to Live #1–3. 2009. Written by Zeb Wells. Illustrated by Paulo Siqueira. New York: Marvel Comics.

The Amazing Spider-Man: Super Special #1. 1995. Written by David Michelinie. Illustrated by Dave Hoover. New York: Marvel Comics.

Ant-Man and the Wasp. 2018. Written by Chris McKenna, Erik Sommers, Paul Rudd, Andrew Barrer, and Gabriel Ferrari. Directed by Peyton Reed. Burbank, CA: Walt Disney Studios.

Astonishing Tales (Vol. 2) #6. 2009. Written by Jonathan Hickman. Illustrated by Rick Pitarra. New York: Marvel Comics.

The Avengers. 2012. Written and directed by Joss Whedon. Burbank, CA: Walt Disney Studios.

Avengers #1. 2012. Written by Jonathan Hickman. Illustrated by Jerome Opeña. New York: Marvel Comics.

——. #31, 34. 2014. Written by Jonathan Hickman. Illustrated by Leinil Francis Yu. New York: Marvel Comics.

——. #37. 2014. Written by Jonathan Hickman. Illustrated by Mike Deodato. New York: Marvel Comics.

——. #44. 2015. Written by Jonathan Hickman. Illustrated by Stefano Caselli and Kev Walker. New York: Marvel Comics.

Avengers: Age of Ultron. 2015. Written and directed by Joss Whedon. Burbank, CA: Walt Disney Studios.

Avengers: Endgame. 2019. Written by Christopher Markus and Stephen McFeeley. Directed by Anthony Russo and Joe Russo. Burbank, CA: Walt Disney Studios.

Avengers: Infinity War. 2018. Written by Christopher Markus and Stephen McFeeley. Directed by Anthony Russo and Joe Russo. Burbank, CA: Walt Disney Studios.

Black Panther. 2018. Written by Ryan Coogler and Joe Robert Cole. Directed by Ryan Coogler. Burbank, CA: Walt Disney Studios.

Captain America: Civil War. 2016. Written by Christopher Markus and Stephen McFeeley. Directed by Anthony Russo and Joe Russo. Burbank, CA: Walt Disney Studios.

Captain America: The Winter Soldier. 2014. Written by Christopher Markus and Stephen McFeeley. Directed by Anthony Russo and Joe Russo. Burbank, CA: Walt Disney Studios.

Contest of Champions #2. 1982. Written by Bill Mantlo, Mark Gruenwald, and Steven Grant. Illustrated by John Romita. New York: Marvel Comics.

Daredevil. "Into the Ring." Season 1, episode 1. Directed by Phil Abraham. Written by Drew Goddard. Netflix. April 10, 2015.

———. "Rabbit in a Snowstorm." Season 1, episode 3. Directed by Adam Kane. Written by Marco Ramirez. Netflix. April 10, 2015.

———. "Stick." Season 1, episode 7. Directed by Brad Turner. Written by Douglas Petrie. Netflix. April 10, 2015.

———. "Speak of the Devil." Season 1, episode 9. Directed by Nelson McCormick. Written by Christos Gage and Ruth Fletcher Gage. Netflix. April 10, 2015.

———. "Nelson v. Murdoch." Season 1, episode 10. Directed by Farren Blackburn. Written by Luke Kalteux. Netflix. April 10, 2015.

———. "The Path of Righteousness." Season 1, episode 11. Directed by Nick Gomez. Written by Steve S. DeKnight and Douglas Petrie. Netflix. April 10, 2015.

———. "Daredevil." Season 1, episode 13. Directed by Steven S. DeKnight. Written by Steven S. DeKnight. Netflix. April 10, 2015.

———. "New York's Finest." Season 2, episode 3. Directed by Marc Jobst. Written by Mark Verheiden. Netflix. March 18, 2016.

———. "Penny and a Dime." Season 2, episode 4. Directed by Peter Hoar. Written by John C. Kelley. Netflix. March 18, 2016.

———. "Kinbaku." Season 2, episode 5. Directed by Floria Sigismondi. Written by Lauren Schmidt Hissrich. Netflix. March 18, 2016.

———. "Regrets Only." Season 2, episode 6. Directed by Andy Goddard. Written by Sneha Koorse. Netflix. March 18, 2016.

———. "Guilty as Sin." Season 2, episode 8. Directed by Michael Uppendahl. Written by Whit Anderson. Netflix. March 18, 2016.

———. ".380." Season 2, episode 11. Directed by Stephen Surjik. Written by Mark Verheiden. Netflix. March 18, 2016.

———. "Resurrection." Season 3, episode 1. Directed by Marc Jobst. Written by Erik Oleson. Netflix. October 19, 2018.

———. "Please." Season 3, episode 2. Directed by Lukas Ettlin. Written by Jim Dunn. Netflix. October 19, 2018.

———. "No Good Deed." Season 3, episode 3. Directed by Jennifer Getzinger. Written by Sonay Hoffman. Netflix. October 19, 2018.

———. "The Devil You Know." Season 3, episode 6. Directed by Stephen Surjik. Written by Dylan Gallagher. Netflix. October 19, 2018.

———. "Aftermath." Season 3, episode 7. Directed by Toa Fraser. Written by Sarah Streicher. Netflix. October 19, 2018.

———. "Upstairs/Downstairs." Season 3, episode 8. Directed by Alex Zakrzewski. Written by Dara Resnik. Netflix. October 19, 2018.

———. "Revelations." Season 3, episode 9. Directed by Jennifer Lynch. Written by Erik Oleson and Sam Ernst. Netflix. October 19, 2018.

———. "Reunion." Season 3, episode 11. Directed by Jet Wilkinson. Written by Jim Dunn and Dara Resnik. Netflix. October 19, 2018.

———. "A New Napkin." Season 3, episode 13. Directed by Sam Miller. Written by Erik Oleson. Netflix. October 19, 2018.

Deadpool's Secret Secret Wars #3. 2015. Written by Cullen Bunn. Illustrated by Matteo Lolli. New York: Marvel Comics.

The Defenders. "The Defenders." Season 1, episode 8. Directed by Farren Blackburn. Written by Lauren Schmidt Hissrich and Marco Ramirez. Netflix. August 18, 2017.

Ditko, Steve, and Stan Lee. 1965. "If Eternity Should Fail!" In *Strange Tales*, Vol. 1, #138. New York: Marvel Comics.

Dr. Strange. 2016. Written and directed by Scott Derrickson. Burbank, CA: Walt Disney Studios.

Dr. Strange: The Oath. 2007. Written by Brian K. Vaughan. Illustrated by Marcos Martin. New York: Marvel Comics.

Excalibur #121. 1998. Written by Ben Raab. Illustrated by Trevor Scott. New York: Marvel Comics.

Fantastic Four #72. 1968. Written by Stan Lee. Illustrated by Jack Kirby. New York: Marvel Comics.

———. #511. 2004. Written by Mark Waid. Illustrated by Mike Wieringo. New York: Marvel Comics.

Fantastic Four Annual #3. 1965. Written by Stan Lee. Illustrated by Jack Kirby. New York: Marvel Comics.

God Loves, Man Kills. 1982. Written by Chris Claremont. Illustrated by Brett Anderson. New York: Marvel Comics.

Guardians of the Galaxy (2013) #21–23. 2015. Written by Brian M. Bendis. Illustrated by Valerio Schiti. New York: Marvel Comics.

Howard the Duck (Vol. 3). 2002. Written by Steve Gerber. Illustrated by Phil Winslade et al. New York: Marvel Comics.

Hulk (2008) #5. 2008. Written by Jeph Loeb. Illustrated by Ed Mcguinness and Chris Giarrusso. New York: Marvel Comics.

Hulk: Let the Battle Begin (Vol. 1) #1. 2010. Written by Jesse Blaze Snider. Illustrated by Steve Kurth. New York: Marvel Comics.

Incredible Hulk #256–57. 1981. Written by Bill Mantlo. Illustrated by Sal Buscema. New York: Marvel Comics.

The Infinity Gauntlet (Vol. 1). 1991. Written by Jim Starlin. Illustrated by George Perez and Ron Lim. New York: Marvel Comics.

The Infinity War. 1992. Written by Jim Starlin. Illustrated by Ron Lim. New York: Marvel Comics.

Iron Man/Captain America: Casualties of War #1. 2006. Written by Christos Gage. Illustrated by Jeremy Haun. New York: Marvel Comics.

Jessica Jones. "AKA Ladies Night." Season 1, episode 1. Directed by S. J. Clarkson. Written by Melissa Rosenberg. Netflix. November 20, 2015.

———. "AKA Crush Syndrome." Season 1, episode 2. Directed by S. J. Clarkson. Written by Micah Schraft. Netflix. November 20, 2015.

———. "AKA It's Called Whiskey." Season 1, episode 3. Directed by David Petrarca. Written by Liz Friedman and Scott Reynolds. Netflix. November 20, 2015.

———. "AKA The Sandwich Saved Me." Season 1, episode 5. Directed by Stephen Surjik. Written by Dana Baratta. Netflix. November 20, 2015.

———. "AKA Ain't We Got Fun." Season 2, episode 8. Directed by Zetna Fuentes. Written by Gabe Fonseca and Jack Kenny. Netflix. March 8, 2018.

———. "AKA Shark in the Bathtub, Monster in the Bed." Season 2, episode 9. Directed by Rosemary Rodriguez. Written by Jenny Klein. Netflix. March 8, 2018.

———. "AKA Three Lives and Counting." Season 2, episode 11. Directed by Jennifer Lynch. Written by Lisa Randolph and Jack Kenny. Netflix. March 8, 2018.

———. "AKA Pray for My Patsy." Season 2, episode 12. Directed by Liz Friedlander. Written by Hilly Hicks Jr. and Raelle Tucker. Netflix. March 8, 2018.

———. "AKA Playland." Season 2, episode 13. Directed by Uta Briesewitz. Written by Melissa Rosenberg. Netflix. March 8, 2018.

Luke Cage. "I Get Physical." Season 2, episode 4. Directed by Salli Richardson-Whitfield. Written by Matthew Lopes. Netflix. June 22, 2018.

———. "On and On." Season 2, episode 7. Directed by Rashaad Ernesto Green. Written by Nicole Mirante Matthews. Netflix. June 22, 2018.

———. "For Pete's Sake." Season 2, episode 9. Directed by Clark Johnson. Written by Matt Owens and Ian Stokes. Netflix. June 22, 2018.

———. "The Main Ingredient." Season 2, episode 10. Directed by Andy Goddard. Written by Written by Akela Cooper. Netflix. June 22, 2018.

———. "They Reminisce Over You." Season 2, episode 13. Directed by Alex Garcia Lopez. Written by Cheo Hodari Coker. Netflix. June 22, 2018.

Marvel Knights: Spider-Man Vol 1 #7. 2004. Written by Mark Millar. Illustrated by Terry Dodson. New York: Marvel Comics.

———. #8. 2005. Written by Mark Millar. Illustrated by Frank Cho. New York: Marvel Comics.

Morrison, Grant. 2015. *The Multiversity Deluxe Edition.* Los Angeles: DC Comics.

New Avengers #1. 2013. Written by Jonathan Hickman. Illustrated by Steve Epting. New York: Marvel Comics.

———. #26. 2014. Written by Jonathan Hickman. Illustrated by Kev Walker. New York: Marvel Comics.

New Warriors #58. 1995. Written by Evan Skolnick. Illustrated by Patrick Zircher. New York: Marvel Comics, 1995.

New X-Men: Childhood's End, Volume 1. 2006. Written by Craig Kyle and Christopher Yost. Illustrated by Mark Brooks. New York: Marvel Comics.

New X-Men: Childhood's End, Volume 2. 2006. Written by Craig Kyle and Christopher Yost. Illustrated by Paco Medina. New York: Marvel Comics.

Secret Wars #8. 1984. Written by Jim Shooter. Illustrated by Mike Zeck. New York: Marvel Comics.

Secret Wars (Vol. 1). 2015–2016. Written by Jonathan Hickman. Illustrated by Esad Ribic. New York: Marvel Comics.

Sensational Spider-Man (Vol. 2) #40. 2007. Written by Roberto Aguirre-Sacasa. Illustrated by Clayton Crain. New York: Marvel Comics.

Smith, Kevin. 2003. "Guardian Devil." In *Daredevil: The Man Without Fear*. Illustrated by Joe Quesada. New York: Marvel Comics.

Spider-Man: Birth of Venom. 2007. Written by Jim Shooter, Roger Stern, Tom DeFalco, John Byrne, Louise Simonson, and David Michelinie. Illustrated by John Byrne, Ron Frenz et al. New York: Marvel Comics.

Spider-Man: Homecoming. 2017. Written by Jonathan Goldstein and John Francis Daley. Directed by Jon Watts. Culver City, CA: Columbia Pictures.

Spider-Man: Venom Returns. 1993. Written by David Michelinie. Illustrated by Erik Larsen. New York: Marvel Comics.

The Superior Spider-Man #1, 4. 2013. Written by Dan Slott. Illustrated by Ryan Stegman. New York: Marvel Comics.

———. #5, 10, 20–21, 30. 2013–2014. Written by Dan Slott. Illustrated by Guiseppe Camuncoli. New York: Marvel Comics.

———. #6–7, 15–16. 2013. Written by Dan Slott. Illustrated by Humberto Ramos. New York: Marvel Comics.

———. #6AU. 2013. Written by Christos Gage. Illustrated by Dexter Soy. New York: Marvel Comics.

———. #22–25. 2013. Written by Dan Slott and Christos Gage. Illustrated by Humberto Ramos. New York: Marvel Comics.

Superman. 1978. Written by Mario Puzo, David Newman, Leslie Newman, and Robert Benton. Directed by Richard Donner. Burbank, CA: Warner Bros. Pictures.

Thanos Annual #1. 2014. Written by Jim Starlin. Illustrated by Ron Lim. New York: Marvel Comics.

Thanos: The Infinity Finale. 2016. Written by Jim Starlin. Illustrated by Ron Lim. New York: Marvel Comics.

Thor. 2011. Written by Ashley Edward Miller, Zack Stentz, and Don Payne. Directed by Kenneth Branagh. Hollywood, CA: Paramount Pictures.

Thor: God of Thunder #6. 2013. Written by Jason Aaron. Illustrated by Butch Guice. New York: Marvel Comics.

Thor: Ragnarok. 2017. Written by Eric Pearson, Craig Kyle, and Christopher L. Yost. Directed by Taika Waititi. Burbank, CA: Walt Disney Studios.

Thor: The Dark World. 2013. Written by Christopher L. Yost, Christopher Markus, and Stephen McFeely. Directed by Alan Taylor. Burbank, CA: Walt Disney Studios.

Troy. 2004. Written by David Benioff. Directed by Wolfgang Petersen. Burbank, CA: Warner Bros.

Ultimates (Vol. 2). 2016. Written by Al Ewing. Illustrated by Kenneth Rocafort et al. New York: Marvel Comics.

Union Jack (2006) #1. 2006. Written by Christos Gage. Illustrated by Mike Perkins. New York: Marvel Comics.

Venom #1–18. 2003–2004. Written by Daniel Way. Illustrated by Francisco Herrera et al. New York: Marvel Comics.

———. #150. 2017. Written by Mike Costa. Illustrated by Tradd Moore. New York: Marvel Comics.

———. #154. 2017. Written by Mike Costa. Illustrated by Paulo Siqueira. New York: Marvel Comics.

Venom (2011) #1–42. 2011–2014. Written by Rick Remender and Cullen Bunn. Illustrated by Tony Moore et al. New York: Marvel Comics.

Venom (2016) #1–6. 2016–2017. Written by Mike Costa. Illustrated by Gerardo Sandoval. New York: Marvel Comics.

Venom (2018) #1–6. 2018. Written by Donny Cates. Illustrated by Ryan Stegman. New York: Marvel Comics.

Venom: Dark Origin #1–5. 2008. Written by Zeb Wells. Illustrated by Angel Medina. New York: Marvel Comics.

Venom: First Host #1–3. 2018. Written by Mike Costa. Illustrated by Mark Bagley and Ron Lim. New York: Marvel Comics.

Venom: The Hunger #1. 1996. Written by Len Kaminski. Illustrated by Ted Halsted. New York: Marvel Comics.

Venom: Lethal Protector #1–6. 1993. Written by David Michelinie. Illustrated by Mark Bagley and Ron Lim. New York: Marvel Comics.

Venom: Sinner Takes All #3. 1995. Written by Larry Hama. Illustrated by Greg Luzniak. New York: Marvel Comics.

Venom: Space Knight #5–9. 2016. Written by Robbie Thompson. Illustrated by Ariel Olivetti et al. New York: Marvel Comics.

Venom: Super Special #1. 1995. Written by David Michelinie. Illustrated by Kyle Hotz, Mark Bagley, and Kevin West. New York: Marvel Comics.

The Walking Dead. "The Big Scary U." Season 8, episode 5. Directed by Michael E. Satrazemis. Written by Scott M. Gimple, David Leslie Johnson, and Angela Kang. AMC Networks. November 19, 2017.

Warlock and the Infinity Watch #1. 1992. Written by Jim Starlin. Illustrated by Angel Medina. New York: Marvel Comics.

Web of Spider-Man #1. 1985. Written by Louise Simonson. Illustrated by Greg LaRocque. New York: Marvel Comics.

X Men II #67, 69. 1997. Written by Scott Lobdell. Illustrated by Carlos Pacheco. New York: Marvel Comics.

X-Men III #31. 2017. Written by Brian Wood. Illustrated by Jorge Molina. New York: Marvel Comics.

X-treme X-Men, Volume 5: God Loves, Man Kills. 2003. Written by Chris Claremont. Illustrated by Igor Kordey. New York: Marvel Comics.

ACADEMIC

Abelard, Peter. 1980. "Epist. Ad Romanus 2." In *The Moral Philosophy of Peter Abelard*, edited by Paul Williams, 156. Lanham, MD: University Press of America.

Abraham, Kochurani. 2014. "Resistance: A Liberative Key in Feminist Ethics." In *Feminist Catholic Theological Ethics: Conversations in the World Church*, 97–107. Maryknoll: Orbis Books.

Abrams, Bryan. 2018. "The Russo Brothers Say *Avengers: Infinity War* Is a Thanos Movie." *The Credits*, April 11, 2018. https://www.mpaa.org/2018/04/the-russo -brothers-say-avengers-infinity-war-is-a-thanos-movie/.

Abrams, M.H., and Geoffrey Harpham. 2008. "Antihero." In *A Glossary of Literary Terms*, 9th Edition. Boston: Cengage Learning.

Alam, Mohammed B. 1992. "Carter, Camp David and the Issue of Palestine." *Pakistan Horizon* 45 (1): 75–83.

Amaya, Erik. 2018. "5 Reasons Jessica Jones Is the Superhero Everyone Needs Right Now." *Rotten Tomatoes*, March 7, 2018. https://editorial.rottentomatoes.com/ar ticle/jessica-jones-is-the-superhero-everyone-needs-right-now/.

Andolsen, Barbara. 1981. "Agape in Feminist Ethics." *Journal of Religious Ethics* 9, no. 1 (Spring): 69–83.

Andrews, Charlotte Richardson. 2016. "Jessica Jones: The Antihero We Need." *BFI*, last modified April 14, 2016. https://www.bfi.org.uk/news-opinion/sight-sound -magazine/reviews-recommendations/tv/jessica-jones-antihero-we-need.

Anselm. 1969. *Why God Became Man and the Virgin Conception and Original Sin*. Translated by Joseph Colleran. Albany: Magi Books.

Arendt, Hannah. 2006. *Eichman in Jerusalem: A Report on the Banality of Evil*. London: Penguin Classics.

Armstrong, Karen. 2009. *The Case for God*. New York: Alfred A. Knopf.

Arnaudo, Marco. 2010. *The Myth of the Superhero*. Translated by Jamie Richards. Baltimore: Johns Hopkins University Press.

Augustine. 1991. *The Confessions of Saint Augustine*. Translated by Edward Bouverie Pusey. New York: Quality Paperback Book Club.

Bady, Aaron. 2017. "The Trouble With Calling Jessica Jones an 'Antihero.'" *Pacific Standard*, June 14, 2017. https://psmag.com/social-justice/what-you-learn-when -you-binge.

Bahlmann, Andrew R. 2016. *The Mythology of the Superhero*. Jefferson, NC: McFarland and Company.

Ballentine, Debra Scoggins. 2015. *The Conflict Myth and the Biblical Tradition*. Oxford; New York: Oxford University Press.

Barkun, Michael. 1997. *Religion and the Racist Right: The Origins of the Christian Identity Movement*. Revised Edition. Chapel Hill and London: The University of North Carolina Press.

Batnitzky, Leora. 2000. *Idolatry and Representation: The Philosophy of Franz Rosenzweig Reconsidered.* Princeton, NJ: Princeton University Press.

Becker, Amy Julie. 2011. "A Christian Response to Overpopulation." *Christianity Today*, May 25, 2011. https://www.christianitytoday.com/ct/2011/mayweb-only/overpopulation.html.

Bennis, Phyllis. 1997. "The United Nations and Palestine: Partition and Its Aftermath." *Arab Studies Quarterly* 19 (3): 47–76.

Ben Zvi, Ehud. 2011. "General Observations on Ancient Israelite Histories in Their Ancient Contexts." In *Enquire of the Former Age: Ancient Historiography and Writing the History of Israel,* edited by Lester L. Grabbe, 21–39. New York: T & T Clark.

Benjamin, Mara. 2009. *Rosenzweig's Bible: Reinventing Scripture for Jewish Modernity.* Cambridge: Cambridge University Press.

Berry, Wendell. 1987. *Home Economics: Fourteen Essays.* New York: North Point.

Bland, Archie. 2016. "Comic Book Superheroes: The Gods of Modern Mythology." *Guardian*, May 27, 2016. https://www.theguardian.com/books/2016/may/27/comic-book-superheroes-the-gods-of-modern-mythology.

Blenkinsopp, Joseph. 1992. *The Pentateuch.* New York: Doubleday.

Boa, Kenneth. 2004. *Augustine to Freud: What Theologians & Psychologists Tell Us About Human Nature and Why It Matters.* Nashville, TN: B&H Publishing Group.

Breznican, Anthony. 2019. "Avengers: Endgame Directors Defend Controversial Black Widow Scene." *Entertainment Weekly*, May 2, 2019. https://ew.com/movies/2019/05/02/avengers-endgame-directors-black-widow-scene/.

Brock, Rita, and Rebecca Parker. 2008. *Saving Paradise: How Christianity Traded Love of This World for Crucifixion and Empire.* Boston: Beacon Press.

Brueggemann, Walter. 2010. *Genesis: Interpretation.* Louisville, KY: Westminster John Knox Press.

Buhring, K. 2008. *Conceptions of God, Freedom, and Ethics in African American and Jewish Theology.* New York: Palgrave Macmillan.

Burley, Ulysses, III, and Nathan Roberts. 2016. "The Biblical Case for Black Reparations." *The Salt Collective*, September 6, 2016. http://thesaltcollective.org/biblical-case-black-reparations.

Carr, David. 1996. *Reading the Fractures of Genesis: Historical and Literary Approaches.* Louisville, KY: Westminster John Knox Press.

Carroll, Michelle. 2018. "Netflix's 'Jessica Jones' Has a Race Problem, But It's Fixable." *Wear Your Voice*, April 5, 2018. https://wearyourvoicemag.com/culture/netflixs-jessica-jones-race-problem-fixable.

Casselot, Marie-Anne. 2016. "Ecofeminist Echoes in New Materialism?" *PhænEx* 11, no. 1 (Spring/Summer): 73–96.

Castle, Gregory. 2001. *Modernism and the Celtic Revival.* Cambridge: Cambridge University Press.

Catholic Church. 1993. *Catechism of the Catholic Church.* Libreria Editrice Vaticana. http://www.vatican.va/archive/ENG0015/_INDEX.HTM.

Center for Disease Control and Prevention. 2017. "National Intimate Partner and Sexual Violence Survey—State Report." Accessed April 5, 2019. https://www.cdc.gov/violenceprevention/datasources/nisvs/summaryreports.html.

Christensen, Terry. 1987. *Reel Movies: American Political Movies from the Birth of a Nation to Platoon*. Oxford: Basil Blackwell.

Clanton, Dan W., Jr. 2008. "Biblical Interpretation and Christian Domestic Terrorism: The Exegeses of Rev. Michael Bray and Rev. Paul Hill." *SBL Forum*. http://sbl-site.org/publications/article.aspx?articleId=788.

Cloud, John. 2011. "Would You Kill One Person To Save Five? New Research on a Classic Debate." *Time*, December 5, 2011. http://healthland.time.com/2011/12/05/would-you-kill-one-person-to-save-five-new-research-on-a-classic-debate/.

Colbert, Stephen, and Josh Brolin. 2018. "Josh Brolin Reads Trump Tweets as Thanos." *YouTube* video, 11:11. June 20, 2018. https://www.youtube.com/watch?v=d853h-8rsPQ.

Collins, John J. 2005. *Does the Bible Justify Violence?* Facets Series. Minneapolis: Fortress Press.

Cone, James Hal. 1997. *God of the Oppressed*. Maryknoll: Orbis Books.

Copan, Paul, and Kenneth D. Litwak. 2014. *The Gospel in the Marketplace of Ideas: Paul's Mars Hill Experience for Our Pluralistic World*. Downer's Grove, IL: InterVarsity Press.

Crawford, Jackson. 2015. *The Poetic Edda: Stories of the Norse Gods and Heroes*. Indianapolis, IN; Cambridge: Hackett.

Cross, Frank Moore. 1998. *From Epic to Canon: History and Literature in Ancient Israel*. Baltimore, MD: Johns Hopkins University Press.

Cuddon, J.A. 2013. "Anti-Hero." In *A Dictionary of Literary Terms and Literary Theory*, 5th Edition, revised by M.A.R. Habib. West Sussex: Wiley Blackwell.

Cunningham, Conor. 2002. *Genealogy of Nihilism*. New York: Routledge Taylor & Francis Group.

Dalley, Stephanie. 1989. *Myths from Mesopotamia: Creation, the Flood, Gilgamesh, and Others*. Oxford: Oxford University Press.

Daly, Mary. 1985. *Beyond God the Father: Toward a Philosophy of Women's Liberation*. Boston: Beacon Press.

Dark, David. 2005. *The Gospel according to America: A Meditation on a God-blessed, Christ-Haunted Idea*. Louisville: Westminster John Knox Press.

Dawn, Marva J. 2001. *Powers, Weakness, and the Tabernacling of God*. Grand Rapids: Eerdmans.

De Geus, C.H.J. 1976. *The Tribes of Israel*. Studia Semitica Neerlandica 18. Assen: Van Gorcum.

Delio, Ilia. 2015. *The Unbearable Wholeness of Being*. Maryknoll: Orbis Books.

Derry, Ken, Matthew J. Cressler, Jon Ivan Gill, Daniel White Hodge, Stanley Talbert, and Laurel Zwissler. 2015. "Bulletproof Love: Luke Cage (2016) and Religion." *Journal for Religion, Film, and Media* 3, no. 1 (May): 123–55.

Detweiler, Craig, and Barry Taylor. 2003. *A Matrix of Meanings: Finding God in Popular Culture*. Grand Rapids: Baker Academic.

Devereaux, Shaadi. 2015. "Netflix, Uncovering Cycles of Abuse and Chill: Jessica Jones and Domestic Violence." *Model View Culture*, November 25, 2015. https://modelviewculture.com/pieces/netflix-uncovering-cycles-of-abuse-and-chill-jessica-jones-and-domestic-violence.

Diamant, Anita. 2007. *Saying Kaddish: How to Comfort the Dying, Bury the Dead, and Mourn as a Jew*. New York: Knopf Doubleday Publishing Group.

Dickens, Charles. 1911. *A Christmas Carol*. London: Hodder and Soughton.

Dionysius the Areopagite. 1897a. *The Celestial Hierarchy*, in *The Works of Dionysius the Areopagite*. Translated by John Parker, 148–99. London: James Parker and Co.

———. 1897b. *On Divine Names*, in *The Works of Dionysius the Areopagite*. Translated by John Parker, 1–127. London: James Parker and Co.

Doniger, Wendy. 2011. *The Implied Spider: Politics and Theology in Myth*. New York: Columbia University Press.

Douglas, Kelly Brown. 1994. *The Black Christ*. Maryknoll, NY: Orbis Books.

Eagleton, Terry. 2016. *Materialism*. New Haven: Yale University Press.

———. 2019. *Radical Sacrifice*. New Haven: Yale University Press.

Elam, J. Daniel. 2019. "Postcolonial Theory." *Oxford Bibliographies*, January 15, 2019. https://www.oxfordbibliographies.com/view/document/obo-9780190221911/obo-9780190221911-0069.xml.

Elvey, Anne. 2009. "Can There Be a Forgiveness that Makes a Difference Ecologically? An Eco-Materialist Account of Forgiveness as a Freedom (ἄφεσις) in the Gospel of Luke." *Pacific* 22, no. 2 (June): 148–70.

Erickson, Millard J. 1998. *Christian Theology*, Second Edition. Grand Rapids, MI: Baker Academic.

Erskine, Noel Leo. 2001. "The Bible and Reggae: Liberation or Subjugation?" In *The Bible in/and Popular Culture*. Edited by Philip Culbertson and Elaine Wainwright, 97–109. Leiden, The Netherlands: Brill.

Evans, C. Stephen. 2005. "Why Should Superheroes Be Good? Spider-Man, the X-Men, and Kierkegaard's Double Danger." In *Superheroes and Philosophy: Truth, Justice, and the Socratic Way,* edited by Tom Morris and Matt Morris, 161–75. Chicago, IL: Open Court Publishing Co.

Farley, Margaret. 2015. *Changing the Questions: Explorations in Christian Ethics*, edited by Jamie L. Manson. Maryknoll: Orbis Books.

Farneti, Roberto. 2015. *Mimetic Politics: Dyadic Patterns in Global Politics*. East Lansing, MI: Michigan State University Press.

Fawaz, Ramzi. 2016. *The New Mutants: Superheroes and the Radical Imagination of American Comics*. New York and London: New York University Press.

Fingeroth, Danny. 2004. *Superman on the Couch: What Superheroes Really Tell Us about Ourselves and Our Society.* New York: Continuum.

Finkelberg, Margalit. 2005. *Greeks and Pre-Greeks: Aegean Prehistory and Greek Heroic Tradition*. Cambridge; New York: Cambridge University Press.

Frye, Northrop. 1982. *The Great Code: The Bible and Literature*. San Diego: Harcourt Brace.

Geisler, Norman. 2004. *Systematic Theology Vol 3: Sin and Salvation.* Bloomington, MN: Bethany House Publishers.

Getz, Gene A. 2012. *A Biblical Theology of Material Possessions*. Eugene: Wipf and Stock Publishers.

Gilders, William. 2004. *Blood Ritual in the Hebrew Bible: Meaning and Power*. Baltimore: Johns Hopkins University Press.

Gil-White, Francisco. 1999. "How Thick Is Blood? The Plot Thickens. . . . If Ethnic Actors Are Primordialists, What Remains of the Circumstantialist/Primordialist Controversy?" *Ethnic and Racial Studies* 22 (5): 789–820.

Girard, René. 1965. *Deceit, Desire, & the Novel: Self and Other in Literary Structure.* Translated by Yvonne Freccero. Baltimore. The Johns Hopkins University Press.

———. 1977. *Violence and the Sacred.* Translated by Patrick Gregory. Baltimore. The Johns Hopkins University Press.

———. 2010. *Battling to the End: Conversations with Benoît Chantre.* Translated by Mary Baker. East Lansing, MI. Michigan State University Press.

Glatzer, Nahum. 1961. *Franz Rosenzweig: His Life and Thought.* Second Edition. New York: Shocken Books.

Gomme, George Laurence. 1908. *Folklore as an Historical Science.* London: Methuen.

Gordon, Peter Eli. 2003. *Rosenzweig and Heidegger: Between Judaism and German Philosophy.* Berkeley, CA: University of California Press.

Gottwald, Norman. 1979. *The Tribes of Yahweh: A Sociology of the Religion of Liberated Israel, 1250–1050 BCE.* Maryknoll: Orbis Books.

Grimm, Jacob. 1882. *Teutonic Mythology.* Fourth Edition. London: G. Bell and Sons.

Gruenwald, Mark, and Alan Zelenetz. 1982. *Thor Annual #10.* New York: Marvel Comics.

Gunkel, Hermann. 1901. *The Legends of Genesis.* Translated by W.H. Carruth. Handkommentar Zum Alten Testament 1. Chicago: Open Court Publishing.

Han, Angie. 2017. "'Thor: Ragnarok' Is About Colonialism." *Mashable*, November 8, 2017. https://mashable.com/2017/11/08/thor-ragnarok-themes-colonialism/.

Handler, Richard. 2002. "Reinventing the Invention of Culture." *Social Analysis: The International Journal of Social and Cultural Practice* 46 (1): 26–34.

Hargrove, Erwin C. 1999. *Jimmy Carter as President: Leadership and the Politics of the Public Good.* Baton Rouge: Louisiana State University Press.

Haynes, Stephen R. 1994. "Christian Holocaust Theology: A Critical Reassessment." *Journal of the American Academy of Religion* 62 (2): 553–85.

Henrichs, Albert. 2010. "What Is a Greek God?" In *Gods of Ancient Greece: Identities and Transformations*, edited by Jan N. Bremmer, 19–42. Edinburgh: Edinburgh University Press.

Holdier, A. G. 2018. "On Superhero Stories: The Marvel Cinematic Universe as Tolkienesque Fantasy." *Mythlore* 132: 73–88.

Holland, Joshua. 2016. "The Average Black Family Would Need 228 Years to Build the Wealth of a White Family Today." *The Nation*, August 9, 2016. https://www.thenation.com/article/the-average-black-family-would-need-228-years-to-build-the-wealth-of-a-white-family-today.

Hout, Bayan Nuwayhed al-. 2004. *Sabra and Shatila: September 1982.* London: Pluto Press.

Howe, Sean. 2012. *Marvel Comics: The Untold Story.* New York: Harper.

James, Alan. 1983. "Painful Peacekeeping: The United Nations in Lebanon 1978–1982." *International Journal* 38 (4): 613–34.

James, Edward. 2003. "Utopias and Anti-Utopias." In *The Cambridge Companion to Science Fiction*, edited by Edward James and Farah Mendelsohn, 219–29. Cambridge: Cambridge University Press.

Jennings, Willie James. 2010. *The Christian Imagination: Theology and the Origins of Race*. New Haven, CT: Yale University Press.

———. 2017. *Acts*. Louisville, KY: Westminster John Knox Press.

Johnston, William. 1980. "Translator's Preface." In *Silence*, by Shusaku Endo, vii–xviii. New York: Taplinger.

Juergensmeyer, Mark. 2003. *Terror in the Mind of God: The Global Rise of Religious Violence*. Third Edition. Berkeley and Los Angeles: University of California Press.

Kadiroğlu, Murat. 2012. "A Genealogy of Antihero." *Ankara University DCTF Journal*, no. 52: 1–18.

Kaplan, Arie. 2008. *From Krakow to Krypton: Jews and Comic Books*. Philadelphia: The Jewish Publication Society.

Kassam, Ashifa. 2017. "Canada Children's Book Recalled amid Accusations of Whitewashing History." *The Guardian,* October 4, 2017. https://www.theguardian.com/world/2017/oct/04/canada-childrens-book-recalled-whitewashing-history.

Kellner, Douglas. n.d. "Cultural Studies and Ethics." Accessed April 3, 2019. https://pages.gseis.ucla.edu/faculty/kellner/papers/CSETHIC.htm.

Kessler, John. 2006. "Persia's Loyal Yahwists: Power Identity and Ethnicity in Achaemenid Yehud." In *Judah and the Judeans in the Persian Period*, edited by Oded Lipschits and Manfred Oeming, 91–122. Winona Lake, IN: Eisenbrauns.

Kierkegaard, Søren. 1949. *Works of Love.* Translated by David F. Swenson and Lillian Marvin Swenson. Princeton, NJ: Princeton University Press.

Kimball, Charles. 2002. *When Religion Becomes Evil: Five Warning Signs*. San Francisco: HarperSanFrancisco.

Koiv, Mait. 2003. *Ancient Tradition and Early Greek History: The Origins of States in Early Archaic Sparta, Argos and Corinth*. Tallinn: Avita.

Kreeft, Peter. 1989. "Unravelling the Mystery of Weakness and Strength." *Christianity Today* 33: 23–25.

Lackey, Emily. 2015. "'Jessica Jones' Is The Female Antihero We Need, Because Complicated Characters Are Real Characters." *Bustle*, November 20, 2015. https://www.bustle.com/articles/125354-jessica-jones-is-the-female-antihero-we-need-because-complicated-characters-are-real-characters.

Lawrence, John Shelton, and Robert Jewett. 2002. *The Myth of the American Superhero*. Grand Rapids: William B. Eerdmans Publishing Company.

L'Engle, Madeline. 1996. "Foreword." In *A Grief Observed*, by C.S. Lewis, xi–xviii. San Francisco: HarperSanFrancisco.

Lewis, C.S. 1970. "Myth Became Fact." In *The Grand Miracle*, edited by Walter Hooper, 38–42. New York: Ballantine Book.

———. 1996. *A Grief Observed*. San Francisco: HarperSanFrancisco.

———. 2001. *Mere Christianity.* New York: HarperCollins.

Lincoln, Bruce. 1999. *Theorizing Myth: Narrative, Ideology and Scholarship*. Chicago, IL: University of Chicago Press.

Linnekin, Jocelyn. 1991. "Cultural Invention and the Dilemma of Authority." *American Anthropologist* 93 (2): 446–49.

Ma, Stella Y. 2003. "The Christian College Experience and the Development of Spirituality Among Students." *Christian Higher Education* 2, no. 4: 321–39.

MacArthur, John. 2018. "Social Injustice and the Gospel." *Grace to You*, August 13, 2018. https://www.gty.org/library/blog/B180813.

Malešević, Siniša. 2004. *The Sociology of Ethnicity*. London: Sage Publications.

Malkin, Irad. 1994. *Myth and Territory in the Spartan Mediterranean*. Cambridge: Cambridge University Press.

Malthus, Thomas R. 1798. *An Essay on the Principle of Population*. Oxford: Oxford World's Classics.

Marx, Karl, and Frederick Engels. 2010. *Marx & Engels: Collected Works—Volume 3, Karl Marx March 1843–August 1844*. London: Lawrence & Wishart.

Marx, Steven. 1994. "Northrop Frye's Bible." *Journal of the American Academy of Religion* 62 (1): 163–72.

McCutcheon, Russell T. 2000. "Myth." In *Guide to the Study of Religion*, edited by Willi Braun and Russell T. McCutcheon, 190–208. London: Cassell.

McDougall, Joy A. 2011. "A Trinitarian Grammar of Sin." *Modern Theology* 27 (1): 55–71.

McDowell, John. 2007. *The Gospel According to Star Wars: Faith, Hope, and the Force*. Louisville, KY: Westminster John Knox Press.

McLoughlin, Kate. 2006. "Dead Prayer?: The Liturgical and Literary Kaddish." *Studies in American Jewish Literature (1981–)* 25: 4–25.

Mendes-Flohr, Paul. 1991. "Franz Rosenzweig and the Crisis of Historicism." In *Divided Passions: Jewish Intellectuals and the Experience of Modernity*. Detroit: Wayne State University Press.

Milbank, John. 2003. *Being Reconciled: Ontology and Pardon*. London: Routledge.

Mohr, Richard. 1982. "The World-Soul in the Platonic Cosmology." *Illinois Classical Studies* 7: 41–48.

Mojsik, Tomasz. 2011. *Between Tradition and Innovation: Genealogy, Names and the Number of the Muses*. Translated by Marcin Fijak. Warsaw: Akme. Studia Historica.

Moltmann, Jürgen. 1974. *The Crucified God*. Translated by R. A. Wilson and John Bowden. New York: Harper & Row.

Morgan, Silas. 2013. "What Marx Can Teach Christian Theology—and the Church—About Being Christian." *The Other Journal*, no. 22: 2–12.

Mroczek, Eva. 2015. "The Hegemony of the Biblical in the Study of Second Temple Literature." *Journal of Ancient Judaism* 6 (1): 2–35.

———. 2016. *The Literary Imagination in Jewish Antiquity*. Oxford; New York: Oxford University Press.

Myers, Ched. 1997. "A Biblical Vision of Justice." *Priests & People*, May 1997.

Nelson-Pallmeyer, Jack. 2003. *Is Religion Killing Us? Violence in the Bible and the Quran*. Harrisburg, PA: Trinity Press International.

Neville, Robert Cummings. 1993. *Eternity and Time's Flow*. Albany: State University of New York Press.

Noth, Martin. 1930. *Das System der zwölf Stämme Israels*. Stuttgart: Kohlhammer.

———. 1972. *A History of Pentateuchal Traditions*. Translated by B.W. Anderson. Englewood Cliffs, NJ: Prentice Hall.

O'Brien, Elmer. 1964. *The Essential Plotinus*. Cambridge, MA: Harvard University Press.

Ordway, Holly. 2015. "Once Upon a Time: The Enduring Appeal of Fairy Tales." *Christian Research Journal* 38 (5): 50–52.

Oring, Elliott. 1986. "On the Concepts of Folklore." In *Folk Groups and Folklore Genres: An Introduction*, edited by Elliott Oring, 1–22. Logan, UT: Utah State University Press.

Oropeza, B. J. 2005a. "'Behold! The Hero Has Become Like One of Us.' The Perfectly Imperfect Spider-Man." In *The Gospel According to Superheroes: Religion and Pop Culture*, edited by B. J. Oropeza, 127–43. New York: Peter Lang.

———. 2005b. "Introduction: Superhero Myth and the Restoration of Paradise." In *The Gospel According to Superheroes: Religion and Pop Culture*, edited by B.J. Oropeza, 1–24. New York: Peter Lang.

Ortlund, Dane. 2010. "'Power Is Made Perfect in Weakness' (2 Cor. 12:9): A Biblical Theology of Strength through Weakness." *Presbyterion* 36: 86–108.

Packer, J. I. 2013. *Weakness Is the Way.* Wheaton, IL: Crossway.

Patterson, Lee E. 2010. *Kinship Myth in Ancient Greece*. Austin, TX: University of Texas Press.

Peppard, Michael. 2011. *The Son of God in the Roman World: Divine Sonship in Its Social and Political Context*. New York: Oxford University Press.

Perman, Matt. 2006. "Did Jesus Teach Pacifism?" *Desiring God*, January 23, 2006. https://www.desiringgod.org/articles/did-jesus-teach-pacifism.

Perry, Tim. 2005. "Mutants That Are All Too Human: The X-Men, Magneto, and Original Sin." In *The Gospel According to Superheroes: Religion and Popular Culture*, edited by B. J. Oropeza, 171–87. New York: Peter Lang Publishing.

Pojman, Louis, and James Fieser. 2009. *Ethics: Discovering Right and Wrong*. Sixth Edition. Belmont, CA: Wadsworth.

Pollock, Benjamin. 2009. *Franz Rosenzweig and the Systematic Task of Philosophy.* Cambridge: Cambridge University Press.

———. 2014. *Franz Rosenzweig's Conversions: World Redemption and World Denial.* Bloomington and Indianapolis: Indiana University Press.

Proclus. 1816. *Platonic Theology*. Translated by Thomas Taylor as *The Six Books of Proclus*. London: A.J. Valpy.

———. 1971. *The Elements of Theology, A Revised Text with Translation, Introduction and Commentary*. Second Edition. Translated by E.R. Dodds. Oxford: Clarendon Press.

Purcell, Lynnie. 2015. "Jessica Jones and the Path to Heroism." *Den of Geek*, December 28, 2015. https://www.denofgeek.com/us/tv/jessica-jones/251612/jessica-jones-and-the-path-to-heroism.

Quandt, William B. 1986. "Camp David and Peacemaking in the Middle East." *Political Science Quarterly* 101 (3): 357–77.

Raphael, Melissa. 2003. *The Female Face of God in Auschwitz: A Jewish Feminist Theology of the Holocaust*. London: Routledge.

Reader, John. 2017. *Theology and New Materialism: Spaces of Faithful Dissent*. Oxfordshire: Palgrave Macmillan.

"*Record Scratch* *Freeze Frame*." 2016. Know Your Meme. 2016. https://knowyourmeme.com/memes/record-scratch-freeze-frame.

Reynolds, Richard. 1992. *Super Heroes: A Modern Mythology*. Jackson: University Press of Mississippi.

Richards, David Adams. 2009. *God Is: My Search for Faith in a Secular World*. N.p.: Doubleday.

Ricoeur, Paul. 1983. *Time and Narrative*. Translated by Kathleen McLaughlin and David Pellauer. Vol. 1. Chicago: University of Chicago Press.

Rohr, Richard. 1995. "The Three P's." In *Radical Grace*, 18. Cincinnati: St. Anthony Messenger Press.

Romanowski, William D. 2001. *Eyes Wide Open: Looking for God in Popular Culture*. Grand Rapids: Brazos Press.

Roosens, Eugeen E. 1989. *Creating Ethnicity: The Process of Ethnogenesis*. Frontiers of Anthropology 5. Newbury Park, CA: Sage.

Rosenberg, Melissa. 2015. "'Jessica Jones' Creator on the 'Tony Soprano' of Female Superheroes." Interview by David Ehrlich. *Rolling Stone*, November 19, 2015. Online. https://www.rollingstone.com/tv/tv-news/jessica-jones-creator-on-the-tony-soprano-of-female-superheroes-33676/.

———. 2018. "Jessica Jones Creator Melissa Rosenberg on Power and Pitfalls of Female Rage." Interview by Nicole Sperling. *Vanity Fair*, March 21, 2018. https://www.vanityfair.com/hollywood/2018/03/jessica-jones-season-2-netflix-marvel-melissa-rosenberg-krysten-ritter.

Rosenzweig, Franz. 1955. *On Jewish Education*. Edited by Nahum Glatzer. Madison: University of Wisconsin Press.

———. 1971. *The Star of Redemption*. Translated by William Hallo. New York, Chicago, and San Francisco: Holt, Rinehart, and Winston, Inc.

———. 1999. *Understanding the Sick and the Healthy: A View of World, Man, and God*. Edited by Nahum Glatzer. Cambridge, MA: Harvard University Press.

———. 2000a. *NinetyTwo Poems and Hymns of Yehuda Halevi*. Edited by Richard Cohen and translated by Thomas Kovach, Eva Jospe, and Gilya Gerda Schmidt. Albany: State University of New York Press.

———. 2000b. "The New Thinking." In *Philosophical and Theological Writings*, edited by Paul Franks and Michael Morgan, 109–39. Indianapolis, IN: Hackett Publishing Company, Inc.

Roser, Max, Hannah Ritchie, and Esteban Ortiz-Ospina. 2019. "Population Growth." *Our World In Data*. May 2019. https://ourworldindata.org/world-population-growth.

Rothstein, Richard. 2018. *The Color of Law: A Forgotten History of How Our Government Segregated America*. New York: Liveright Publishing Corporation.

Rozsa, Matthew. 2018. "'Avengers: Infinity War': Not Just a Mediocre, Muddled Mess—but Possibly a Dangerous Precedent." *Salon*, April 27, 2018. https://www.salon.com/2018/04/27/the-avengers-infinity-war-not-just-a-mediocre-muddled-mess-but-possibly-a-dangerous-precedent.

Sallust. 1793. *On the Gods and The World*. Translated by Thomas Taylor. London: Edward Jeffrey.

Saunders, Ben. 2011. *Do the God's Wear Capes? Spirituality, Fantasy, and Superheroes.* New York: Continuum.

Schwartz, Regina M. 1997. *The Curse of Cain: The Violent Legacy of Monotheism.* Chicago: University of Chicago Press.

Sela, Avraham. 2000. "The 1973 Arab War Coalition: Aims, Coherence, and Gain-Distribution." In *Revisiting the Yom Kippur War*, edited by P. R. Kumaraswamy, 36–69. New York: Frank Cass Publishers.

Selengut, Charles. 2003. *Sacred Fury: Understanding Religious Violence.* Walnut Creek, CA: AltaMira Press.

Shriver, Donald. 2008. "Forgiveness: A Bridge across Abysses of Revenge." In *Forgiveness & Reconciliation: Public Policy & Conflict Transformation*, edited by Raymond G. Helmick and Rodney Petersen, 151–79. Philadelphia: Templeton Foundation Press.

Slack, Jennifer Daryl, and Laurie Anne Whitt. 1991. "Ethics and Cultural Studies." *Cultural Studies*, edited by Lawrence Grossberg, Cary Nelson, and Paula Treichler, 571–92. New York: Routledge.

Smith, James K. A. 2010. *Thinking in Tongues.* Pentecostal Manifestos 1. Grand Rapids, MI: Eerdmans Publishing Co.

———. 2014. *How (Not) to Be Secular: Reading Charles Taylor.* Grand Rapids: Eerdmans.

Smith, Jonathan Z. 1982. "In Comparison a Magic Still Dwells." In *Imagining Religion: From Babylon to Jonestown*, 19–35. Chicago, IL: University of Chicago Press.

Smith, Travis. 2018. *Superhero Ethics.* West Conshohocken, PA: Templeton Press.

Sorensen, Sue. 2014. *The Collar: Reading Christian Ministry in Fiction, Television, and Film.* Eugene, OR: Wipf and Stock.

Springfield! Springfield!. 2018. "Marvel's Luke Cage (2016) Season 2 Episode Scripts." Accessed January 23, 2019. https://www.springfieldspringfield.co.uk/episode_scripts. php?tv-show=marvels-luke-cage-2016&season=2.

Staley, Oliver. 2017. "The Tragic Twilight of the Forgotten Comic-Book Mastermind Who Created Cloak and Dagger." *Quartz.* May 4, 2017. https://qz.com/972793/the-sad-storyof-the-comic-book-writer-who-created-rocket-raccoon/.

Stanton, Elizabeth Cady. 1993. *The Woman's Bible.* Boston: Northeastern University Press.

Status of Women in the States. 2019. "Violence and Safety." Accessed April 5, 2019. https://statusofwomendata.org/explore-the-data/violence-safety/.

Stewart, Rebecca. 2016. "Editor's Introduction." In *Crime Uncovered: Antihero*, edited by Fiona Peters and Rebecca Stewart, 7–15. Bristol, UK: Intellect.

Stone, Michael. 2018. "Secretary of State Mike Pompeo: 'We Will Continue To Fight . . . Until the Rapture.'" *Patheos*, December 28, 2018. https://www.patheos.com/blogs/progressivesecularhumanist/2018/12/secretary-of-state-mike-pompeo-we-will-continue-to-fight-until-the-rapture.

Strömberg, Fredrik. 2001. "'Yo, rag-head!': Arab and Muslim Superheroes in American Comic Books after 9/11." *Amerikastudien/American Studies* 56 (4):573–601.

Sturluson, Snorri. 1916. *The Prose Edda.* Translated by Arthur Gilchrist Brodeur. Scandinavian Classics 5. New York: The American-Scandinavian Foundation.

Suurmond, Jean-Jacques. 1992. "The Church at Play: The Pentecostal/Charismatic Renewal of The Liturgy as the Renewal of the World." In *Pentecost, Mission, and Ecumenism: Essays on Intercultural Theology*, edited by Jan A. B. Jongeneel et. al., 247–59. Frankfurt: Peter Lang.

Svetelj, Tone. 2012. "Rereading Modernity—Charles Taylor on Its Genesis and Prospects." Boston College.

Sykes, Shawnee M. Daniels. 2014. "A Feminist Ethical Perspective on Women/Girls as Oppressors: The Cycle of Oppressor-Internalized Oppression." In *Feminist Catholic Theological Ethics: Conversations in the World Church*, 269–79. Maryknoll: Orbis Books.

Taylor, Charles. 1989. *Sources of the Self: The Making of the Modern Identity*. Cambridge: Harvard University Press.

———. 2004. *Modern Social Imaginaries*. Durham: Duke University Press.

———. 2007. *A Secular Age*. Boston: Harvard University Press.

———. 2011. *Dilemmas and Connections*. Cambridge: Harvard University Press.

Terry, Janice J. 1990. "The Carter Administration and the Palestinians." *Arab Studies Quarterly* 12 (1/2): 153–65.

Theodossopoulos, Dimitrios. 2013. "Laying Claim to Authenticity: Five Anthropological Dilemmas." *Anthropological Quarterly* 86 (2): 337–60.

Tobolowsky, Andrew. 2017. *The Sons of Jacob and the Sons of Herakles: The History of the Tribal System and the Organization of Biblical Identity*. Forschungen Zum Alten Testament 2. Tübingen: Mohr Siebeck.

Tolkien, J.R.R. 2001. "Mythopoeia." In *Tree and Leaf*, 83–90. New York: HarperCollins.

Travers, Julia. 2016. "Jessica Jones: An Imperfect, Bitter, and Strong Anti-Hero." *Medium*, February 8, 2016. https://medium.com/legendary-women/jessica-jones-an-imperfect-bitter-and-strong-anti-hero-5fb14dee865.

Tutu, Desmond. 1999. *No Future Without Forgiveness*. New York: Doubleday.

Vanhoozer, Kevin. 2010. *Remythologizing Theology: Divine Action, Passion, and Authorship*. New York: Cambridge University Press.

Vayntrub, Jacqueline. 2019. *Beyond Orality: Biblical Poetry on Its Own Terms*. The Ancient Word. London; New York: Routledge.

Vondey, Wolfgang. 2010a. *Beyond Pentecostalism: The Crisis of Global Christianity and the Renewal of the Theological Agenda*. Pentecostal Manifestos 3. Grand Rapids, MI: Eerdmans Publishing Co.

———. 2010b. "Does God Have a Place in the Physical Universe? Physics and the Quest for the Holy Spirit." In *Science and the Spirit*, 75–91. Bloomington: Indiana University Press.

———. 2018. "Religion as Play: Pentecostalism as a Theological Type." *Religions* 80, no. 9: 1–16.

Waldmeir, Patti. 1998. *Anatomy of a Miracle: The End of Apartheid and the Birth of the New South Africa*. New Brunswick: Rutgers University Press.

Wallis, Jim. 2017. *American's Original Sin*. Ada, MI: Brazos Press.

Wariboko, Nimi. 2012. *The Pentecostal Principle: Ethical Methodology in New Spirit*. Pentecostal Manifestos 5. Grand Rapids, MI: Eerdmans Publishing Co.

West, M.L. 2003. *Greek Epic Fragments From the Seventh to the Fifth Centuries BC*. Cambridge, MA: Harvard University Press.

———. 2013. *The Epic Cycle: A Commentary on the Lost Troy Epics*. Oxford: Oxford University Press.

Wiech, Kahane, Farias Shackel, and Tracey Savulescu. 2013. "Cold or Calculating? Reduced Activity in the Subgenual Cingulate Reflects Decreased Aversion to Harming in Counterintuitive Utilitarian Judgment." *Cognition* 126 (3): 364–72.

Williams, Delores. 2013. *Sisters in the Wilderness: The Challenge of Womanist God-Talk*. Maryknoll: Orbis Books.

Willmington, Harold L. 2011. *Willmington's Guide to the Bible*. Carol Stream, IL: Tyndale House Publishers.

Wink, Walter. 1998. *The Powers That Be*. New York: Galilee Doubleday.

Wright, N.T. 2007. "On Earth as in Heaven." *NTWrightPage*, May 20, 2007. http://ntwrightpage.com/2016/03/30/on-earth-as-in-heaven.

Yoder, John Howard. 1994. *The Politics of Jesus*. Grand Rapids: Eerdmans.

Yong, Amos, and James K. A. Smith, eds. 2010. *Science and the Spirit: A Pentecostal Engagement with the Sciences*. Bloomington: Indiana University Press.

Young, Robert. 2003. *Postcolonialism: A Very Short Introduction*. Brantford, Ont.: W. Ross MacDonald School Resource Services Library.

Zurara, Gomes Eanes De. 2010. *The Chronicle of the Discovery and Conquest of Guinea*. Cambridge: Cambridge Library Collection.

Index

About the Contributors

Matthew Brake is the series editor for Lexington's Theology and Pop Culture series. He has master's degrees in interdisciplinary studies and philosophy from George Mason University. He also has a Master of Divinity from Regent University. He has published numerous articles in the series *Kierkegaard Research: Sources, Reception, Resources*. He has chapters in *Deadpool and Philosophy*, *Wonder Woman and Philosophy*, and *Mr. Robot and Philosophy*. He also co-edits a series for Claremont Press on Religions and Comics with A. David Lewis.

Dan W. Clanton, Jr. (PhD) is an associate professor of religious studies at Doane University in Crete, Nebraska. A researcher of aesthetic interpretations of biblical literature and the intersection between religion and (popular) culture, he has edited or co-edited *The End Will Be Graphic: Apocalyptic in Comic Books and Graphic Novels*; *Understanding Religion and Popular Culture*; and is currently co-editing the *Oxford Handbook of the Bible in American Popular Culture*. Since 2017, he is the program chair of the Society of Biblical Literature's National Bible and Popular Culture Section. He enjoys spending time with his family, collecting jazz and classical music on vinyl, reading comics, and watching far too much television.

Daniel D. Clark is an associate professor of English at Cedarville University where he teaches courses about the graphic novel, contemporary world literature, and film. Before teaching at Cedarville, he lived in Okinawa, Japan, where he taught various courses for the Okinawa Prefectural Language Center, the Okinawa Prefectural Nursing School, and the University of Maryland on U.S. military installations. Clark has published several articles on graphic novels and manga for Salem Press and the *International Journal of Comic Art*.

Austin M. Freeman has a PhD in systematic theology from Trinity Evangelical Divinity School. He publishes on the theology of fantasy literature, including American comics and J.R.R Tolkien. He is primarily a DC fan but likes being ecumenical. He teaches Greco-Roman, medieval, and British literature at a classical school in Dallas, Texas, where he resides with his wife Mandi and their dog Henry.

Amanda Furiasse received her PhD in religion and graduate certificate in museum studies from Florida State University and currently teaches courses at Florida A&M University. Her research is aimed at understanding how subjugated communities can use art and ritual practice to redress violence and trauma with a specific focus on the ritual practices of Jewish communities from the Global South. She is currently working on a digital museum and archive preserving material evidence of women's ritual practices in historically underrepresented communities.

Kristen Leigh Mitchell received her MDiv from Union Theological Seminary in New York City in 2014 with a concentration in theology and the arts. She holds a BA in communication studies from University of North Carolina at Greensboro, and is currently working toward a second bachelor's degree in music. Kristen is a freelance scholar, writer, spiritual director, and indie-folk singer songwriter (www.kristenleighmusic.com) currently based in the NC Piedmont region. In her spare time, she enjoys playing video games, practicing traditional longbow archery, and discussing nerd culture and theology with her husband Joe.

Levi Morrow is a PhD candidate at Tel Aviv University, where he wrote his MA thesis on the afterlife of Franz Rosenzweig's early twentieth-century-German Jewish theology in the writings of the twenty-first-century Religious Zionist Rabbi Shimon Gershon Rosenberg (Shagar), examining Shagar's turn to Rosenzweig as an alternative to Religious Zionist theological doctrine, the rather Hegelian nature of which made Rosenzweig a fitting alternative. Levi has also done extensive work translating Shagar and other Religious Zionist authors for English-speaking audiences. Born in the United States, he now lives in Israel with his wife and two daughters.

Kevin Nye (MDiv) works in homeless services and advocacy in Los Angeles. A graduate of Fuller Theological Seminary, Kevin also writes on the intersections of theology, justice and equity, and pop culture, for various outlets including *Reel Spirituality* and his own blog. Kevin is formerly a licensed minister in the Church of the Nazarene, and continues to write and work for the love of the Church and the sake of God's world.

Taylor J. Ott is a PhD candidate at Fordham University in theological and social ethics. Her doctoral work is on the role of conflict (or more often, the lack thereof) in Catholic social thought, and engages intersectional feminist ethics as a resource for thinking through the presence of conflict in the process of social transformation. She holds a master's in theology from St. John's University in Queens and a bachelor's in psychology from Michigan State University.

Tim Posada is the chair of journalism and new media at Saddleback College. His writings have appeared in *The Journal of Popular Culture* and edited volumes on digital fandom, hysteria in horror, race and gender in science fiction, and transmedia storytelling. He is currently working on a book for Lexington/ Fortress on depictions of the body, soul, and spirit in popular culture. He holds a PhD in cultural studies from Claremont Graduate University, writing his dissertation on the emerging language of superhero media. He is also the film critic for the *Beverly Press*.

Jeremy E. Scarbrough holds a PhD in music (emphasis in philosophy), an MA in Christian apologetics, an MA in theological Studies, a Master of Music Education, and a BA in music. He has taught music and philosophy at the high school and undergraduate levels. He also founded the Ole Miss chapter of Ratio Christi, where he taught Christian apologetics. Dr. Scarbrough currently resides in Tampa, Florida, with his wife and two children. He serves as instructor of philosophy, specializing in moral philosophy, for Pasco-Hernando State College. His research emphasizes interdisciplinary connections between philosophy, theology, pop culture worldviews, and the arts.

Gregory Stevenson is professor of New Testament at Rochester University in Rochester Hills, Michigan. He has a PhD from Emory University and an MDiv from Harding School of Theology. He is the author of *A Slaughtered Lamb: Revelation and the Apocalyptic Response to Evil and Suffering*, *Televised Morality: The Case of Buffy the Vampire Slayer*, and *Power and Place: Temple and Identity in the Book of Revelation*. He has also published numerous articles and essays on both biblical studies and the intersection of religion and popular culture.

Andrew D. Thrasher is a post-graduate researcher at the University of Birmingham, U.K., and adjunct professor of religious studies at George Mason University and Tidewater Community College. He holds a post-graduate Master of Theology (ThM) from Regent University (2017) and a Master of Arts from George Mason University (2014). He is a contributor to *Theology and Game of Thrones*, *Theology and Black Panther*, and a festschrift, *Raimon*

Panikkar: A Companion to His Life and Thought. He has a background in comparative theology and philosophical theology and is currently researching post-secular theology for his doctorate.

Andrew Tobolowsky is an assistant professor at the College of William and Mary in the religious studies department. His work focuses on the Bible, Greek mythology, myth generally, and history. He is the author of *Sons of Jacob and the Sons of Herakles*, published by Mohr Siebeck in 2017, and a number of articles dealing with mythic and historical phenomena from the Ancient Near East to the Mediterranean world.